THE ULTIMATE TIMELINE

THE ULTIMATE SUMMARY OF WORLD HISTORY

BY AARON MAJIFER

GW00382067

This book is dedicated to Ms. S. B. Baker. Thank you for your kindness, support and enthusiasm every day (and for letting me hog the laptop).

INTRODUCTION

Understanding history in itself will not solve all of the world's problems. But it can at least educate us in understanding how we got to where we are today and help us steer our world in the direction we want it to head in. We are all a product of history but also its creators.

This book started off not being a book at all. It actually was not the original intention. A couple of years ago, I started compiling some rough notes for my own research: I wanted to create my own timeline that would help me piece together historical events, starting from the dawn of civilisation to the present day. I wanted to not just learn these events in isolation but how they are all connected: how each event unfolded and led to the next. Fast forward a couple of years and what started out as a side hobby had burst into a full-blown history project. It unleashed the inner nerd in me I knew deep down always existed. My rough notes somehow eventually evolved into what I hope has become a more refined and cohesive narrative: and the end result is this book.

What do I hope to achieve from this?

Of course, timelines are nothing new. There are many brilliant versions out there and they come in different shapes and sizes. Some are interactive and others are highly informative. Some are short and concise - like the ones you read in museums - and others are long and encyclopedic. Mine does not claim to be any better. What I hope to achieve with this book, though, is to create a continuous narrative where the reader can not only unfold history from one event to the next but appreciate how and why situations turned out the way they did.

You can, of course, always search on Google via your phone when the Great Pyramid of Giza was built or ask your home smart speaker when and where Napoleon died. That's fine. I don't know about you, though, but my memory is like a sieve and, very quickly after searching for a piece of information online, I tend to forget it in the long term. Hopefully this timeline can be used as a "search tool" of sorts - and act like a point of reference - whilst also helping to reinforce and retain knowledge. It has worked for me.

What can this book do for you?

Maybe history is your hobby as it is mine and you simply want to better understand, like me, how historical events unfolded over time. Perhaps you are looking for a summary of events surrounding a particular period you are studying at school, college or university. Or perhaps, for some of you, this inspires you to compile your own set of notes or create a timeline of your own. Or you might want to use this to brush up for that next work quiz night to impress your colleagues. Maybe for some of you, after reading this, it will spark your interest in a certain topic leading you to research it further or read or write more about it. Whoever you are, I hope you get something out of it.

Disclaimers

With the last few points above in mind, this leads me neatly on to a few disclaimers. Whilst it is a general world history timeline, this book certainly does not claim to cover every single event in world history. That would be near to impossible or it would just take me a lot longer (forever probably?) to write. Therefore, there may be some disappointment if you are looking to find entries regarding a certain country, civilisation or event and they are not covered. For that, I apologise. My aim was never to cover everything but to create a narrative to help us understand how we got to where we are. This is why I say that I hope this inspires you to create your own timeline: a timeline that covers a period of time, country or topic that is personal to you in some way. My ignorance can be your gain. You will of course find, through reading this book, the kinds of topics or countries that are of interest, or importance, to me (which in turn might give away something about who I am and what interests or motivates me). Unfortunately, anybody writing about history will have some degree of bias, which is why I hope this encourages you to develop your own voice and opinions.

Those of you looking out for key events in British history may also be disappointed. For example, (arguably) the most important date in

English history, 1066 CE, has been skipped. I did this intentionally. This is because I am planning my next book and timeline dedicated entirely to British history, which I am excited to publish as well one day. British history is to some degree covered in this book but only in the context of the rest of the world. For example, you cannot cover the history of India - which I do explore in some detail - without exploring British colonialism. I also intend to release an in-depth timeline that covers events which specifically took place around the Second World War.

What did I use to help write this book?

I gathered the information to write this book from a wide variety of sources. I took inspiration from books, TV documentaries, museums, podcasts and also a little something called...the Internet. Below are some of the superb books, which helped my timeline (though the list is non-exhaustive):

The Timetables of History by Bernard Grun (the initial book that inspired me to write my own timeline)

Sapiens: A Brief History of Humankind by Yuval Noah Harari

The Shortest History of Europe by John Hirst

Rubicon: The Triumph and Tragedy of the Roman Republic by Tom Holland

A History of India by Hermann Kulke and Dietmar Rothermund

The Silk Roads: A New History of the World by Peter Frankopan

I gained a lot from listening to some insightful podcasts. There are three that stood out. The first is *The History of Rome* podcast series written and presented by Mike Duncan. The second is a brilliant podcast series on the history of the Byzantine Empire delivered by Lars Brownworth. The third is *The Ancient World* series by Scott Chesworth. They are all free to download. Some of you might also be familiar with the numerous *Crash Course* history videos on YouTube presented by John Green, which have been thoroughly entertaining and very informative for me.

There are some great documentaries, particularly about some of the significant moments in the history of the United States. They are *The Civil War*, *The Vietnam War* and *The West* (the first two directed by, and the latter produced by, esteemed filmmaker Ken Burns).

I picked up a lot of information from various museums in places I've visited in recent years: the *Natural History Museum* in London, the *War Remnants Museum* in Ho Chi Minh City, the *National Museum of American History* in Washington DC, the *Museum of the City of New York*, the *Gruuthusemuseum* in Bruges, and the *Museo Historico Nacional* in Buenos Aires all stood out for me.

Enough about me. I hope you enjoy reading this.

YEAR (BCE)	EVENT
6.5 million years ago	Archaeologists have discovered the skulls of **Hominins** (or the Hominini) dating back to 6.5 million years ago. The closest living relatives of Hominins are the Gorillini from which chimpanzees, bonobos and apes all derive. Both the Gorillini and Hominini have a common ancestor: the Hominidae family. The Hominini tribe is large and consists of a number of species. Within it, scientists have placed Hominins into different groups based on how closely they believe those Hominins are related to each other. Each group is known as a *genus*, and modern humans belong to the genus **Homo** (which means "man" in Latin). The Hominini tribe includes all of the human species that ever existed. There have been many Hominins that have existed throughout the history of the planet but only one human species exists today – Homo sapiens (that's us). Other human species, grouped in the Homo genus, are now extinct. The earliest Hominin fossil found so far was discovered in Chad. Other fossil finds show that, 4 to 6 million years ago, a number of different Hominin species, like the well-studied Ardipithecus ramidus, existed in Africa.
2 million years ago	Over the past 2 million years there have been at least 8 species of the Homo genus living in Africa, Asia and Europe. These were species that derived from the Hominins. Many of these Homo species survived over hundreds of thousands of years in fierce competition with other Homo species and in the face of adversely changing climates. Some of the older human species were the **Homo rudolfensis**, **Homo erectus** and **Homo habilis**.

Numerous partial skulls and teeth belonging to Homo erectus, spanning more than 1 million years in age, have been found across many different parts of the world. Both |

Homo rudolfensis and Homo habilis have been identified as possible species from which we – Homo sapiens – evolved. Both species lived between 1 to 2 million years ago, one larger-bodied and larger-brained, the other smaller. Homo erectus may have also lived around the same time. The body shape and limb proportions of Homo erectus were similar to modern humans from hot and dry environments but their brains were smaller. They probably walked and ran very much like Homo sapiens do. Their long legs would suggest they were adapted for endurance running. This running style could be linked to persistent hunting techniques where hunters run down their prey until exhausted, making them easier to kill. This technique is still followed by humans in some parts of the world. These species co-existed with other Hominins, such as Paranthropus boisei.

1 million years ago

The **Homo heidelbergensis** species is thought to have evolved from the Homo erectus and fossils of this species have been found in Africa and Eurasia. Homo heidelbergensis fossils show a mix of Homo erectus features and later human characteristics. These species had established large populations in Africa and Europe by around 600,000 BCE.

Homo neanderthalensis (or **Neanderthals**) evolved around this time as well. They are one of the closest human relatives to Homo sapiens. Their remains have been found across Europe and West Asia and scientists know more about them than any other extinct Homo species. They were shorter and stockier than most Homo sapiens today, had powerful muscular bodies and similar-sized brains, albeit shaped differently. Their faces had hefty brow ridges and large noses. Their bodies evolved in a time dominated by cold but they also thrived in warmer times. Remains of animal bones and tools show us they were successful hunters who developed new stone technology. From fossils found in a Siberian cave, scientists also have the genome of another extinct human species closely related to Homo sapiens and the Neanderthals: the **Denisovans**.

All of these early human species had learned how to **domesticate fire** by about **300,000 BCE**. Fire allowed these human species to create a source of light and fight off predators. Arguably the most important activity the domestication of fire led to was **cooking**. Now, foods such as wheat and rice (which are hard to digest raw) could be eaten and digested easily. Cooking also killed harmful bacteria. About a million years ago, humans started developing more of the salivary amylase gene (amylase being an enzyme which catalyses the breakdown of starch into sugars). Humans evolved to possess many copies of the gene, which equipped them better to digest starch. As they started cooking starch-rich foods, having multiple copies of this gene became significantly advantageous for humans, which sucked up the energy from these foods turning them into sugars. Over time, as the theory goes, humans' intestines became shorter (they required less energy to digest food), they spent less time chewing and more energy went to their brains which increased significantly in size.

200,000   The earliest finds of **Homo sapiens** skeletons come from East Africa and date to around 200,000 years ago. Homo sapiens are therefore believed to have evolved around this time with their journey beginning in Africa. Scientists believe that Homo sapiens evolved from Homo heidelbergensis, the same species Neanderthals evolved from.

120,000   Researchers attribute this time to the first wave of migration of Homo sapiens out of Africa. However, this wave is believed to have died out somewhere in the Middle East.

70,000-30,000	During this time, Homo sapiens would invent boats, oil lamps, arrowheads and harpoons. They would also begin to create art. Researchers believe that, to enable all of this, a revolution occurred within the cognitive abilities of Homo sapiens, perhaps due to genetic mutations in the brain. The consequence of this was that Homo sapiens were able to communicate vast quantities of information about their surroundings allowing them to plan and carry out complex actions. They could also form large social networks -by cooperating with strangers in numbers - and use their imaginations to create fictions (such as gods and spirits) shown to us as sculptures of things that do not exist in this world. These concepts have made us remarkably successful as a species. They set us apart from the other human species, giving us the ability to spread throughout the world, to adapt and to make our homes in a range of different environments.
60,000	The Homo sapiens from Africa began to migrate to Asia. This is considered by researchers to be the second wave of migration, which would turn out to be more successful than the first.
45,000	Homo sapiens began to settle in Australia having travelled by sea, perhaps from the Indonesian archipelago.
	The first Homo sapiens to populate the Americas arrived from Asia after crossing the Bering Strait.
40,000	The Neanderthals are thought to have become extinct around this time. Possible factors that have contributed to their extinction are an unstable climate — where severe changes in temperature can happen rapidly, sometimes within a lifetime — and competition for survival from other human species, like Homo sapiens, which had become the most resourceful, innovative and adaptable species of all the humans.

30,000	Homo sapiens began to settle in India.
20,000	Homo sapiens began to settle in Greece.
14,000	Homo sapiens settling in the Andes from South America are traced back to around this time.
13,000	Dogs became the first animals to be domesticated by humans.
11,000	The **Homo floresiensis** became extinct around this time. Homo sapiens were now the only surviving human species.
11,000-7,000	Historians refer to this approximate period as the birth of the **Agricultural Revolution** or the beginning of the **Neolithic Age** (replacing the older Paleolithic Age which, up to this point, covered human history from the time humans were developing stone tools). Traditional hunter-gatherers tended to live in small bands (of up to several hundred individuals) roaming from one place to another hunting animals and gathering plants to survive. However, during the Agricultural Revolution, this lifestyle would be swept aside in favour of establishing permanent settlements and creating a reliable food supply from them. Within these permanent settlements, cultivation of plants such as wheat and rice (or, in the case of Mesoamerica, maize) began alongside domestication of cattle, goats, sheep and pigs. With agriculture, there was more food available in one hectare of land than out in the forest. With a food surplus, more people could be fed. The more people that can be fed, the more likely it is that people can survive and reproduce to have children. Agriculture therefore gave way to a human population explosion. Surplus of crops and population would eventually lead to more sophisticated trade networks, communities and stronger armies. Some of the earliest known settlements can be found in places like Jericho, Damascus and Aleppo in the Middle East.

5000- 4000	Civilisations – more complex human societies – began developing in the land of **Mesopotamia**, which represents an area in the Middle East between the rivers Tigris and Euphrates (now situated in modern Syria, Iraq and Kuwait). The region's stable climate, rich soil and steady supply of fresh water made it ideal for agriculture to develop and thrive. It was in Mesopotamia that settlements blossomed into some of the world's first cities. This collection of cities was specifically located in southern Mesopotamia in the ancient region of **Sumer** and consisted of Eridu, Ur and Uruk (with Kish, Nippur and Lagash to follow). Over the next millennium, some of these cities, like Uruk, would grow into city-states. By the beginning of the 3rd millennium BCE, Uruk may have had between 50,000 to 80,000 residents which would have made it the largest city in the world at the time. In order to organise the mass gatherings of construction workers, farmers, architects, priests and merchants within a city, an administrative class emerged, which probably led to the notion of the first kings, each protected by an army, to rule over these cities.

Elsewhere, the early "**Indus Valley civilisation**" began to form around the valleys of modern-day Pakistan. It started off in the plains of the Indus River valley, irrigated by the snow melts of the mountains and plenty of rainfall, making it a very fertile base for large-scale agricultural settlements.

In **China**, many early villages and farming communities were forming around the Yellow River Valley.

4200	The city of **Susa** was founded in the region of **Elam**, an area close to the Persian Gulf, now covered by modern Iran. Susa was culturally closely tied with Sumer.

3761	According to Jewish tradition, the Hebrew calendar started at the time of the creation of the world, which took place on 7 October 3761 BCE.

| 3500-3000 | **Writing had been invented by Sumerians** to document food and drink transactions, facilitate long-distance communication and make other mathematical calculations needed in order for complex societies to function. Alongside writing, Sumerians introduced barley as a universal measure for the value and exchange of goods and services: arguably the world's first ever money system. Eventually, grams of silver were used as currency. However, coinage would not be invented until King Alyattes of Lydia oversaw the world's first coins in the 7th century BCE.

Also, the oldest surviving potter's wheel, freely spinning on an axle, was found in Ur, dating to approximately this period. |

| 3500 | Huaricanga was the earliest city founded by the Norte Chico civilisation, situated in modern Peru's north central coast. Other settlements would form and thrive in the same area. Over time, their settlements would shift from the coast to more internal regions. |

| 3300 | Sumer, with its cluster of city-states, became the first region to enter the so-called **Bronze Age**, the period associated with the first use of bronze (an alloy consisting primarily of copper and tin). The region now known as Greece would enter the Bronze Age in around 2700 BCE. |

| 3000-2500 | During this period, the Sumerian language system, which first took shape approximately one millennium previously, developed into a full written language called **cuneiform**. Sumerian kings would soon use this language to issue decrees and priests would use it to record religious teachings. |

3150-
2890

King Narmer (or **Menes**) is credited as the unifier of the region in what is now **Egypt** and founder of the 1st **Egyptian dynasty**. **Hor-Aha** is considered to be the second king of the 1st dynasty. Prior to this time, ancient Egypt was a collection of small independent cities (including Heliopolis, Memphis and Thebes) located along North Africa's Nile river. The Nile had a natural cyclical flooding pattern which early farmers took advantage of. The Niles's flooding brought with it rich silt that helped restore the soil whenever it flooded and made it exceptionally fertile allowing crops to grow in abundance. Prior to the unification of Egypt, the city states which grew around the Nile Valley were divided into two regions based on the flow of the Nile: Upper Egypt in the south and Lower Egypt in the north.

During the first and second Egyptian dynasties, around the same time as cuneiform came into existence, **hieroglyphics** would develop as a written language for the ancient Egyptians.

2900-
1800

Many cities, similar to those in Sumer, were forming along the Indus River with populations of between 30,000 and 40,000. Their inhabitants probably traded with people in other ancient settlements via land and sea. The most prominent cities belonged to the **Mohenjo Daro** civilisation – situated in the lower Indus where the Sindh province is – and the **Harappan** civilisation – located by the Ravi River where the Punjab province is.

The people of Mohenjo Daro are credited as having developed the first sewage system. Using the power of the Indus River, they created covered sewers, indoor wells and private restrooms. They also developed their own unique written language, which has never been deciphered. By around the 18th century BCE, the Indus Valley civilisations would fall into decline, perhaps as a result of changes in environmental conditions, such as reduced rainfall, which occurred in around 2000 BCE. Towards the 17th century BCE, the areas around the Indus Valley remained productive but major cities had been abandoned and long distance trade with outside cities had declined.

2890-2686   The period of the **2nd Egyptian Dynasty**.

2800-2500   **Gilgamesh** ruled as King of Uruk. The fictional *Epic of Gilgamesh*, which was written a couple of centuries later and based on him, is considered one of the earliest works of literature.

2700   The combined state of Elam formed around this time.

2700-1450   The **Minoan** civilisation existed on the island of Crete and thrived during this period. The term "Minoan" refers to the mythical King Minos of Knossos. Historians refer to the writing system developed by the Minoans as Linear A as it is considered the precursor to Linear B, which was the writing system used by the Mycenaeans (the precursor to the ancient Greeks).

2686-2613   During the period of the **3rd Egyptian Dynasty**, the **Step Pyramid at Saqqara** was built for the burial of King **Zoser** (or **Djoser**). The ancient Egyptians built pyramids in order to prepare kings for their journey into the afterlife. The Step Pyramid was the first Egyptian pyramid and the first monumental building constructed solely of stone.

2613-2498   The period of the **4th Egyptian Dynasty**.

2589-2566   The **Great Pyramid of Giza** was constructed. There are several pyramids at Giza but only one pyramid is identified as the "Great Pyramid" of Giza and on the list of the **Seven Wonders of the Ancient World**: that is the Pyramid of Khufu, built sometime during the reign of **King Khufu** (or **Cheops** according to the Greeks). It has a flat – not pointed – top and is 481 feet (146 metres) tall. It consists of an estimated 2.3 million stone blocks. Until the Lincoln Cathedral in England eventually overtook it in 1311 CE, this pyramid was the tallest human-made structure in the world.

2570   The **Great Sphinx of Giza** was constructed around this time during the reign of King Khafra (Khufu's son).

2498-
2345   During the **5ᵗʰ Egyptian Dynasty**, Ra the sun god, became one of the foremost gods worshipped in ancient Egypt. King Unas was the last ruler of this dynasty. In preparation for his death, he had the burial chamber in his pyramid inscribed with spells for the afterlife: these are referred to as the **Pyramid Texts**.

2345-
2181   During the **6ᵗʰ Egyptian Dynasty**, King Pepi II reigned from the age of 6. He is believed to have lived and ruled until he was 94, although this is disputed among Egyptologists. If correct, however, this would make Pepi II the longest reigning monarch in history to date.

2334-
2278   **Sargon the Great** ruled as King of Akkad, another principal Sumerian city. According to legend, Sargon's mother, a high priestess, placed Sargon in a reed basket and abandoned him to a river that carried him to a person who would adopt him and raise him to become a gardener. He eventually became a cupbearer to the King of Kish, Ur-Zababa, whom he overthrew. At the same time, the King of Umma, King Lugalzagesi, had conquered all of the Sumerian cities. But his success was short-lived because Sargon defeated him and, in doing so, captured all of his subjugated Sumerian cities allowing him to rule over all of southern Mesopotamia. Sargon is then said to have conquered or taken tribute from cities as far as the

eastern Mediterranean and Cyprus to the region of Elam. He had also taken the region of Mari, part of modern Syria. He is credited for having forged history's first known empire: the **Akkadian Empire**. This empire helped to spread the Akkadian written language, which developed around 2,500 BCE and was based on the old Sumerian cuneiform writing system.

2200-2000   Prior to this time, the Akkadian Empire suffered an invasion by, and had fallen to, the Gutians, a group of nomadic people from in and around the Zagros mountain range (mainly where Iran is now). But the kingdom of Ur soon conquered the Gutians and drove them out of Mesopotamia. From this, the **Third Dynasty of Ur** (or **Ur III**) was founded, during which time the Ziggurat of Ur was built. However, this dynasty was short-lived as it would suffer invasions by King Kandattu's Elamite army as well as the Amorites, a civilisation originating from the region of Syria. The Amorite and Elamite kingdoms would soon jostle with one another for control of southern Mesopotamia.

Towards the beginning of the 20th century BCE, a new kingdom was gaining momentum in the city state of Assur in north east Mesopotamia and would continue to grow in stature: the **Assyrian** kingdom. Also, in Anatolia (which makes up the majority of modern Turkey), a civilisation known as the **Hittites** was developing.

1900   Around the 19th century BCE, **Babylon**, originally established as a major city by the Amorites, declared itself as an independent state and a Babylonian kingdom would begin to form.

1809-1776   During the reign of Shamshi-Adad I, the Assyrians conquered vast territories, including much of Syria, Anatolia and all of Mesopotamia north of Babylon.

1792- 1750	**Hammurabi** became King of Babylon. During his reign, he would conquer the entire region of southern Mesopotamia creating a powerful Babylonian Empire. His armies would push back the influence of the Elamites, conquer Mari and force the Assyrians to pay tribute. He is perhaps best known for introducing a new code of law, one of the first written laws in history, which would set a template for later legal systems.
1700- 1600	In around 1700 BCE, there was a natural disaster in Crete, perhaps an earthquake. Minoan palaces, such as Knossos and Phaistos, were destroyed but the Minoan people had them rebuilt and a general regeneration ushered in a Minoan Golden Age of art and architecture. One example of their art is the famous fresco of the boxing twins. During the Minoan Golden Age, the palaces at Knossos, Phaistos, Mallia and Zakros were all standing. In around 1600 BCE, however, a huge volcano on the nearby island of Thera erupted, devastating the Minoan civilisation. Meanwhile, in mainland Greece, a new civilisation was developing: the **Mycenaeans**.
1650- 1550	A group of raiders from western Asia known as the Hyksos moved into the Nile Delta, conquered the 13th and 14th Egyptian dynasties and founded the **15th Egyptian Dynasty**, marking the beginning of an intermediate period where there was no outright ruler of Egypt due to its division. The power vacuum allowed for the rise of the **16th Egyptian Dynasty**, which was founded in Thebes. It was eventually replaced by a new dynasty, the **17th Egyptian Dynasty**, which existed concurrently with the 15th Dynasty. During this time, the Hittites formed an empire at Hattusa in Anatolia.
1595- 1155	Babylon was sacked by King Mursili of the Hittites, leading to a dark age for the Babylonians. Taking advantage of

the destruction, the Kassites (relatively recent immigrants from the near East) took control of Babylon and ruled over it until 1155 BCE.

1550-1292	This period covers the **18th Egyptian Dynasty,** which was founded by Ahmose I when he expelled the last king of the Hyksos from Egypt. The new dynasty sparked the beginning of a New Kingdom of Egypt. Ahmose I and his successor, Amenhotep I, led great military conquests. They were succeeded by Thutmose I and Thutmose II respectively and, following them, Queen Hatshepsut I ruled Egypt between 1479 and 1458 BCE. King Thutmose III succeeded Hatshepsut. He was later nicknamed as the "Napoleon of Egypt" and led military expeditions that brought the eastern coast of the Mediterranean and Nubia under Egyptian rule.

Akhenaten, who ruled Egypt between 1353 and 1336 BCE, is known for having established a new religious order around worshipping the sun god Aten. Queen Nefertiti, Akhenaten's wife, may have ruled in her own right for a brief period. King **Tutankhamun**, Akhenaten's son, ruled between 1335 and 1323 BCE but died when he was around 18 or 19 years old, ending his royal family line.

1500-1300	A kingdom called **Mitanni,** north of Mesopotamia and in southern Anatolia, was founded by a group of people called the **Hurrians,** who would dominate Assyria for the next two hundred years. Mitanni's downfall would eventually come from the invading Hittites and Assyrians, reducing it to a vassal state.
1500	Around this time, a group of light skinned Indo-European nomadic people from the north, which would later refer to themselves as **Aryans,** invaded the Indus Valley having entered through the Khyber Pass — a mountain pass in modern Pakistan bordering modern Afghanistan. The so-called Aryans are likely to have originated from central

Asia and southern Russia near the Caucasus mountains and between the Black and Caspian Seas. They are believed to have spoken a proto Indo-European language which would form the bases for later prominent languages such as Latin, Greek and Sanskrit (the latter of which would eventually become one of the main languages of ancient India). They introduced to India two-wheeled chariots and horses and worshipped Indra (god of storm and war) as their chief god and other deities such as Agni (god of fire). Widespread use of iron tools and weaponry allowed the Aryans to eventually expand from the upper Indus into the Ganges river valley. The new more settled agricultural lifestyle that resulted eventually led to an amalgamation into larger political units called **Janapadas**.

The most important sources of information about the early Indo-Aryans who settled in northern India are the **Vedas** (meaning **"Knowledge"**), which were orally transmitted verses originating from divine inspiration and passed down from one generation of priests (or "rishis") to the next. Hence the Vedas are "sruti" (Sanskrit for "that which is heard") and the most sacred of all the Hindu scriptures. There are four Vedas: the Rig Veda (the Veda of hymns) consisting of the most prominent of all sruti literature, the Yajur Veda (the Veda of worship) containing the rules (like a handbook) on how to perform rituals, the Sama Veda (the Veda of songs) containing a collection of chants, and the Atharva Veda which was added to the other three Vedas at a later date. Each Veda consists mainly of: Samhitas (hymns, prayers and chants), Brahmanas (directions on rituals), Aranyakas (mantras and interpretations of rituals) and Upanishads (esoteric philosophical teachings).

The followers of these philosophical beliefs would become known as **Hindus** (most probably a name adopted by the Persians when they invaded India in the 6th century BCE and who derived the name from "Indus" after the river).

Many claim the original name of the religion to be "Sanathana Dharma" (loosely translated to "righteousness forever" or "eternal duty").

1500   Villages along the rivers leading to the Gulf of Mexico formed the **Olmec** civilisation. The Olmecs used pictographs called glyphs, which developed into arguably the first written language in Mesoamerica.

1500-
1000   The prophet **Zoroaster** or **Zarathustra** is believed to have lived around this period but historians dispute the exact timing. He founded the religion of Zoroastrianism, which would eventually be followed as the main religion in ancient Persia. A key element of the religion is the worship of the god Ahura Mazda as the highest deity ("Ahura" meaning "lord" and "Mazda" meaning "wisdom").

1450-
1300   The **Mycenaeans** (the precursor civilisation to the ancient Greeks) invaded Crete and conquered the Minoans, leading to their eventual downfall. The Mycenaeans were trading and raiding across the Aegean Sea and had already set up settlements in Thebes, Athens, Mycenae and Pylos. They were not a unified empire but a conglomerate of numerous kingdoms each with their own fortresses. The most impressive fortress was the impregnable acropolis at Mycenae (in addition, in around 1250 BCE, the famous Lion Gate at Mycenae was constructed). The Mycenaeans used as their written language what historians refer to as Linear B (developed from the Minoan Linear A), which is the earliest known form of Greek.

1365-
1330   During the reign of King Ashur-uballit I, the Assyrians broke free from the control of the Hurrians and began the development of a new Assyrian empire.

1300-
1200   A group of distinct nomadic dessert tribes known as the **Hebrews** (or the Twelve Tribes which, according to the

Hebrew Bible, descend from Jacob (later renamed Israel)) settled in the region known as **Canaan** in around the 13th century BCE. Canaan is a region in the coastal plains of the Levant, consisting of present-day Lebanon, Syria, Jordan and Israel. The ancient Greeks would later refer to Canaanites as "Phoenicians". The Canaanites developed the first alphabetic writing system (that is, a writing system based on alphabetic characters). During the Bronze Age, cities would grow in the region and trade routes would develop with neighbouring civilisations. But their geographical position would make them vulnerable to warring states (such as the Hittites, Mitanni and Egyptians) contesting for their land.

1292-
1189

Rameses I founded the **19th Egyptian Dynasty**. He was succeeded by his son, Seti I, and then by his grandson, **Rameses II** (or Rameses the Great), who reigned from 1279 to 1213 BCE. Rameses II led several military expeditions into the Levant as well as into Nubia. The early part of his reign was focussed on building cities, temples, and monuments. He established the city of Pi-Rameses (near Avaris) as his new capital.

1274

The **Battle of Kadesh**: Rameses II led his forces to Kadesh where they met a Hittite army. Here, it is believed that the largest ever chariot battle was fought, involving between five and six thousand chariots. The results of the battle are not clear though the Hittites and Egyptians eventually signed a peace treaty (the Treaty of Kadesh) in 1258 BCE.

1235

The Assyrian King Tukulti-Ninurta I conquered Babylon and declared himself King of Babylon.

1200

Around this time, an early proto-Celtic culture, the **Halstatt** culture, first emerged where Germany is now and then spread westward as far as Iberia (modern Spain), Britain and Ireland.

The Bronze Age Collapse

The Bronze Age collapse is the term given to a supposed cultural, societal and economic collapse of several major prominent Bronze Age kingdoms - including the Mycenaean kingdom and the Hittite empire - interrupting trade, art and culture and generally plunging a large portion of the ancient world into a dark age period.

Historians debate as to what caused the Bronze Age collapse. Theories range from one or a combination of the following: collapse in economies, breakdowns in complex trade networks, overspending in financing wars, failing bureaucracies, famine and overpopulation. The catalyst for the collapse may have been a mysterious group of outsiders - known simply as the "Sea People" - which invaded and sacked numerous cities. **Rameses III**, a **20th Egyptian Dynasty** king who reigned between 1186 and 1155 BCE, is said to have fought the Sea People at the Nile Delta and forced them to retreat into the Levant.

Between the late 13th and early 12th century BCE, every single Mycenaean palace was destroyed and ancient Greece entered its dark age. One explanation offered for the upheaval in Greece is that it was triggered by a potential invasion by the Dorians: one of the four major ethnic groups of classical Greeks, the other three being the Aeolians, Achaeans and Ionians. The latter group made up much of the mainland Greek population but began to migrate west to the coast of Anatolia and settle in places like Miletus, Ephesus and Troy.

After the Bronze Age collapse, northern independent city states in the Levant, namely Byblos, Sidon and Tyre (all today part of Lebanon) would prosper from trade with other civilisations and embark on a new bold era of maritime expansion and colonisation. We conveniently give the people of this collection of cities the term "**Phoenicians**", a name later given by the Greeks due to their monopoly in the purple dye trade (the ancient Greek word for the colour was "phoinikes"). The Phoenician alphabet, which was a continuation of the Canaanite script, was developed around this time. Due to its geographical position and extensive trade networks, the Phoenician script would spread beyond the Canaanite region and became the first widely used alphabetic script. Egyptian, Akkadian, Linear B and other written scripts in the region took a professional scribe a long time to learn and master. By comparison, the beauty of the Phoenician alphabet, with its easy-to-learn 22 consonants, was that it made written communication accessible to the masses. The Phoenicians carried their language with them to their colonies and trading posts, allowing it to be widely adopted.

Also taking advantage of the chaos that ensued from the Bronze age collapse was a group of people called the **Philistines** who arrived and settled in the southern Levant during the 12th century BCE (and who may have derived from the mysterious Sea People). Additionally, a nomadic group called the **Arameans** emerged, firmly establishing themselves in the region of Syria (originally known as Aram) where the state of Aram Damascus was founded. They brought with them the Aramaic written language, which was adapted from the Phoenician alphabet. Although almost all of the Hebrew Bible (known in Judaism as the "Tanakh" and in Christianity as the "Old Testament") was written in ancient Hebrew (a separate but related language), a couple of minor parts were also written in Aramaic.

In addition, some historians connect the collapse of the Hittite civilisation with the arrival of a new tribe from the Balkans which invaded Anatolia: the **Phrygians**.

1115- 1077	The Assyrian king Tiglath-Pileser I reigned during this time allowing a new Assyrian Empire to become a major force in the ancient Near East. Whilst numerous civilisations suffered as a result of the Bronze Age collapse, Assyria survived it and capitalised on the chaos. The Assyrian elite cultivated a ruthless warrior mentality, intent on destroying its neighbours.
1000	The world population was an estimated 50 million at this time.
1000- 900	According to tradition, during the second half of the 10th century BCE, the Kingdom of **Israel** formed in the Canaanite region, alongside the Phoenicians and the Philistines who were already occupying the area. The kingdom of **Judah** - where Jerusalem is based – formed shortly afterwards. According to the Biblical account, Israel started with three celebrated rulers: **Saul, David** and **Solomon**. Saul was considered to be the first King of a unified Israel and Judah having been anointed by the prophet Samuel. David (the same David who defeated Goliath according to the Bible story) succeeded Saul. David then appointed his son, Solomon, as his successor. After Solomon's death, the kingdom was again split into Israel (with Samaria as the capital) and Judah (with Jerusalem as the capital).
1000- 900	Around this time, **Sparta** was settled by Dorian Greeks and would firmly establish itself as a city-state by the following century.
945-720	The **22nd Egyptian Dynasty** was founded by King Shoshenq I. Shortly after coming to power, Shoshenq launched a successful military campaign against Judah and Israel. According to the Hebrew Bible, Rehoboam, the son of Solomon and King of Judah, gave to Shoshenq all of the treasures of Solomon's Temple (also known as the

First Temple) in Jerusalem in order to prevent the sacking of the city.

900-700   The region where **Greece** is now began to move away from its dark ages ushering in what is referred to as the **Archaic Period**. Athens, which had already been a well-established city before the Bronze Age collapse, would soon thrive again. Renewed Greek culture would allow other city-states (or "poleis") like Corinth, Thebes, Sparta and Miletus to grow in stature, eventually turning into strong political institutions or military powerhouses. Despite frequent conflict among each of the city-states, a common language, culture and religion bound these people together in shared Greek identity. The people in this region would collectively refer to themselves as **Hellenes**. Non-Hellenes (that is, non-Greeks) were known as "barbari" (where we get the word "barbarian"). Competition with the Phoenicians for trading posts around the Mediterranean would increase due to the eagerness of the Greeks to colonise in order to support their growing population. As examples, Hellenes from the island of Euboea (Greece's second largest island after Crete) colonised Al-Mina, a trading post on the coast of northern Syria. Another group would colonise Pithecusa (now the Italian island of Ischia). Greek Corinthians established Syracuse on the island of Sicily. Then there were the settlements in the southern part of mainland Italy, which would come to be known as "Magna Graecia".

Competition from the Greeks did not stop the Phoenicians, which would establish trading colonies of their own: in the (now Italian) islands of Sardinia and Sicily and the (now Spanish) southwestern Iberian cities of Tartessos and Cadiz (the latter being considered one of the oldest cities in Western Europe). The southwest region of what is now Spain was ruled by a group called Tartessians, at least before the Greeks, Phoenicians and Romans would arrive. The Spanish east coast was ruled by Iberians, the Basque region by the Aquitani and a large portion of the remainder by Celts.

A civilisation known as the **Etruscans** appeared on the scene in around the 9th century BCE. They were the successors of the early Iron Age Villanova culture of Etruria located in modern Tuscany in Italy. The region had bountiful farmland, copper, iron deposits and well-positioned natural harbours.

Also, by the 9th century BCE, there was a migration of people who entered the Zagros mountains into the region of Persis (now the Fars province in southwestern Iran). This tribe of people would come to be known as the **Persians**. Another tribe had entered the region of Media (now in northwestern Iran). They became known as the **Medes**.

People in the Peruvian highlands, north of modern day Lima, began building a ceremonial site at Chavín De Huantar. This group has been given the name **Chavín**. Civilisations which would follow in the Andean region include the **Nazca** (which developed in around 200 BCE) and the **Moche** (in around 100 CE).

The 9th century BCE in India also correlates to the beginning of the **Late Vedic Period**. During this time, skin colour (**Varna**) had become established as a badge of distinction between the invading Aryans and the conquered indigenous people. Varna soon assumed the definition "caste" and the Aryans used it to categorise people into a societal caste system. A hymn in the Rigveda recognised four castes (in order of importance in the eyes of the Aryans): Brahman, the caste for the priests, Rajanya (or Kshatriya), the warrior caste, Vaishya, the caste for farmers, traders and merchants and Shudra, the caste for workers and artisans.

There also developed an "untouchables" caste (also known

as Dalits) for the very lowest of society and who kept the more undesirable jobs.

883-859   Ashurnasirpal II reigned as King of Assyria and contributed to the expansion of the Assyrian Empire. During his reign, he had built a new capital city called Kalhu (also called Nimrud).

859-824   Ashurnasirpal's son, Shalmaneser III, became the next King of Assyria. His long reign saw a constant series of military campaigns against the likes of Babylon, Aram Damascus and Urartu, the latter being a region located between Anatolia, Mesopotamia and the Caucasus mountains. During Shalmaneser III's reign, a black obelisk was built in Nimrud depicting his successes. In particular, the King of Israel at the time, King Jehu, is shown to be bowing to Shalmaneser and paying tribute to him.

814   **Carthage**, based in North Africa where Tunisia is now, was founded by the Phoenicians (according to tradition, at the direction of the King of Tyre, Pygmalion). The city would flourish and become one of the most prosperous trading hubs in the ancient world.

800-700   By the 8th century BCE, the Etruscans were sharing the Italian peninsula with two other groups of people. The first were the **Italics** who were divided into several main tribal groups and had migrated into the north and centre of the peninsula in around 1000 BCE. The second were the **Messapians** who had migrated from coastal Illyria at approximately the same time and settled at the "heel" of Italy.

Around this period, **Lycurgus** reigned as lawgiver of Sparta. With numerous reforms, he would change the city from unruly and chaotic to strong and disciplined. Sparta would become a militaristic state where boys, via the infamous "agoge" system (often credited to Lycurgus), were trained up at an early age to be warriors.

800-400   The great religious and literary Sanskrit works, the *Upanishads*, *Mahabharata* and *Ramayana*, all may have originated from this period. All of these works were traditionally communicated orally, passed down from generation to generation, before eventually being written down. The Upanishads laid out the fundamentals of Hindu philosophy, which include the concepts of **Samsara** (reincarnation), **Karma** (action: all actions have consequences), **Dharma** (duty), **Moksha** (liberation), **Atman** (the individual soul) and **Brahman** (a term that is ineffable and goes to the root of the universe).

776   The **first Olympic Games** took place in Olympia. They were dedicated to Zeus, the king of gods of ancient Greece. At first, the games consisted of only one event, the "stadion", which was a foot race measuring approximately 200 yards. However, the programme would soon expand to include boxing, wrestling and chariot racing. The games also had a political element to them: the Greek city-states held a truce not to wage war against each other whilst the games were taking place. They were an opportunity for each city to show clout and assert political dominance.

770-750   The first signs of Greek writing and poetry were identified on pottery shards. The Greek written script was adapted from the then-contemporary Phoenician script. Thanks to the simplicity of the Greek alphabet, the ancient Greeks would use their written language to pave the way for significant progress in the fields of science, philosophy, art and of course literature. The compositions of **Homer's** *Iliad* and **Odyssey**, the famous ancient Greek epics originally passed down verbally from one generation to the next, would soon be written down in this popular new language.

753   <u>The Birth of Rome</u>

The founding of **Rome** is traditionally dated to 753 BCE. According to Roman mythology, the story of Rome's origins are as follows:

A vestal virgin named Rhea Silvia from Alba Longa (an ancient city in Latium, part of the Italic kingdom) became pregnant, which was considered sacrilege to local custom. She claimed the war god Mars had impregnated her. But the king at the time, Amulius, did not believe Rhea and had her locked away. Notably, she was the daughter of Amulius' brother, Numitor, whose throne Amulius had recently usurped. Rhea's life was spared but her twin sons - **Romulus** and **Remus** - were kidnapped at birth and hurled into the Tiber river. When they washed up, they were suckled by a she-wolf to survive. Local villagers then raised the twins who, when they had grown up to adulthood, were told of their real origins. True to their heroic status, they raised an army and marched on Alba Longa. Amulius was slain in battle and Numitor was restored to his throne. The twins then decided to found a new city close to where they had been washed ashore (that is, along the banks of the Tiber). However, they disputed which hill their city should be built on. Romulus favoured the Palatine and Remus preferred the Aventine. Romulus killed Remus in the dispute and established his new city the way he wanted. He named it Rome after himself and is considered Rome's first king.

744-727   The **Assyrian Empire** strengthened once again under the rule of **Tiglath-Pileser III** (a former general of the province of Nimrud). He reformed the army and increased the frequency of military campaigns, defeating the kingdom of Urartu, old enemies of the Assyrians, subduing Syria and expanding into the region that is now Iran by conquering the Medes and Persians. He also subjugated Judah, Israel and the Phoenician cities. He then put down a revolt in Babylon and declared himself "King Pulu of

Babylon". When he died in 727 BCE, Tiglath-Pileser was succeeded by his son, Shalmaneser V, who continued and maintained his father's powerful empire.

725   **King Hoshea**, who is considered to be the last King of Israel, halted all tribute payments to Assyria, perhaps under the assumption he would be supported by Egypt. He was captured and arrested by the Assyrians and then taken to Nimrud where he was thrown in prison. Shalmaneser V ordered his armies to besiege Samaria.

722-705   **King Sargon II** succeeded his older brother Shalmaneser V - possibly by usurping his throne - to become new King of Assyria. His armies finally captured Samaria, ending the siege. **The Kingdom of Israel had fallen** to the Assyrians. Sargon II then turned his armies to the south and began fighting the combined Chaldean and Elamite forces rising up in Babylon. Initially, the Assyrians were pushed back and unable to reclaim Babylon. In 709 BCE, however, Sargon II eventually recaptured the city and pronounced himself Babylon's king.

716-673   Romulus died in 716 BCE. A Sabine nobleman called **Numa Pompilius** succeeded him. The foundation of the office of Chief Priest (or **Pontifex Maximus**) in Rome is attributed to his rule as well as the introduction of the Vestal Virgins (a tradition already recognised in Alba Longa). Numa Pompilius also had the temple of Janus built, which began the tradition of keeping its doors open during wartime and shut during times of peace.

705-681   Sargon II died in battle and **Sennacherib** became the new King of Assyria. He commissioned ambitious building projects during his reign, including the enhancement of Nineveh, which he made Assyria's new capital. In 703 BCE, he put down another revolt in Babylon and installed a puppet king to keep the peace. He then turned his attention to Judah where King Hezekiah was refusing to pay tribute to the Assyrians. By 701 BCE, Sennacherib had conquered Judah. However, although he had captured numerous cities in the region - including Byblos, Tyre and Sidon - he did not manage to capture the heavily fortified city of Jerusalem (thanks to divine intervention, according to the Biblical account). The rest of Sennacherib's reign was dominated by putting down revolts by the Elamites and Babylonians before he was assassinated in 681 BCE.

700-600   During this time, the Etruscans had emerged as the leading civilisation in the Italian peninsula, developing close trading networks with the Greeks and Phoenicians. They were divided into independent states ruled by kings. Meanwhile, the city of Rome was beginning to take shape.

By this time, the Greeks and Phoenicians were using the newly invented technology-savvy Trireme to push their seafaring exploits. The Greeks established the colony of Massilia (now modern Marseille) in southern France in around 600 BCE (Nikaia – modern Nice – by contrast is likely to have been established much later, perhaps in the 4th century BCE).

During this period, the Medes established an independent kingdom of their own. Also around this time, **Achaemenes**, a ruler of Parsua – originally a vassal state of the Median kingdom – began what would soon become the historically significant **Achaemenid** dynasty. Although not much is known about Achaemenes, he is considered to be the founder of the **Persian** royal line.

Meanwhile, the western Anatolian kingdom of **Lydia**, which is believed to have started following the decline of the Hittite civilisation from the Bronze Age collapse, would grow in both power and size, particularly under the legendary King Gyges.

681-669   Esarhaddon succeeded Sennacherib as the new Assyrian king. In 671 BCE, his armies successfully marched on Egypt and captured the Egyptian capital of Memphis. He died, however, in the middle of an attempt to try and put down a rebellion in Egypt.

673-642   **Tullus Hostilius** succeeded Numa Pompilius as the next Roman King. His reign is best known for his campaigns against, and destruction of, the people of Alba Longa.

669-631   **Ashurbanipal** succeeded his father, Esarhaddon, to become King of Assyria at 17 years old (some consider him to be the last great Assyrian king). He picked up where his father left off and quelled rebellions in Egypt, establishing a puppet king to rule there. The Assyrian army would eventually withdraw from Egypt in 664 BCE so, even though the king in Egypt was technically a puppet ruler, due to Ashurbanipal's attention being drawn elsewhere in the empire, he could effectively rule Egypt independently, thus beginning the **26th Egyptian Dynasty**.

In 652 BCE, the King of Babylon – brother of Ashurbanipal – declared Babylon independent and gathered anti-Assyrian forces. Ashurbanipal led forces into Babylon and their armies fought for four years after which Babylon would eventually fall to the Assyrians in 648 BCE. Ashurbanipal also led campaigns against the Elamites, once and for all destroying its cities, including Susa, in 647 BCE, and deporting their people. However, by the time Ashurbanipal died in around 627 BCE, the Assyrian Empire would break into civil war, marking its eventual downfall. The subsequent instability would allow rival kingdoms, such as the Medes and Persians, to exploit the power vacuum.

Many people within the Assyrian Empire were speaking Aramaic at this time. As early as the mid-10th century BCE, the Assyrian kings adopted the practice of deporting people from conquered colonies on a mass scale. This is the probable reason for Aramaic, a popularly spoken language in the region, spreading throughout the empire. The language had an alphabet, derived from the Phoenician alphabet, which made it easy to speak and write. It was gradually replacing Akkadian as the main language of the empire. This may have been why Ashurbanipal established a vast and impressive library in Nineveh - arguably his greatest achievement - in an attempt to preserve Akkadian culture. Aramaic prevailed, though, and within a century or so, would displace ancient (or Biblical) Hebrew as the main language of the Jews. So widespread was Aramaic in the Middle East during the 1st century CE, it is most likely to be the language spoken by Jesus.

664-525   As mentioned above, the 26th Egyptian Dynasty was initially installed as a puppet government by the Assyrians but it then effectively became independent. In 653 BCE, with the help of the Lydians, the Egyptian king drove the Assyrian armies out of Egypt and established his new capital at the city of Sais. One of the last great rulers of this Dynasty, Ahmose II, is known for forging trading alliances with the ancient Greeks. Naucratis was set up as a Greek colony on the Nile to help foster this relationship.

650-600   **Draco**, the lawgiver of Athens, is believed to have lived during this time. He was known for implementing a legal system with harsh and repressive measures. The word "draconian" derives from Draco's stringent legal code.

650-500   In the Indian subcontinent, the first territorial kingdoms were beginning to take shape in the central region of the Gangetic Plain. From the numerous small tribal kingdoms, known as **Janapadas** (which themselves developed from semi-nomadic tribes called Jana), sixteen major kingdoms, called **Mahajanapadas**, would emerge. Some of the noteworthy kingdoms were Gandhara - the western most and an important location for trade with Persia and central Asia – and Magadha - the origin of two great future ancient Indian empires: the Maurya and Gupta Empires. The other kingdoms were Kamboja, Kuru, Surasena, Panchala, Vatsa, Kashi (with its capital at Varanasi), Kosala, Matsya, Malla, Vajji, Anga, Assaka, Avanti and Chetya.

642-617 **Ancus Marcius** became the next Roman King. The population of Rome had grown significantly after the invasion of Alba Longa under the previous king, Tullus Hostilius. Under Ancus Marcius, the Romans expanded their population further by defeating the Latins (a tribe from the region of Latium near Rome) and resettling them.

625-585 **Cyaxares** became **King of the Medes**. He is credited for uniting the tribes of the Zagros, predominantly the Medes and Persians. He also forged an alliance with the newly established King of Babylon, **Nabopolassar,** by marrying his daughter Amytis to Nabopolassar's son, the future Nebuchadnezzar II. Nabopolassar took back control of Babylon from the Assyrians and crowned himself king, marking the beginning of a neo-Babylonian Empire. The Babylonian-Median alliance would then go on to conquer Assur and, by 612 BCE, Nineveh had fallen. **The Assyrian Empire had fallen** and Ashur-uballit II, who reigned during the fall of Nineveh, is considered to be the last King of Assyria.

617-579 **Lucius Tarquinius Priscus** became King of Rome by election (and the first Etruscan Roman king). During his reign, he defeated the neighbouring Sabines and captured half a dozen Latin cities. He is said to have had constructed Rome's great sewage system, the Cloaca Maxima, chariot racing stadium, the Circus Maximus, and a stone wall fortifying the city. He also laid the foundations for a temple on the Capitoline Hill in honour of the chief Roman god Jupiter.

610-560   **King Alyattes** reigned over Lydia. Under his reign, the world's first coins were minted and mass-produced. They were composed of copper and electrum (a naturally occurring alloy of silver and gold) and were stamped with a lion's head. Before this, gold and silver rings or ingots were commonly used as currency for commercial transactions. However, they had to be weighed and checked in order to determine their value. Now, the weight and design of each coin was standardised so as to allow trade to take place more efficiently and confidently. The stamp on the coin would prove its validity, material and value. The Pactolus River (now in Turkey) is said to have naturally supplied the electrum needed to mint the coins. According to myth, the reason for this is that the legendary King Midas of Phrygia – who had a "golden touch" allowing him to turn anything he touched to gold – washed away his power in this river.

604-562   Nabopolassar died and was succeeded by **Nebuchadnezzar II** as King of Babylon. Under the new king's ruthless government, the Babylonian Empire reached its peak. He had built the 91 metre-high **Great Ziggurat of Babylon** (or Etemenaki), dedicated to the chief Babylonian god Marduk, and the grand Ishtar Gate, dedicated to the goddess Ishtar. The former has been associated with the Tower of Babel. No trace remains today because Alexander of Macedon (traditionally known as Alexander the Great) would eventually dismantle it for reconstruction.

Legend has it that King Nebuchadnezzar II had the **Hanging Gardens of Babylon** – one of the **Seven Wonders of the Ancient World** – constructed for his Median wife Amytis because she was homesick. Some historians debate whether they were actually built in Babylon, as there is strangely very little mentioned about them by a king who was renowned for boasting about his triumphs. They could instead have been built in Nineveh by Assyrian King Sennacherib (see above). Or they could have just been pure legend. Originally, the walls of Babylon were on the list of the Wonders of the Ancient World but were taken off. The list was actually compiled by a variety of Greek writers centuries later.

599-527   **Vardhamana** (or **Mahavira**) is believed to have lived during this time. Born into a warrior caste, he was dissatisfied with life around him and so he gave up his possessions, fasted and meditated. Through this, he gained full enlightenment and became a **Jaina** (conqueror) and founded the religion **Jainism**, which introduced, among other things, the doctrine of **Ahimsa**: non-violence against any living thing.

594   **Solon**, credited by historians as having laid the foundations for **Athenian democracy** with his reforms, was appointed archon, the highest governmental position of Athens. He declared Draco's laws null and void and cancelled all debts in order to improve the economy. He implemented a legal written code that allowed for access to justice for the poorer classes in society. Solon's reforms also included reshaping the **ecclesia** (the people's assembly) which became open several times a month to all 30,000 Athenian male citizens who could participate in politics and decide on key issues of policy. Around 6,000 would typically attend an assembly meeting. The **boule**, a council of 400 members, was created as a separate institution to the ecclesia. Members of the boule met everyday and carried out the day-to-day administrative functions of the government. The boule also set the agenda for discussion and approval in the assembly and evaluate the assembly's proposals.

After his reforms, Solon embarked on a ten-year voyage where he was said to have visited Cyprus, Lydia, Miletus and Egypt.

589   After a campaign against Judah, Nebuchadnezzar II surrounded and laid siege to Jerusalem, culminating in the destruction of the city and its temple in the summer of 587 or 586 BCE. Thousands of Jews were deported to Babylon. Judah was subsequently annexed to the Babylonian Empire.

585   The warring Medians, under King Cyaxares, and Lydians, under King Alyattes, met at the **Battle of Halys** on 28 May 585 BCE. But the battle abruptly stopped after the occurrence of a solar eclipse which both sides saw as a sign to cease fighting and negotiate a truce. According to Greek historian Herodotus, it was Greek philosopher Thales who had predicted that solar eclipse. Cyaxares died shortly after the battle and his son **Astyages** succeeded him as King of the Medes.

     Thales was a philosopher, mathematician and astronomer from Miletus and one of the **Seven Sages of Greece**, which were a prestigious group of wise men who lived during the 6th century BCE. The other six were Solon (mentioned above), Cleobulus from Lindos, Chilon from Sparta, Bias from Priene, Pittacus from Mytilene and Periander from Corinth. The famous philosopher and mathematician Pythagoras also lived around the 6th century BCE.

580   Cambyses, a descendent of Achaemenes, succeeded his father Cyrus I and became **King Cambyses I of Anshan**, a city of ancient Elam between the lower Zagros mountains and the Persian gulf. Cambyses I was married to the daughter of Median king Astyages and his rule was effectively overseen by the Medes. According to the mythological account of Herodotus, Astyages wanted to have Cambyses' infant son Cyrus - his own grandson - killed because he had premonitions about the boy growing up and destroying his empire. He sent his general Harpagus to kill Cyrus but the mission did not succeed. Cyrus was subsequently raised in secrecy by shepherds.

When Astyages later found out about Harpagus' failed attempt, he had Harpagus' son killed, chopped up, and served on a platter to him.

579-535   The unscrupulous sons of Ancus Marcius, the previous Roman King, successfully ordered for the assassination of Lucius Tarquinius Priscus, whose wife then orchestrated for the popular **Servius Tullius** to be the next King of Rome. Servius Tullius' two daughters were married to Lucius Tarquinius Priscus' two sons, Lucius Tarquinius and Arruns Tarquinius.

During his reign, Servius Tullius ordered a census, requiring all Roman citizens to register their tribe, age, social status, household, property and income. Each social rank was divided into a group of roughly one hundred citizens then further divided by age. The census would establish each individual's tax obligations, requirements for military service and voting rights.

563-483   **Siddhartha Gautama** (or **Shakyamuni**) is believed to have lived around this time. He was born as the son of a Shakya prince in a Himalayan region, which is now part of Nepal. Growing up, he witnessed the suffering of people around him. Not just physical suffering, such as poverty or disease, but suffering of the mind. He saw how people chased knowledge, money and material possessions but were never truly content. In search of a higher truth, he left his family aged 29 and spent many years as a wandering ascetic. Then, after many years of deep meditation, according to his followers, he experienced enlightenment (or Nirvana) sitting down under a tree. The experience gave him an insight into the causes of human suffering and how to overcome them. He became known as "**Buddha**" (which means "Enlightened One"). He then preached his first sermon in a place called Sarnath (near Varanasi) and toured many parts of what is now Bihar and eastern Uttar Pradesh in India, spreading his teachings and attracting more followers. He even met the high nobility of his time, some of whom too became his followers. Buddha's original quest for rationally enlightened experience is documented by his explanation of the "four noble truths" and of the "eightfold path".

561   **Peisistratus,** a politician who represented a very popular political faction in Athens, seized control of the Acropolis at the city and ruled as a tyrant (in ancient Greece, a **"tyrant"** was considered to be a ruler who would take power by force without any constitutional right).

After a rebellion, however, Peisistratus was forced to flee the city. He would return in 556 BCE, only to be exiled again, and then again in 546 BCE. Apparently one eventful return involved him riding a chariot accompanied by a woman dressed as Greek goddess Athena.

560   **Croesus** became **King of Lydia** following the death of his father, Alyattes. During his reign, Croesus funded the reconstruction of the Temple of Artemis in the city of Ephesus. One of the **Seven Wonders of the Ancient World**, it was apparently 120 metres long, made entirely of marble and contained within it a great statue of Artemis (the Greek goddess of hunting). In 356 BCE, an alleged pyromaniac called Herostratus burned the temple down. It was reconstructed again but stood only until 262 CE when the Goths raided Ephesus and used the materials from the temple to rebuild its city after an earthquake.

Also, under the reign of Croesus, the Lydians had discovered how to separate gold from silver to produce coins of solid gold and take the kingdom's wealth to new heights (hence the old expression "rich as Croesus" to describe immense wealth).

559   Cyrus succeeded his father Cambyses I to become **King Cyrus II of Anshan**. Due to his soon-to-be significant

achievements, he would later become known as **Cyrus the Great**.

556-539   After Nebuchadnezzar II died in around 562 BCE, a few rulers reigned over Babylon for a short while until **Nabonidus** took the throne. He is considered to be the last King of Babylon prior to its fall.

550   Astyages marched his army on Cyrus in order to remove him as a potential threat to his kingdom. However, Harpagus, originally Astyages' trusted general, betrayed the Medes and turned his armies against them, allowing Cyrus to defeat and capture Astyages. The victory meant that Cyrus controlled the Median vassals and marked the beginning of the first **Persian** (or **Achaemenid**) **Empire**.

547-546   Cyrus waged a military campaign against Croesus' Kingdom of Lydia. Eventually, Sardis (Lydia's capital) fell after a long siege. Croesus was apparently executed. Harpagus, now a general of the Persians, was sent to conquer Anatolia, including the kingdoms of Lycia and Cilicia. Phoenicia was also conquered and divided into the four new Persian vassal kingdoms of Sidon, Tyre, Arwad and Byblos. Cyrus also had constructed a new capital city - **Pasargadae** - for the newly founded Achaemenid Empire.

540-490   During the 5th century BCE, Kosala and Magadha followed particularly ruthless policies that involved invading their neighbouring territories. **King Bimbisara of Magadha** (who reigned between approximately 540 BCE to 490 BCE) may have been one of the instigators who laid the foundations for the rise of Magadha as a great power in India.

539   Cyrus marched his vast army to the eastern bank of the Tigris and met the Babylonians at the city of Opis. Cyrus overthrew Nabonidus whose fate was unknown. Upon

entering Babylon, **Cyrus declared himself as Great King of Anshan, Persia, Media, Babylon, Sumer and Akkad.** As a ruler who was historically celebrated for religious and cultural toleration, Cyrus apparently freed the Jews who had been captured under the reign of Nebuchadnezzar II.

During the reign of Cyrus the Great, the Persians had no written language of their own just yet and continued to use the Elamite script. For the administrative arm of the Persian Empire, Aramaic (widely spoken in the region) was chosen as their main language, confining Akkadian to scholars and priests in Babylon and Assyria. Even the Jews, after the Babylonian exile, were said to have adopted Aramaic in place of ancient Hebrew.

535   Cyrus the Great led his armies over the Hindu Kush and encountered the Gandhara and Kamboja kingdoms in India, perhaps forcing them to pay tribute.

535-509   Lucius Tarquinius, encouraged by Servius Tullius' younger daughter, went to the house of the Roman Senate and convinced the senators to remove Servius Tullius as king. Following this, Lucius Tarquinius had his men murder him and then took the throne for himself. His so-called wicked deed earned him the nickname **King Tarquin the Proud (or Arrogant).** During Tarquin's reign, the construction of the Temple of Jupiter on the Capitoline Hill was completed. In doing so he had to rid of the Tarpeian Rock (traditionally where accused murderers, traitors and liars were ritually executed). He also led successful military campaigns, which included wars against the Sabines.

According to Roman legend, Tarquin was visited by a Greek oracle (or sibyl) who offered to sell 9 books. Tarquin refused to buy them so she burned 3 yet offered the remaining 6 at the original price. Tarquin refused again so she burned 3 more and offered the remaining 3, again, at the original price. Tarquin then accepted and these books were kept in the Temple of Jupiter. The books are said to be the famous Sibylline Books consulted by Roman leaders in great time of need.

530-522   Cyrus died in around 530 BCE, allegedly in the midst of battle. His tomb still stands today in the ruins of Pasargadae. His son, **Cambyses II**, succeeded him. In 525 BCE, Cambyses II marched to Egypt. In the decisive **Battle of Pelusium**, his Persian army defeated the Egyptians and soon went on to conquer the rest of their kingdom, ushering in the **27th Egyptian Dynasty**: a dynasty ruled by the Persians. During his reign, according to legend, Cambyses II lost 50,000 of his men in a sandstorm (the men referred to as the "Lost Army of Cambyses"), although this may have been due to a defeat in battle.

527   After Peisistratus died, he passed his rule to his sons, **Hippias and Hipparchus**. However, in 514 BCE, Hipparchus was assassinated amidst a personal dispute and, in 510 BCE, Hippias was overthrown by the powerful King of Sparta, Cleomenes.

522-486   When Cambyses II died from an illness, with no children to succeed him, his brother **Bardiya** inherited the throne. However, a claimant to the Achaemenid royal line called Darius would soon overthrow Bardiya and take the Persian throne for himself to become **Darius I** (later known as **Darius the Great**). According to traditional accounts, the so-called Bardiya was an imposter and actually a priest. However, this may have been a cover up story fabricated by Darius to justify his rebellion.

Darius' reign marked the peak of the Persian Empire. He successfully put down revolts in Babylon and Assyria. In 515 BCE, Darius conquered the Indus Valley and controlled the region stretching from Gandhara to modern Karachi, imposing Persian administration. He then appointed Scylax, a Greek explorer, to embark on a grand mission to explore the Indian Ocean, Arabian Sea and Red Sea. In 513 BCE, he fought and defeated the Scythians, a nomadic group of people originating from southern Siberia which had settled around the Black Sea. Following this, Darius' armies conquered Thrace (which is between modern Greece and Turkey) and subjugated neighbouring Macedonia. He also installed pro-Persian tyrants in Ionian Greek cities, bringing them under heavy Persian influence.

At home, Darius built an impressive palace complex at Susa (the former Elamite capital) and ordered the construction of a new royal capital: **Persepolis** (known to the Persians as **Parsa**). He established the Behistun Inscription: a rock relief containing text in three different cuneiform script languages — Old Persian, Elamite and Akkadian — boasting Darius' military victories. By the time of his death in 486 BCE, just under 50 million people - at the time around 45% of the world population - lived under Persian rule making it the largest empire in world history by share of global population.

509   <u>The Birth of the Roman Republic</u>

The foundation of the Roman Republic is traditionally attributed to the year 509 BCE, though this date is disputable. It is possible that Roman historians, seeking to out-do their Greek counterparts, changed the timing of the abolition of the Roman monarchy to slightly predate the establishment of true democracy in Athens in 508 BCE. It is therefore difficult to know for certain when exactly monarchy in Rome was abolished and perhaps the transition from monarchy to republic was much more gradual than has been made out.

Nevertheless, here is the traditional account. By way of background, it helps to introduce Tarquin the Proud's nephew, **Lucius Junius Brutus**, whose father was married to Tarquin's sister Tarquinia. Tarquin allegedly had Brutus' elder brother killed and his father's fortune seized. Brutus, perhaps mistaken by Tarquin for being a dullard and therefore insignificant, was spared and instead offered a position close to Tarquin. Brutus soon worked his way up to the prominent position of tribunus celerum, a commander of the King's bodyguard and second only to the King.

As the story goes, in 509 BCE Tarquin's youngest son Sextus made advances on Lucretia, the wife of the renowned officer **Lucius Tarquinius Collatinus**, and then raped her after she refused him. Afterwards, Lucretia confessed the rape and then committed suicide out of shame of the incident. Collatinus and Brutus – both holding grudges for the deaths of their respective loved ones - publicly denounced Sextus' deed, inciting anger among the Roman people. Following this, Brutus proposed the radical notion of abolishing the monarchy and for Roman government to become a "matter for the public" (or **res publica**). The proposal was that Rome was to be governed by a pair of leaders (or **consuls**) elected by the public for an annual term. Having two consuls would mean each would check the other's power and having one-year terms meant that consuls could not stay in power for too long. In times of emergency, a "dictator" could be appointed to take full authority, though only for a maximum 6-month term. The consuls were to be advised by the already existing **Senate**, an institution as old as the city itself consisting of a body of people from a group of elite families. The Senate played the role of legislator and advisory council.

Brutus and Collatinus were elected as Rome's first two consuls. However, due to a decree being ordered that all Tarquins be expelled, Collatinus – who was himself related to Tarquin – was expelled and replaced by

Publius Valerius. Tarquin himself was eventually forced to flee for good. The new republic fought to put down counter-rebellions attempting to restore the monarchy. In and amongst these uprisings, Brutus would end up being killed.

When the republic was founded, the population of Rome was about 130,000 divided into patricians (a small elite group of nobles who could allegedly trace their roots to the hundred senators appointed by Romulus) and plebs (free Roman citizens, who were not patricians, forming the majority of the population). The patricians consisted of some of the wealthiest in Rome who held enough votes between them to keep out any opposition from power. Therefore, at the beginning of the republic, Rome was realistically an oligarchy designed to keep the wealthy few in power.

508-507   The Beginnings of Democracy in Athens

After the Spartans had overthrown Hippias, two people fought for rule over Athens: Cleisthenes and Isagoras. With the help of the Spartan king Cleomenes, Isagoras initially prevailed, forcing Cleisthenes to flee Athens. However, the Athenian citizens rebelled against the tyrannical rule of Isagoras and Cleomenes, besieging them in the Acropolis before allowing their escape. Cleisthenes was subsequently welcomed back to Athens.

Cleisthenes then implemented political reforms (building on Solon's previous reforms of 594 BCE) leading to a political institution vastly different to oligarchy, monarchy or tyranny and which has since been associated with the beginnings of democracy. Under Solon, the poorest classes were prevented from participating in the 400-member boule. After Cleisthenes' reforms, though, the boule was extended to 500 members, divided into 10 groups of 50. These 500 members were chosen by lot (not elected) to serve for one year. Each group represented each of the newly created 10 Athenian tribes. Each tribe was established according to collated areas of residence (or demes) and were weighted such that no tribe had no more or no less power than another and was diversely represented. One tribe - represented by its 50 members in the boule - would hold the position of executive of the boule for one tenth of the year before rotating to another tribe, thus ensuring that every tribe had the executive function once a year.

The new system also introduced ostracism where Athenian citizens would vote in the assembly to exile a particular person considered to be a threat to the democracy. The term comes from the Greek word "ostraka", meaning the pottery shard on which a citizen would inscribe the name of the person he wanted exiled.

Women, slaves and foreigners were denied participation in Athenian politics so Athenian government was by no means a true democracy applying today's standards. In fact, excluding that demographic, as well as those too young to serve, only about 20% of the population could actually participate.

500   The world population was an estimated 100 million at this time.

499   The **Ionian Revolt**: the Greek cities of Ionia rebelled against the pro-Persian tyrants who ruled over them, launching the Greeks and the Persians into their first major conflict. Athens and Eretria sent armies to support the revolt. The rebellion was eventually put down by the Persians but not before the Persian city of Sardis was burned down.

494   **Secession of the Plebs**: Rome had in place a debt bonding law where, if a debtor could not pay his creditor,

he became a slave to the creditor until the debt was repaid. This particularly affected soldiers (the majority of which were plebs) who, upon returning from war, were faced with huge debts. The plebs rebelled, particularly by refusing to enroll for military duty when Rome was facing attack from outsiders. Eventually, a compromise was reached and a new office of the Tribune of the Plebs was created allowing two plebian men to check the powers held by the consuls.

490   Darius I dispatched an armada of ships in the Aegean in order to destroy or subjugate several Greek islands and city states. Their main targets, though, were Athens and Eretria. The Persians captured Eretria and then sailed for Attica, landing about 25 miles north of Athens in a place called Marathon. The Athenians travelled to Marathon to meet the Persians in battle. At the **Battle of Marathon**, the Greeks defeated the Persians, successfully repelling their attempted invasion of Greece.

486   Darius I died and his son **Xerxes I** succeeded him as the King of Persia.

480   Xerxes I continued his father's attempts to invade the Greek mainland. At the **Battle of Thermopylae**, a small group of Spartan soldiers led by King Leonidas repelled the Persians for as long as possible before succumbing to defeat. Athens was then attacked and destroyed. However, in what is famously called the **Battle of Salamis**, in the Saronic Gulf near Athens - between the mainland and island of Salamis - a fleet of Greek allies decisively defeated a larger Persian-led fleet. This defeat halted any further Persian conquest and is considered the turning point in the war between the Greeks and Persians.

479   At the **Battles of Plataea** and **Mycale**, further Greek victories effectively brought the Persian conquest of Greece to an end. The defeat of the Persian invasion was

followed by **Athens' Golden Age**. 5th century BCE Athens had philosopher Socrates and his student Plato, the playwrights Aeschylus, Sophocles, Euripides and Aristophanes, the historians Herodotus and Thucydides, Hippocrates – who made huge advancements in medicine – Pericles – the statesman who commissioned much of the art, literature and sculptures that adorned Athens – and Phidias – the sculptor responsible for the design of the statues of Zeus in Olympia and Athena in the Parthenon.

478   The Athenians formed the Delian League in order to defend against further Persian invasion.

471   Construction started on the Temple of Zeus at Olympia and was completed in 457 BCE. It would be credited as one of the **Seven Wonders of the Ancient World**. The statue of Zeus inside the temple was apparently made of ivory and gold, holding a statue of Nike (goddess of victory) in one hand and a sceptre in the other.

465   Xerxes was assassinated. His son, **Artaxerxes I**, succeeded him.

451   Roman law was officially codified into the Twelve Tables. Prior to this, the legal framework was a nebulous body of written and oral traditions lacking in precedent and consistency.

447-438   Construction on the **Parthenon** began in 447 BCE before it was completed in 438 BCE. It was built to house a colossal gold and ivory statue of the Greek goddess of wisdom and warfare, Athena.

431   **The Peloponnesian War**, fought between Athens' Delian League and Sparta's Peloponnesian League, began.

425-423   Xerxes, son of Artaxerxes I, succeeded his father and became **King Xerxes II** of Persia. However, Xerxes II ruled

47

only for 45 days before being assassinated by his brother **Sogdianus** who himself only ruled for 6 months before being murdered by his illegitimate brother Ochus who in turn took the throne and adopted the title **Darius II**.

404   Darius II died. His son, **Artaxerxes II**, succeeded him and would rule for 45 years, the longest by any Persian king.

Following the death of Darius II, Amyrtaeus of Egypt led a revolt against Persian authority and successfully reclaimed the throne from Persian rule, forming the **28th Egyptian Dynasty**, which lasted until 399 BCE. Artaxerxes II was, at the time of the revolt, too distracted by infighting with his brother, Cyrus the Younger.

Meanwhile, the Peloponnesian War ended with Sparta and the Peloponnesian League victorious.

399   Socrates, disliked by his contemporaries and an outspoken critic of Athenian democracy, was put on trial for impiety and corrupting the youth. He was found guilty and executed.

387   Rome was sacked by Celtic people who had settled in the region now covering France, Luxembourg and Belgium (known to the Romans as **Gaul**).

359   A man of nobility called Philip inherited the throne of Macedon, a kingdom to the north of the Greek city states, to become **King Philip II of Macedon**.

358   **Artaxerxes III** succeeded his father to become King of Persia. In 343 BCE, he campaigned in Egypt and successfully overthrew the Pharaoh, establishing the **31st Egyptian Dynasty**, once again ruled by the Persian Achaemenid Empire. However, this dynasty would only last until 332 BCE when Alexander would conquer Egypt.

356	**Alexander** (known in the western world as **Alexander the Great**), the son of Philip II, was born in Pella, the capital of the kingdom of Macedon. During his teenage years, Alexander was a tutor of **Aristotle** (himself a student of Plato).
351	Construction had been completed on one of the **Seven Wonders of the Ancient World**: the Mausoleum at Halicarnassus (which is now modern Bodrum in Turkey). It was built as a tomb for Mausolus, a member of the Hecatomnid dynasty which governed Caria in southwest Anatolia. When Mausolus came to power in 377 BCE, Caria was a distant part of the Persian Empire. He established a new capital at Halicarnassus. The mausoleum itself (the name of which originates from this ruler) was apparently 140 feet (43 metres) high. Construction was not finished before Mausolus' death but was continued by his sister and wife, Artemisia (who may also have died before its completion).
343-341	The first Samnite War was fought in the Italian peninsula between the Romans and Samnites, a warlike tribe which resided in Italy's Apennine mountains.
338	The armies of Philip II of Macedon defeated a coalition of Athens and Thebes at the Battle of Chaeronea. In 337 BCE, he helped unite the rulers of most of the Greek city-states (except for Sparta) by gathering them in Corinth and establishing a federation known as the League of Corinth, with Philip at the head.
338	Artaxerxes III died and was succeeded by his son Arses (or **Artaxerxes IV**).
336	Artaxerxes IV was killed by a prominent Persian official called Bagoas who installed Artaxerxes IV's cousin, **Darius III**, on the Persian throne.

Meanwhile, in Macedon, Philip II, while attending his daughter's wedding, was killed by one his bodyguards. The reasons behind the assassination are not known, although Alexander, Philip's son, blamed Darius III. Following his father's death, Alexander (historically referred to as **Alexander the Great**) became **King of Macedon** at the age of 20. He intended to avenge Philip's death and continue his expansionist policy, embarking on a remarkable series of campaigns in a short time. Before his conquests outside the Greek mainland, Alexander consolidated his power in Macedon and Greece (including by putting down revolts in Thebes, Thessaly, Athens and Thrace).

334   Alexander's armies crossed the Hellespont and embarked upon his bold Persian campaign. That summer, he tracked down and defeated the Persian Achaemenid armies at the river Granicus, east of Troy. This opened up Anatolia for Alexander, who continued to release the Greek cities of the west coast from Persian rule.

333   The Persians were defeated again at the **Battle of Issus**, which would mark the beginning of the end of Persian rule.

332   Alexander advanced on Egypt and captured it without a fight. Here, he founded the city of Alexandria.

331   Alexander returned from Egypt to Persia and crushed the last stand of Darius III's armies at the great **Battle of Gaugamela** in the plain of Mesopotamia. Darius fled the battle – but would later be killed by his dissenters - whilst Alexander advanced to, and captured, Babylon and Susa.

330   Alexander went on to capture Persepolis, which signified the **fall of the Persian Achaemenid Empire**.

329   Alexander conquered Samarkand (now in present-day Uzbekistan). The Greeks called it Maracanda.

327-326	Alexander crossed the Hindu Kush mountains to begin his campaign in India. After seizing Gandhara – previously under Persian rule – he and his armies moved to the Punjab. At the battle of Hydaspes, he defeated the army of King Porus of the Pauravas dynasty (which had around two thousand elephants). Porus was subsequently converted as Alexander's ally. Alexander was determined to keep going and cross the Ganges for further conquests but his soldiers, who were growing restless, refused to obey his orders. He finally turned back and proceeded with his troops along the river Indus where they faced battles with the tribes of that area.
326-304	The Romans fought with the Samnites again in a second Samnite War.
324	Alexander returned to Susa in Persia where he married his second wife, the princess Stateira, daughter of Darius III, thus marrying into the Achaemenid dynasty.
323	After a series of swift and successful campaigns which resulted in a vast empire, **Alexander died** in Babylon, possibly of a fever. After his death, a succession crisis ensued which would eventually lead to the divide of his newly-acquired empire. This marked a new era commonly referred to as the **Hellenistic Age**.

At the time of Alexander's death, there were two possible legitimate heirs. One was his half brother, Philip Arrhidaeus, and the other was his posthumous son, named Alexander IV, son of Alexander's first wife, Roxana of Bactria. However, neither of these legitimate heirs could in practice exercise power: Arrhidaeus was considered mentally unfit and Alexander was just a baby. This gave way for the **Diadochi**, Alexander's generals and claimants to be successors (including Perdiccas, Ptolemy, Antigonus, Lysimachus, Leonnatus, Eumenes and Seleucus Nicator), all |

of whom tried to capitalise on the opportunity. Ptolemy was the one who successfully retrieved Alexander's dead body and declared himself to be its official guardian, staking his claim to be successor.

In the decades that followed, the race for the legitimacy to succeed Alexander saw the founding of numerous self-proclaimed kingdoms which would eventually weaken one by one. One of them was the **Seleucid Empire**, which grew over time following Seleucus' acquisition of Babylonia in 321 BCE and lasted until 64 BCE. He expanded his dominions to include much of Alexander's near-eastern territories. At the height of its power, the Seleucid Empire included central Anatolia, Persia, the Levant, Mesopotamia, and what is now Kuwait, Afghanistan, and parts of Pakistan and Turkmenistan.

Another was the **Ptolemaic Kingdom** based in Egypt and ruled by Ptolemy (the general who had initially retrieved Alexander's body).

320   An army leader by the name of **Chandragupta Maurya**, whose military career is said to have begun by fighting against the garrisons that Alexander had left along the river Indus, seized the throne of the Indian Kingdom of Magadha. In the years that followed, he consolidated his control over the army and focussed on the administration of his newly founded **Maurya Empire**. By 317 BCE, the Greek outposts in India had been abandoned allowing Maurya to assert control over his new empire and making Alexander's legacy in India a brief episode in Indian history.

305   Seleucus Nicator and his armies crossed the Hindu Kush mountains in order to try and continue Alexander's legacy in India. Chandragupta Maurya's armies met him in the Punjab and prevented any further march eastward. In the subsequent peace treaty, Seleucus ceded to

Chandragupta all territories to the east of Kabul as well as Baluchistan. In return, he received five hundred war elephants.

298-290 A third Samnite War ended with the Romans controlling most of the central part of the Italian peninsula.

293-273 Chandragupta's son **Bindusara** inherited the Maurya Empire in around 293 BCE, following his father's death, and ruled until around 273 BCE.

284 Construction began around this time by the Ptolemaic Kingdom on the Lighthouse of Alexandria based in the island of Pharos in Alexandria, Egypt. Listed as one of the **Seven Wonders of the Ancient World,** it was said to have been between 350 and 450 feet (or between 106 and 137 metres) in height.

280-279 The Romans clashed with the Greek city of Tarentum in the southern part of the Italian peninsula. The people of Tarentum hired the armies of Pyrrhus, the King of Epirus (a region partly covered by modern day Albania) and a cousin of the late Alexander the Great. Whilst Pyrrhus defeated the Romans in two engagements, his armies suffered severe losses in each battle (hence, where we get the term "Pyrrhic victory"). The Romans would eventually defeat Pyrrhus and go on to conquer Magna Gracia.

280 The Colossus of Rhodes, one of the **Seven Wonders of the Ancient World**, was built. It was a statue of the Greek sun god Helios standing at 108 feet (or 33 metres) high.

275-272 By 275 BCE, the Romans had conquered every Greek city in the southern Italian peninsula besides Tarentum. Eventually, after a series of inconclusive victories, Pyrrhus abandoned Italy and, in 272 BCE, Tarentum fell to the Romans. Pyrrhus later died whilst fighting in the Greek mainland. Most of the Italian peninsula was now under the control of the Romans. The so-called Pyrrhic Wars represented the last chance for the Greeks to repel Rome's advances and brought attention to the might of the Romans.

268   Bindusara's son Ashoka (later to be known as **Ashoka the Great**) ascended the throne of the Maurya Empire. Upon his ascension, the Maurya Empire extended as far south as the present state of Karnataka. In 261 BCE, after conquering Kalinga in the east, Ashoka controlled the entire Indian subcontinent except for the southernmost region. However, apparently after seeing the suffering and cruelness of war during the campaign against Kalinga, Ashoka abandoned his expansionist policy, converted to Buddhism and, in turn, declared India as a Buddhist state. In subsequent years, he began large-scale missionary projects to spread Buddhism beyond India. From southern India and Sri Lanka, Buddhism would travel to southeast Asia and, from northwest India, it spread into central Asia from where it eventually reached China in the 1st century CE via the Silk Roads and became mainstream in that region in the following centuries. Buddhism then arrived in Japan via Korea in around the 6th century CE and spread to Tibet about a century or so later.

Another key part of Ashoka's legacy is the writing produced during his reign - particularly on the **Ashoka Edicts** (or Ashoka Inscriptions) - making his reign the first fairly well-documented period in Indian history. The Ashoka Edicts remain the earliest evidence for an Indian written script (aside from the currently undecipherable script of the Indus civilisation). The writing systems used were Brahmi, which was adopted throughout the Indian subcontinent including in the south where Tamil was spoken, and Kharosthi, used in the northwest and most likely originated from the Aramaic script, the official writing system of the Persian Achaemenid Empire. The earliest datable writing systems for Sanskrit are the Brahmi script.

The later-developed Devanagari script, which descends from the Brahmi writing system, would be adopted for Sanskrit and is used today for modern Indian languages like Hindi and Marathi.

264-241   Rome and Carthage had now grown to be the two big powerhouses in the Mediterranean. Through its wealth amassed over the centuries from trading settlements, Carthage controlled most of northern Africa, the southeastern region of Iberia (modern Spain) and several of the major islands in the Mediterranean. **The First Punic War** broke out in 264 BCE over control of the island of Sicily. After 23 years of battles, during which period the Romans learnt lessons in naval warfare for the first time, Carthage finally capitulated and Rome annexed Sicily as a province. The term "Punic" originates from the name the Romans gave to the Phoenicians.

250-200   The origin of Paris can be dated back to around this period when a Celtic tribe called the Parisii founded a town on the banks of the river Seine. It became an important settlement for the tribe due to its strategic location and easy defensibility.

247   Around this time, a central Asian nomadic tribe called the Parni, ruled by King Arsaces, invaded the Seleucid-dominated region of Parthia which was already in rebellion against Seleucid rule. The Seleucids at the time were caught up in a war with Ptolemaic Egypt allowing the Parni tribe to cement their hold over Parthia. The invasion marked the beginning of the **Parthian Empire**.

233   Ashoka the Great died. Following his death, the Maurya Empire fell into decline and eventually ended when the last ruler of the dynasty, Brihadratha, was assassinated in 185 BCE by his general, Pushyamitra Shunga, who founded the Shunga dynasty (which itself lasted for 112 years).

218-201	The Romans declared war on Carthage (beginning the **Second Punic War**) after Carthage's aggressive expansionist policy in Iberia, which Rome saw as a threat to its dominance. Whilst Rome sent an army to Iberia, the great Carthaginian military commander **Hannibal** daringly marched his army across the Alps in an attempt to invade Italy. Despite early victories for Hannibal, the Romans would eventually fight back and win the war.
	As part of the war, in 213 BCE, the Romans besieged the Carthaginian-aligned city of Syracuse, home to the renowned Greek mathematician Archimedes (who had on one occasion apparently exclaimed *"Eureka!"* whilst running down the streets naked after having discovered the scientific law of buoyancy in his bath tub). Despite Archimedes' clever inventions which helped defend the city, the Romans eventually captured it in 212 BCE and Archimedes was killed.
	As Roman success continued in the Second Punic War, Carthaginian presence in Iberia effectively ended in 206 BCE after Roman victory at the Battle of Ilipa. After the Second Punic War, a large portion of former Carthaginian lands in Iberia (on the south and east coast) now formed part of the Roman Empire. The Romans would refer to this territory as Hispania (where the name "Spain" originates).
200	The Nazca civilisation, responsible for the mysterious Nazca lines in Peru and known also for their fine ceramics, may have formed around this time.
171-132	Mithridates I became king of the Parthian Empire. An ambitious king, he led campaigns that turned Parthia into a major force in the east, occupying key territories in Mesopotamia - including Babylon - and Persia.

167-160   In 198 BCE, the Seleucid Empire had taken control of Judea from the Ptolemaic Empire. The new ruler, Antiochus IV, persecuted the Jews and forbade them from practising their religion, instead imposing Hellenistic influence on Jewish life, which included forcing Jews to worship Greek gods. This sparked the **Maccabean Revolt**, a Jewish rebellion led by the Maccabees against the Seleucid Empire lasting from 167 to 160 BCE. The revolt was successful and led to Judean sovereignty, which later developed into the independent Hasmonean dynasty. **Hanukkah** is celebrated by Jews today as the rededication of the Temple of Jerusalem during the revolt. According to tradition, the Maccabees could only find a small flask of pure oil to light the menorah in the Temple, which would only be enough to burn for a day. But, by miracle, the menorah burned for eight days, allowing sufficient time to find fresh pure oil.

149-146   The Romans finally conquered Carthage in the **Third Punic War**, which resulted in the **sacking and burning of Carthage** and the enslaving of all of its inhabitants. Rome then declared its new province of Africa in the region.

146   Following Rome's annexation of Macedon as a province, the Greeks effectively fell to Roman control after their defeat at the Battle of Corinth, ushering in a period of Roman hegemony over Greece.

138   General Zhang Qian of China's Han Dynasty was sent on a diplomatic mission to create economic and cultural ties with Central Asia. He is often credited for opening up the so-called **"Silk Roads"**, the term given to the network of transcontinental trade routes that stretched thousands of miles connecting China with the West. As well as goods, like silk and precious metals, travelling along these routes over many centuries, so did knowledge, ideas and religions.

100	**Julius Caesar** was born at this time into a wealthy Roman patrician family.
88	Roman politician Lucius Cornelius Sulla was elected as consul in Rome, albeit amidst civil unrest between political factions. Meanwhile, King Mithridates VI of Pontus (a region neighbouring the Black Sea), considered one of Rome's greatest enemies, invaded the Roman province of Asia (now western Turkey) and organised a massacre of around 80,000 Roman settlers remaining in several Anatolian cities. This essentially eliminated Roman presence in the region and Greek cities defected to the side of Mithridates. Sulla responded to the Greek uprising by brutally sacking Athens in 87 BCE.
85	Julius Caesar's father died at a time of civil war between Caesar's uncle and Sulla, his political rival. When Sulla emerged victorious (eventually assuming dictatorship in 82 BCE) and ordered a purge of his enemies, Caesar went into exile and ended up joining the military. Sulla eventually died in 78 BCE, paving the way for Caesar to return to Rome where he would work his way up the political system.
73	In India, the last king of the Shunga dynasty was murdered by a slave girl at the order of the king's Brahmin minister, Vasudeva. The short-lived Kanva dynasty, which was founded by Vasudeva after the Shunga dynasty, would oversee the decline of Magadha, relapsing to its earlier position of one Mahajanapada among several others.
73	A former gladiator called **Spartacus** raised an army of around a hundred thousand men and incited a slave rebellion against Roman oppression. Roman general Marcus Licinius Crassus was called upon to put down the revolt. At the Battle of Silarius, Crassus' army defeated Spartacus and his army, although Spartacus' body itself was never identified. Meanwhile, another celebrated

general, **Pompey Magnus**, keen to take credit for victory in the war against the slave rebels, ordered his army to find escapees of the battle and kill them. Despite little involvement in the battle, Pompey shrewdly took all the credit for defeating Spartacus and sought to use the victory for political gain.

64-63   Pompey and his armies campaigned in Syria, capturing its capital Antioch and deposing the last Seleucid king, ending Seleucid domination. He had also defeated Mithridates VI of Pontus. Rome subsequently annexed Syria and Pontus as provinces. The armies of Pompey also besieged and captured Jerusalem, bringing Judea under Roman control with a puppet ruler installed. After the eventual deaths of Pompey and Caesar (further explained below), Mark Antony and Octavian would continue Rome's tight grip on the region of Judea.

59-52   With the backing of Pompey, Caesar was elected to the position of proconsul. To cement his power, Caesar also brokered an alliance between Pompey and Crassus, Pompey's political enemy, by agreeing to help pass through legislation in both their favour (generous tax cuts for Crassus and land promised to Pompey's veterans). The alliance is referred to as the **Triumvirate**. To solidify this alliance, Caesar arranged for Pompey to marry his daughter Julia (though she tragically died in 53 BCE in childbirth).

Thus, with a combination of Caesar's political shrewdness and intimidation tactics adopted by his supporters, the Senate passed his legislation in favour of the Triumvirate. The Senate also granted Caesar governorship of three provinces, one of which was Transalpine Gaul (correlating to southern France). Caesar subsequently embarked upon a series of military campaigns to boost his prestige. In the years that followed, he conquered most of what is modern day France. In 55 and 54 BCE, Caesar and his armies crossed into Britain but only managed to establish alliances with local tribes - not invade - before returning to Gaul.

In 53 BCE, Crassus' military campaign in Parthia resulted in one of the worst defeats in Roman history and led to his death. The Triumvirate had effectively come to an end. In 52 BCE, Caesar suffered a setback when he lost to the formidable Gallic chieftain, Vercingetorix, at the Battle of Gergovia. However, he responded by besieging and defeating Vercingetorix's men in the Battle of Alesia, one of Caesar's greatest military achievements. Gaul was entirely under the control of Rome and was now a Roman province.

50-45   An anti-Caesar Senate, backed by Pompey, fearful of his ambitions and his threat to the Roman Republic, ordered Caesar to surrender command of his legions or else be considered an enemy of Rome. In January 49 BCE, Caesar crossed the Rubicon river (the boundary between Gaul and Italy) with his 13th legion and triggered civil war. Upon hearing of this, Pompey retreated south to raise an army. At the Battle of Pharsalus in 48 BCE, the armies of Pompey and Caesar met. Caesar won the battle but Pompey retreated to Egypt where he pleaded to King Ptolemy XIII for aid. Ptolemy was a 14-year old and in the throes of a civil war with his sister **Cleopatra VII**. Ptolemy, seeking Caesar's assistance in his civil war, had Pompey killed and apparently had his head presented to Caesar when he arrived in Egypt. Caesar was said to be horrified at Pompey's undignified death and had the assassins killed. Caesar would ally with Cleopatra against Ptolemy and have an affair with her (she allegedly gave birth to Caesar's only biological son, Caesarion). Ptolemy's men were defeated and Cleopatra was installed as Pharoah.

In Rome, with effective authority over the Senate, Caesar

had himself declared dictator for an unprecedented ten years. With power firmly in his hands, he ruled autocratically. Keen to secure his legacy, he began numerous projects, including the construction of the Basilica Julia in the Roman forum, and made reforms such as the introduction of the Julian calendar, which is very close to the calendar we follow today. Before the Julian calendar was introduced, the system for measuring time was incoherent and unreliable, often manipulated by the nobility for political gain.

44 Caesar cast himself as **dictator for life**, further cementing his autocratic rule. He then planned an invasion of Parthia, a decision that was unpopular among some senators. On 15th March (known as the **Ides of March**), during a session of the Senate, a group of conspirator senators (including the noteworthy Marcus Brutus and Gaius Cassius) brutally stabbed Caesar to death.

Caesar's assassination created a political vacuum. When his will was read, it transpired that he had left much of his fortune to his 19 year-old nephew Gaius Octavius. Caesar had also adopted Octavius posthumously. Octavius would change his name to Gaius Julius Caesar but would be referred to by historians as Octavianus (or simply **Octavian**). His adoption and name change would encourage the Roman legions, which were loyal to Caesar, to get behind him. One of Caesar's allies, Marcus Antonius (or **Mark Antony**), using his political ties, tried to win favour with the legions also, which would eventually cause Octavian and Antony to become rivals in fierce competition with one another.

43-40 The advocates of Caesar - Octavian, Mark Antony and Marcus Lepidus - formed the Second Triumvirate. Octavian's armies joined forces with those under Antony and together they campaigned against, and ultimately defeated, the armies of Brutus and Cassius at the **Battle of Philippi**. Both Cassius and Brutus committed suicide.

Antony and Octavian signed an agreement granting Antony control east of the Adriatic and Octavian the west. Lepidus would soon be pushed out of the picture and the Triumvirate would effectively turn into a "bi-umvirate". Antony meanwhile began an alliance, a relationship and, eventually, a family with Cleopatra in Egypt. In 40 BCE, Antony married Octavian's sister, Octavia, in an attempt to cement an alliance between himself and Octavian. Despite this, however, he continued his relationship with Cleopatra and this heightened tension between him and Octavian.

37   After brief Parthian-backed rule, Judea was recaptured by the Romans to become a client state. **King Herod** was installed as a puppet ruler. Meanwhile, Octavian married Livia Drusilla after she had been forced to divorce her then-current husband (with whom she had a son: the future emperor Tiberius).

34-30   Tension between Octavian and Antony worsened after the so-called Donations of Alexandria where Antony and Cleopatra distributed lands held by Rome and Parthia amongst Cleopatra's children. Each child was granted a title, particularly Caesarion – alleged son of Julius Caesar and Cleopatra - who would receive the title King of Kings and King of Egypt. Cleopatra was proclaimed Queen of Egypt. Most important of all, Caesarion was declared legitimate son and heir of Caesar, a move that Octavian saw as a major threat to his power.

        Following this, the Triumvirate would dissolve and a propaganda war ensued, leading to Octavian and Antony publicly declaring each other enemies. Antony accused Octavian of being a usurper to Caesar's command. Octavian accused Antony of being corrupted by the east and more loyal to Cleopatra than to Rome. Eventually, the Senate declared war on Cleopatra in 32 BCE. In 31 BCE, at the **Battle of Actium**, Octavian's armies defeated Antony's resulting in Antony and Cleopatra fleeing to Alexandria. Octavian, on the front foot, then arranged an invasion of Egypt and, in August 30 BCE, captured Alexandria.

According to legend, Cleopatra hid herself in a tomb and sent an attendant to inform Antony that she was already dead. Antony then stabbed himself in a suicide attempt but the self-inflicted wound did not kill him. Antony's body, still alive, was dragged to Cleopatra's hiding place. Antony then died in Cleopatra's arms. Octavian spared Cleopatra's life but she soon killed herself by poking a snake until it struck her. Octavian had her son Caesarion executed (prompting the famous line "two Caesars are one too many").

27-12   Today, we recognise Octavian as **Rome's first emperor**, signaling a departure from the traditions of the Roman Republic, which had been the institution in Rome for the last 500 or so years. The road to becoming emperor cannot be explained by a single event but instead a collection of steps taken by Octavian who exercised clever diplomacy and political prudence in order to transform Rome from a republic to an autocracy.

The Senate granted Octavian the title of **Caesar Augustus** during a constitutional settlement. In practice, he asked to be referred to as **"Princeps"** (first citizen) so as not to appear power grabbing. He accepted a ten-year term during which he would oversee certain provinces, which comprised much of the conquered Roman world and included all of Hispania, Gaul, Syria, Cilicia, Cyprus and Egypt. Command of these provinces meant that Octavian (now Augustus) had control over the majority of

Rome's legions: control of the army was a major factor behind his consolidation of power. Command over Egypt was particularly crucial too: the wealth from this province bankrolled the imperial regime and its ample grain supplies fed the Roman people.

Augustus' influence in political affairs was another factor behind his rise to power. After surviving a near fatal illness in 23 BCE, Augustus decided to amend his constitutional settlement with the Senate. He would resign the consulship. However, he retained control over his imperial provinces. Instead of consul, he would be named Tribune in perpetuity. A Tribune had the right to attend senatorial sessions and propose and veto legislation.

Augustus established the Praetorian Guard (though it took its roots from the days of the Republic): a mini army of around 4,500 men to protect him and his royal family. The Praetorian Guard would play a decisive role in the often dangerous game of Roman politics throughout Roman history. Augustus also brought in administrative reforms. He improved bureaucracy by introducing a rigorous tax collection system, creating new government jobs and generally improving state administration. He was incredibly wealthy from his control of the provinces and having inherited Caesar's fortune. He could easily underwrite, and attach his name to, infrastructure projects (he funded the construction of the Pantheon, for example) to gain public favour. In addition, around this time, the poet Virgil was commissioned by Augustus to write the epic **Aeneid**, widely considered as one of the greatest works of Latin literature.

Upon the death of Marcus Lepidus, Augustus also added Pontifex Maximus (chief priest) to his list of titles. With his titles and demonstrable powers, he had control over religious, state and military affairs.

After the war was won against Antony and Cleopatra, Augustus' reign brought with it a period of peace and prosperity, a welcome relief to the Roman people who had to put up with many years of civil war.

YEAR (CE)	EVENT
2-4	Lucius and Gaius, Augustus' grandsons and adoptive heirs, both died. Tiberius, Livia Drusilla's son (and Augustus' stepson), was adopted by Augustus to be his heir. However, Tiberius was required in turn to adopt as his heir his nephew **Germanicus**, who was the grandson of Mark Antony and Octavia (Augustus' sister) and who would soon be married to Augustus' granddaughter Agrippina. Germanicus would become renowned for leading successful campaigns against the Germans on the Rhine. His general success and popularity would soon become the cause for Tiberius' jealousy.
6	Judea was brought under direct Roman administration and became a province of the Roman Empire.
9	The Romans were soundly defeated by a group of Germanic tribes at the Battle of the Teutoburg Forest. They had failed to annex the region of Germania.
12	Gaius, future emperor and son of Germanicus, was born. His sister Agrippina the Younger was born 3 years later. When Gaius was a toddler living with Germanicus whilst on his military campaigns in Germania, he would dress up in a little army outfit and the soldiers nicknamed him "**Caligula**" which means "Little Boots". The nickname only came back into use after his death and is used by historians today.
14	Augustus died of natural causes. Speaking of his reforms, his last words were apparently that he found Rome as a city of brick and left it as a city of marble. The Senate hailed **Tiberius** as Rome's new emperor.
19	Germanicus died under mysterious circumstances. Sources suggest an assassination plot hatched by the envious Tiberius.

23   Tiberius' biological son Drusus the Younger died from poisoning, perhaps at the hands of Lucius Sejanus, who was supposedly Tiberius' trusted advisor and who had been elevated to Praetorian Guard. Sejanus' influence in Rome grew exponentially and he would effectively become one of the most powerful men in the empire.

26   Growing more and more distant from his imperial duties, Tiberius retired from Rome to an imperial villa-complex on the island of Capri to live a decadent lifestyle. He would never set foot in Rome again for the rest of his life. Sejanus effectively became Rome's de facto ruler.

27-33   The Birth of Christianity

The story of **Jesus' crucifixion** is referred to as **The Passion** (derived from the Latin word "to suffer"). If Jesus was crucified, it was likely to have taken place around this approximate period. During this time, Judea was a Roman province governed by Pontius Pilate, a Roman Prefect (which was essentially a military officer responsible for governing a particular province). The capital of Judea was the thriving coastal city of Caesarea. By contrast, the city of **Jerusalem** - the scene of The Passion - was at the time considered less important to the Romans and was effectively marginalised from any major economic activity.

According to the New Testament, Jesus was a Jewish preacher from Galilee. He became renowned in the region for his inspirational parables and miracle workings, gathering along the way a group of 12 dedicated followers called Disciples. Due to his growing influence posing a threat to well-established Jewish custom, Jesus was arrested by Jewish priests, put on trial, sentenced by Pilate and crucified by the Romans. He is then believed to have risen from the dead a week later before ascending to heaven. After the crucifixion and resurrection of Jesus, the Twelve Disciples, now Apostles, continued to pray in the way they were taught by Jesus and began to convert their fellow Jews to his teachings. "Christ" comes from the Greek word "christos", meaning "anointed one", and was the title given to Jesus. By the turn of the century, followers of Jesus Christ were referred to as Christians.

A key figure in the spread of Christianity was Saul of Tarsus (later to be known as **Saint Paul**). According to tradition, he initially persecuted the early Christians until, whilst travelling to Damascus one day, he experienced a vision in which he saw and spoke to the resurrected Jesus. After this episode, he converted, and dedicated his life, to the Christian cause.

Originally, Christianity started out as an exclusively Jewish sect practised in Judea. Every Christian was a Jew, albeit a Jew who believed in the teachings of Jesus. However, Saint Paul played a significant role in opening up the religion, and making it inclusive, for Gentiles (that is, non-Jews). This was in spite of those in the Christian community who wanted membership to be exclusive. Inclusiveness won the day and, with that, Christianity expanded and spread throughout the Greco-Roman world through a series of missionary journeys. It would grow to become a separate religion, distinct from Judaism, in its own right.

By the time of the reign of Roman Emperor Nero, a small community of believers had established a Christian foundation in Rome itself. According to Christians, those in Rome were led by Saint Peter, one of the Twelve Apostles and considered the first Bishop of Rome (or Pope). However, the Christians in Rome, consisting of a predominantly lower class Greek or Aramaic-speaking minority, were looked down upon, and often persecuted, by the Romans.

29   To remove them as political threats, Tiberius had the wife of the already-deceased Germanicus, together with her two eldest sons, sent into exile during which they would eventually die. The eldest daughter, Agrippina, was forced to marry her cousin. The youngest son, Caligula, was spared.

31   Sejanus, accused of plotting to overthrow Tiberius, was arrested and murdered. The emperor's growing cruelty and paranoia culminated in treason trials, which involved purging any suspected enemies. Meanwhile, Caligula, whose family had died at the hands of Tiberius, was called to the island of Capri and effectively held as a prisoner by the emperor at his villa. Tiberius' young grandson Gemellus also resided at the villa. Both would compete for the role of successor emperor.

37   Tiberius died. According to one theory, he was murdered either by Caligula or the Praetorian Prefect, Macro, under Caligula's direction. In his will, Tiberius had left his powers jointly to Caligula and Gemellus, his intention being that they would be co-emperors. However, Caligula and Macro successfully convinced the Senate to throw out the will. The co-heir plan was abandoned and Caligula had secured his position as sole emperor. Caligula spared Gemellus and instead adopted him as his son and heir to the throne. Although he initially enjoyed a popular and successful reign, later in 37 CE, Caligula slipped into a coma either through illness or being poisoned. Three months later he would recover and, soon after this, he had Gemellus executed for suspected treason whilst Macro was forced to commit suicide.

38   Drusilla, Caligula's closest sister and supposed lover, died of fever. Caligula, descending further into madness, declared her a goddess after her death. Caligula's other sisters, Agrippina and Livilla, were exiled in 39 CE after the discovery of an alleged plot to overthrow him as emperor (known as The Plot of the Three Daggers).

40   Caligula allegedly attempted, but failed, to invade Britain. There is a story that he dressed up Roman soldiers as prisoners of war and paraded them in Rome to make it look like the invasion was successful.

41	Caligula was assassinated by Cassius of the Praetorian Guard as part of a plot hatched by rebel senators. **Claudius**, Caligula's uncle and Germanicus' younger brother, was declared the new emperor. Agrippina was returned from exile to be reunited with her estranged infant son Lucius Domitius Ahenobarbus (the future emperor Nero).
43-47	Claudius, with the help of his general, Plautius, began the Roman **conquest of Britain**. After the Battle of Medway, the Romans pushed the Britons back to the Thames river before pushing further into their home territory and securing the south east of the island. The Romans would establish their new capital at Camulodunum (today Colchester in Essex). They then pushed further in their campaign and, within four years, were firmly in command of the territory roughly south east of an imaginary line between the Severn and Humber estuaries.
48-53	After having his third wife (Messalina) executed for supposed infidelity and treason, Claudius then married his niece Agrippina and adopted her son, who changed his name to Nero Claudius Caesar Drusus Germanicus. When Nero was 14, he was elevated to be co-heir alongside Claudius' son Britannicus and his position was further strengthened by a marriage to Claudius' daughter, Octavia.
54	Claudius died, most probably via poison administered to him by his wife Agrippina, who was supposedly concerned by Claudius' preference for his son Britannicus to become the next emperor instead of Nero. After Claudius' death, **Nero** was confirmed as new emperor. Britannicus was removed from Claudius' will and soon also poisoned to death.
59	After several years of intense rivalry between mother and son, Agrippina was killed, probably on the orders of Nero. Several years later, Nero began purging his enemies by conducting treason trials.

60-61   Despite an uprising led by Boudica, Queen of the Celtic Iceni tribe, the Romans defeated the Britons at the Battle of Watling Street. The battle was said to have been so crucial that, had it been lost by the Romans, there is a possibility that they would have had to withdraw from Britain completely.

64   A fire started at the Circus Maximus in Rome and quickly raged out of control, burning most of the city continuously for 5 to 7 days. After the so-called **Great Fire of Rome**, 3 of the city's 14 districts had been destroyed and another 7 were badly damaged. The rumour was that Nero himself started the fire, however he was apparently not even in Rome when it broke out. Seeking an easy scapegoat, Nero blamed the then-minority Christians for the fire. He had them captured and tortured for confessions. Some were fed to dogs and others were crucified or burnt alive. According to Christian tradition, Saint Peter was among those crucified.

66   The Jewish Revolt (or **Roman Jewish War**) broke out in Judea. One of the main causes of the revolt, aside from fundamental religious differences between Jews and Romans, was harsh tax policy. Nero appointed his general Vespasian to put down the uprising and reassert Roman dominance in Judea.

68-69   As Nero's erratic behaviour escalated, more of those close to him began to turn against him. After a palace coup, Nero committed suicide in 68 CE. Upon Nero's death, **Galba**, the governor of Hispania, ascended to the throne after being declared emperor by his army and the Senate. The so-called **"Year of the Four Emperors"** then followed in 69 CE: in January, Galba was assassinated and replaced by the emperor **Otho**. Within three months, Otho committed suicide after a revolt by **Vitellius**, a general commanding armies in the Rhineland. Vitellius then succeeded Otho as emperor. However, the armies in the east proclaimed their general, Vespasian (who had been tasked by Nero to put down the Jewish Revolt), as a rival emperor. After Vespasian's armies had seized Rome in December, Vitellius was soon overthrown and eventually killed. **Vespasian** was declared the new emperor by the Senate.

70   As part of the Roman Jewish War, Vespasian's son Titus oversaw the siege, and eventual capture, of Jerusalem by the Romans. The capture of Jerusalem resulted in the Temple of Jerusalem being destroyed and hundreds of thousands Jewish deaths.

73   The Roman Jewish War ended with the Romans crushing Judea. After the war, those Jews who survived and were not taken prisoner fled their ruined homes for a new life elsewhere in the empire where they continued to face persecution.

79   Vespasian died of an illness and was succeeded by his son **Titus**. Later that year, **Mount Vesuvius erupted**. The volcano, located on the Gulf of Naples, catapulted out a cloud of molten rock, ash and gases which fell back to the Earth as a pyroclastic flow and buried several Roman cities, including **Pompeii** and **Herculaneum**. Around 20,000 people are believed to have lost their lives.

80   Construction in Rome of the Flavian Amphitheatre - better known as the **Colosseum** - which originally began under Vespasian was completed under Titus.

81   Titus died of an infection. His younger brother **Domitian** succeeded him. Later that year, Domitian had built an arch (the Arch of Titus) in honour of his older brother and to commemorate Rome's recent victory in the Roman Jewish War. Later in his reign, he completed the Temple of Jupiter and another temple dedicated to both Titus and Vespasian.

96   Domitian was assassinated by a group of conspirators. The Senate appointed his advisor, **Nerva**, as the successor emperor.

97   Old and without any children, Nerva adopted the popular Spanish-born general, Trajan, as his heir.

98   Nerva died of an illness. **Trajan** succeeded him, becoming the first provincial emperor of Rome.

105- Trajan fought two wars against the Dacians, the first of which
106   started in 101 CE. The Dacians hailed from the region of Dacia (now predominantly modern-day Romania and Moldova). When the Dacians broke their peace terms of the First Dacian War, a Second Dacian War followed in 105 CE. Prior to the second war, and in preparation for the invasion, Trajan appointed renowned architect Apollodorus to construct a bridge (known as Trajan's Bridge) over the Danube. The bridge was over 1,100 metres long, 15 metres wide and 19 metres tall. It is considered to be one of the most impressive engineering marvels of the ancient world. Trajan's armies defeated the Dacians in 106 CE, annexing part of their kingdom to form the new Roman province of Dacia.

113   Apollodorus designed a number of building projects for Trajan. Trajan's Column was completed in 113 CE to commemorate the emperor's victory over Dacia. In addition, Trajan's Forum and the Baths of Trajan were all built during the emperor's reign.

114   Trajan invaded Armenia after the Parthians installed a king not acceptable in the opinion of the Romans. The Armenian king was overthrown and Trajan added Armenia to Rome's list of provinces.

115- Trajan's armies emerged from the mountains of Armenia into
116   the deserts of Mesopotamia where they launched themselves against the Parthian Empire (vulnerable at the time due to internal political fractures). By 116 CE, Trajan already controlled enough territory to organise a new province between the Tigris and the Euphrates rivers that he named Mesopotamia. He then sent two legions south to secure key cities with one legion eventually capturing the ancient city of Babylon. Trajan then seized the Parthian capital, Ctesiphon, and annexed a large portion of Parthian territory.

Meanwhile, another major Jewish revolt broke out when, in 115 CE, a Jewish leader named Lucuas from Cyrene (a province neighbouring Egypt) declared war on the Romans. Greek and Roman temples were sacked and many inhabitants were killed. The revolt stretched to Egypt, then to Cyprus and then to Mesopotamia. According to reports, the Jews killed over 400,000 Greco-Romans as part of the uprising. Whilst Cyprus was reclaimed by the Romans, the fighting in Egypt was much tougher, though it too was eventually re-conquered in 117 CE. Lucuas and other Jewish commanders were eventually executed.

117   Trajan died at 63 years old. His first cousin **Hadrian**, the governor of Syria, was secured as the new emperor. Just days after becoming emperor, concerned the Roman Empire lacked the necessary resources, Hadrian ordered the legions to begin withdrawing from the territories in the east which Trajan had conquered, namely Mesopotamia, Armenia and Dacia. He instead focussed his reign on securing the empire's borders (Hadrian's Wall in Britain being an example) and trying to secure peace within it. In doing so, he would spend a large part of his reign touring the empire and its provinces.

132-
135   Another Jewish uprising (sometimes referred to as the **Bar Kokhba Revolt**) had begun. The revolt was this time led by Jewish military leader, Simon bar Kokhba. However, within four years, the Romans had entirely suppressed the rebellion. Approximately 600,000 Jews were killed and around a thousand villages and 50 fortified towns were decimated. Hadrian, in an attempt to erase Jewish history, renamed the province of Judea as "Syria Palaestina" and banned Judaism in the region, executing scholars and enslaving many Jews. From 135 CE onwards, Judea would no longer be the cultural or religious hub for Judaism until the modern era.

Up until the Roman Jewish Wars, Jerusalem had acted as the natural de facto capital of the new religion, Christianity.

However, since the fall of the city to the Romans in 70 CE, the church gradually began to separate itself permanently from Judaism. With no recognised capital, Christianity became far more decentralised. By the time the 2nd century CE arrived, The New Testament (most likely originally written in ancient Greek) is said to have been completed by this time, though the original Apostles and Gospel writers were no longer alive. An independent Christianity soon flourished with its own hierarchy of command distinct from all other religions in the Roman Empire.

The local leadership of each of the Christian centres would run their parishes as they decided. Each city would have its own chain of hierarchy, with deacons at the bottom attending to the sick and poor, then presbyters (today known as priests). At the top was the bishop, the supreme religious authority in his district, clarifying the differences between a true and a false teaching. The differences in opinion as to what was a true and false teaching were frequently, passionately - and often violently - disputed between different bishops.

Perhaps naturally, the bishops in the larger cities - like Rome, Antioch and Alexandria - would have greater influence. The bishop of Rome (eventually recognised as the Pope) in particular exerted an even higher authority due to Rome being the capital of the Roman Empire and because his seat was said to have been founded by Saint Peter himself.

138   Hadrian named a senator, Antoninus, as his heir and adopted him. As a stipulation of appointing him as heir, Hadrian required Antoninus to adopt teenager Marcus (soon-to-become the renowned "philosopher emperor" Marcus Aurelius) and child Lucius (later the emperor Lucius Verus) as his heirs. Hadrian then died in 138 CE, probably from heart disease, and **Antoninus** succeeded him as emperor as had been planned. He assumed the title "Antoninus Pius" during his reign to reflect his supposed clemency and just rule. Antoninus' reign is often pointed to as the golden age of the Roman Empire where Rome

was at the height of its power and there were no major wars or scandals. At the time of his reign, the provinces of the Roman Empire were (until re-organised much later under the emperor Diocletian):

- Italia (modern Italy)
- Sicilia (modern Sicily) (claimed after the conclusion of the Punic Wars)
- Corsica and Sardinia
- Gallia Transalpina (stretching from the Alps in the east to the Pyrenees in the west. It was referred to by the Romans as Our Province and today covers the region of Provence in France)
- Gallia Cisalpina (northern Italy)
- Gallia Lugdunensis (central and northern France)
- Gallia Aquitania (southwest France)
- Gallia Belgica (which forms the Low Countries, correlating roughly to Belgium, Luxembourg and parts of the Netherlands)
- Germania Inferior (northern Germany)
- Germania Superior (southern Germany)
- Britannia (modern England and Wales)
- Hispania (modern Spain)
- Mauretania (north Africa)
- Africa (claimed after the final destruction of Carthage in 146 BCE and correlating to Tunisia and Algeria)
- Creta (Crete) and Cyrenaica (present-day Libya)
- Aegyptus (modern Egypt) with its capital at Alexandria
- Arabia (the former Nabataean Kingdom in Jordan where the famous **Petra** is located)
- Judea (renamed Syria Palaestina)
- Syria, with Antioch as its capital
- The provinces of Anatolia (modern Turkey) consisting of Bithynia and Pontus (which ran the southern Black Sea coast), Galatia, Cilicia and Cappadocia. The rest of the west coast of Anatolia consisted of the province of Asia

- Thracia (north-eastern Greece)
- Achaia (southern and central Greece)
- Moesia (eastern Europe)
- Dacia (modern Romania and Serbia)
- Macedonia (the separate province of Epirus was later carved out of this)
- Illyricum (later split into Dalmatia – modern Croatia – and Pannonia – modern Austria)
- Noricum (central Austria)
- Raetia (modern Switzerland)

161   Antoninus Pius died from illness aged 74. The Senate was prepared to transfer sole authority of the emperorship to **Marcus Aurelius** but he demanded that power be shared with his adopted brother **Lucius Verus**. In practice, though, Marcus was the more powerful of the two and effectively acted as sole ruler. A keen student in philosophy, he was a follower of the works of Epictetus, a leading Stoic philosopher from around that period.

161-166   King Vologases IV of Parthia led his armies into Armenia, deposed the Roman-approved king and imposed one of his own countrymen as ruler. The Romans eventually recaptured the Armenian capital from the Parthians and went on to defeat them, sacking Seleucia and Ctesiphon in the process. Vologases was forced to surrender. Soon after the successful campaign, however, a plague (known historically as the **Antonine Plague**) spread throughout the Roman Empire, killing at least 5 million people. It is believed to have originated from China and spread along the Silk Roads before reaching the Roman military, which came into contact with the disease whilst besieging Seleucia. They then carried it to the rest of the empire on their return from campaign.

169   Lucius Verus died from disease, possibly from contracting the Antonine Plague.

177	Marcus Aurelius elevated his 16 year-old son, Lucius Aurelius **Commodus**, to the position of co-emperor.
180	Marcus Aurelius dedicated much of his reign to campaigning in Germania. Despite success in battle, he died (perhaps from the plague also) before full victory could be achieved. Commodus became sole emperor at the age of 19. Despite his father's wishes, and against the advice of his military advisers, Commodus put an end to the war with the Germanic tribes and swiftly made peace with them. He then withdrew his soldiers from the Danube.
	Commodus is generally regarded as an infamously incompetent emperor who cared more for lavish living than running an empire. Apparently seeing himself as the reincarnation of Hercules, he was a keen gladiator (something that was frowned upon due to the low social status attached to gladiators). His opponents in combat would be set up to lose from the outset, or were physically handicapped, so as to make Commodus seem invincible when he defeated them. In another display of power, later in his reign, he changed the name of Rome to "Colonia Commodiana".
182	There was a failed assassination attempt on Commodus allegedly orchestrated by his elder sister Lucilla and senator Quintianus (who tried to deliver the final blow). But when the plot failed, Lucilla was exiled to Capri and later executed. Quintianus was also put to death. A paranoid Commodus then began a series of bloody purges of his suspected enemies, a theme which ran throughout his reign.
188	Cleander, a freedman previously promoted by Commodus to be his trusted advisor and "favourite", sold public offices and entry to the Senate. This was a significant change because, since the foundation of the Republic, seats of the Senate had been reserved for the elite (only those of Senate lineage were eligible for service). Instead, membership of the Senate would pass to those who Cleander preferred. Commodus, in the

meantime, would use the money to fund his lavish lifestyle and leave public duties in the hands of his advisors.

190   Cleander was blamed for stockpiling grain imported from Egypt, creating a grain shortage that devastated the empire. He was soon assassinated.

192   Commodus' inner circle plotted to assassinate him. The first attempt failed: Commodus' mistress, Marcia, tried to poison him but he managed to vomit up the substance. However, in the second attempt, the conspirators sent Commodus' fighting partner Narcissus to murder him. Solider and politician, **Pertinax**, stepped in as emperor but only reigned for 86 days.

193   Pertinax was murdered by the Praetorian Guard and the emperorship was auctioned off to the highest bidder. After buying the imperial throne, Didius Julianus became emperor but only lasted 66 days before being ousted by **Septimius Severus**. He was declared emperor by the Senate but each of the armies of Clodius Albinus and Pescennius Niger declared them to be emperor. Hence, 193 CE has been called the **Year of the Five Emperors** and Rome was in civil war. In the upcoming years, however, Septimius Severus defeated both Pescennius Niger and Clodius Albinus to become undisputed emperor.

200   The world population was an estimated 200 million at this time.

211   Septimius Severus died whilst campaigning in Britain, leaving the Roman Empire to his sons.

224   Persian noble Ardashir I overthrew the last Parthian king, ending the Parthian dynasty and founding the **Sasanian Empire**. He would re-use the former Parthian capital, Ctesiphon, as the empire's own capital. At its peak, the Sasanian Empire would control lands extending from western Anatolia to modern-day Pakistan and were a major military rival to Rome. It would be the final kingdom of the Persian

Empire before the rise of Islam.

235   Upon the assassination of Roman Emperor Severus Alexander, the Roman Empire went through an economic and political crisis where, over the next 50 years, around 40 different individuals were either emperor or claimed to be emperor.

283   When Roman Emperor Carus died, his sons Carinus and Numerian succeeded him for a short while. Carus' death is a mystery (but he probably died of natural causes unlike the legend which claims he was struck by lightning).

284-   After the death of Numerian, the popular military commander
303   Diocles was proclaimed emperor by his army. As emperor, Diocles changed his name to Diocletianus (better known to us as **Diocletian**). Soon after becoming emperor, Diocletian defeated Numerian's brother and co-emperor, Carinus, who supposedly died in battle. Having consolidated his position as sole emperor, Diocletian, recognising that the Roman Empire was too large to be ruled by one person, divided it in two. He appointed his fellow officer Maximian to the rank of "augustus", effectively making him co-emperor (though Diocletian would maintain his position as "senior" emperor). Maximian was given the Latin-speaking West and Diocletian kept the more prosperous Greek-speaking East.

In 293 CE, Diocletian split the empire again. He and Maximian invited accomplished military commanders Constantius (father of the renowned Constantine) and Galerius to be "caesars" (their juniors or sons-in-law), forming what we call the "tetrarchy", a name given retrospectively to this power structure. Under the tetrarchy, the Roman Empire was essentially divided into four quarters: Constantius inherited Gaul and eventually Britannia (he was appointed as caesar with the tough assignment of recapturing Britannia which he did), Maximian was in charge of Spain, Africa and Italy, Galerius was given the Danube provinces and Diocletian took the far East.

Under Diocletian, the role of emperor had shifted from "princeps" (first citizen) to "dominus" (master of the empire). He considered himself a living god, demanding that his subjects prostrate themselves in front of him and kiss the hem of his robe. He hardly left his palace, perhaps to create an aura of divinity around him. By assuming godlike titles ("Iovius" for Diocletian and "Herculius" for Maximian) and staging ceremonies, the co-emperors - akin to their Persian counterparts - were to be seen as the representatives of the gods.

It came as no surprise, therefore, that Diocletian despised the growing monotheistic Christian community, which forbade the worship of Greco-Roman deities. Christianity willingly embraced the politically and economically downtrodden within the empire's cities, namely slaves, women and the poor. In doing so, it posed a threat to Roman stability.

During the past couple of centuries, emperors would adopt different policies on how to 'deal' with the Christians: some were tolerant of them and others persecuted them. Diocletian fell into the latter camp. Before his reign, churches were being built freely and persecution was not wide scale. This changed when, in 303 CE, Diocletian initiated the last and most severe of the **Christian persecutions**. The Church of Nicomedia (a Greek city in Bithynia) was ordered to be razed to the ground. Then, an Imperial Edict ordered every citizen in the empire to make a pagan sacrifice and that every church in the empire was to be destroyed. Scriptures were to be burned and Christians were not allowed to assemble in one place. Their property and wealth were confiscated. They were rounded up and tortured for information about their fellow members. Many were burned alive, particularly in the provinces under the control of Galerius, a strong supporter of Diocletian's anti-Christian policy. According to legend, during the persecutions, a Roman soldier (now Saint George, the patron saint of England), was martyred for not recanting his Christian faith.

During the course of his reign, Diocletian overhauled the government (including the Senate), transforming it into a centralised bureaucracy run by career civil servants who ensured tax revenue was collected more efficiently and accurately. He would make a number of reforms to all aspects of the Roman Empire, including administration, the military and re-districting the provinces. The newly created provinces were divided into 12 dioceses run by vicars who were in charge of enacting policy. This model would be kept until the emperor Justinian - who would later rule the eastern part of the empire - returned to the provincial governor model. But in the west, the Diocese were taken over by the clergy and formed the basis of Catholic administration in Europe which exists to this day.

301   After being baptized as Christian, King Tiridates III of Armenia declared that his kingdom would adopt Christianity as its official religion. Armenia was therefore the first kingdom in history to recognise Christianity as its state religion.

304   Diocletian and Maximian voluntarily and simultaneously abdicated the throne and retired, handing over their power to Galerius and Constantius as augusti. Diocletian entrusted two generals, Maximinus Daia and Flavius Valerius Severus, to be the new caesars. Maxentius, Maximian's son, and Constantine, Constantius' son, were cast aside but their omission would spark a bitter power struggle.

306-   When Constantius died, the army stationed in York in Britain
310   proclaimed his son, **Constantine**, the new augustus. Galerius refused to accept this. Severus, a friend of Galerius, was elevated to augustus instead. Meanwhile, a group of officers in Rome turned to Maxentius and proclaimed him as the new augustus. Galerius again refused to accept this and ordered Severus to defeat Maxentius. Severus' army marched on Rome to fight Maxentius but the city was well fortified and was able to fend off Severus' men. Subsequently, Maximian (Maxentius' father) came out of retirement in aid of his son. His army marched to Ravenna (where Severus had retreated) and

captured it. Severus was executed soon afterwards. However, Maximian then switched sides and joined Constantine in opposition against Maxentius (his own son). Constantine had recently married Maximian's daughter, Fausta.

In 308 CE, the retired Diocletian stepped in to broker an agreement between the warring emperors in an attempt to restore peace. He gave Galerius his blessing to elevate his ally, Licinius, to augustus to rule the western part of the empire (with Constantine to be Licinius' caesar in the West). Galerius and Maximinus Daia would continue their roles in the East. Maximian was sent back into retirement and Maxentius was left out of the treaty altogether In 310 CE, Maximian, setting his sights on regaining his power once more, betrayed Constantine and declared himself augustus. However, he was captured and forced by Constantine to commit suicide.

311   Galerius died of ill health. Maximinus Daia then agreed a territorial alliance with Licinius. However, when Constantine and Licinius began to forge an alliance of their own, Maximinus Daia and Maxentius allied with one another to counterbalance them.

312   Constantine, sensing the opportunity to overthrow Maxentius, set on a bold campaign to conquer Italy. He marched his army across the Alps with the intention of capturing Rome. Prior to the pivotal **Battle of Milvian Bridge** (where Maxentius' and Constantine's armies would meet) Constantine allegedly experienced holy visions promising him victory if he embraced Christianity. His revelations told him to adopt the Chi Rho symbol (Chi and Rho are the first two Greek letters that spell the word "Christ") and display it on the military standard of his army (known as a labarum). There is very little evidence of this story happening and Constantine may have fabricated it as propaganda later in his reign when he would fully embrace Christianity. At Milvian Bridge (near Rome), though, Constantine indeed defeated Maxentius' army and Maxentius himself died in the battle (allegedly drowning in the Tiber).

After Milvian Bridge, Constantine would increase his patronage of Christianity: he sponsored the building or rebuilding of churches and exempted clergymen from tax obligations. Whilst he still accepted pagan worship, he would become more open to the Christian ways of doing things. It is likely he believed that the Christian god, rather than the Roman gods, could better protect him and his empire.

313   In an unprecedented act, Constantine and Licinius issued a joint resolution recognising the legal status of Christians in the Roman Empire: it officially established the Christian right to worship. Conversion to Christianity would increase as a result. Christians who endured the recent persecutions would be compensated for properties confiscated from them. The resolution is historically referred to as the **Edict of Milan**, although whether any formal edict was enacted is disputed. It is also debated whether the act was Constantine's recognition of his Christian faith or a political move, perhaps to provoke and isolate his political enemy, Maximinus Daia, known for his anti-Christian agenda.

Licinius' army eventually defeated Maximinus Daia, who died later in 313. After his death, Constantine and Licinius carved up the Roman Empire with Constantine controlling the West and Licinius the East. To cement their alliance, Constantine offered to Licinius his half-sister, Constantia, for marriage.

316   Diplomatic relations between Constantine and Licinius broke down to the point that their armies would meet in several battles. Whilst the battles ended in peace, tension continued between the two factions.

320   Chandragupta of the **Gupta dynasty** in northern India was crowned Chandragupta I. He married a Lichchhavi princess. The marriage probably contributed to the rise of the Gupta dynasty in India because the Lichchhavis were a mighty clan that controlled most of north Bihar since the time of Buddha.

324   War between Licinius and Constantine flared up again. When their armies met at the Battle of Adrianople, there was no decisive outcome. The fighting continued (during which Crispus, one of Constantine's sons, would play a key role), and culminated in the Battle of Chrysopolis where Licinius was finally defeated, forced to surrender and eventually executed.

Constantine was now the undisputed ruler of the Roman Empire. Later in 324 CE, he made a trip to the formerly ancient Greek city Byzantium in Anatolia (modern Turkey) and decided that it would become the empire's new capital city. Byzantium would be renamed "Constantinople" (today Istanbul).

325   There were deep-rooted divisions in the church within which complex theological matters were being debated passionately among religious leaders. A particular topic that polarised opinion was the doctrine of Arianism - popularised by a priest called Arius - which was spreading in the east. Those who supported it argued that, since Christ was the begotten son of God, there must have been a time when Christ did not exist. Therefore, according to the Arian doctrine, though both were divine, Christ was subordinate to God. Those who disagreed with Arianism claimed that God and Christ were whole and equally divine. This divided the Christian community and stood in the way of Constantine's attempts to unite it.

To settle matters, Constantine ordered that a council be held in Nicaea (in Anatolia) and attended by Christian representatives from across the empire. The purpose was to settle all schisms within the church with Constantine playing the role of mediator. Around 300 bishops attended and discussed many things such as when Easter was to be celebrated. In particular, though, anti-Arianism won the day and the council issued a statement that became known as the **Nicene Creed**, reflecting what had been agreed. Other points of canon law were decided, including that the bishops of Rome, Alexandria and Antioch had superior authority above other bishops.

326 Constantine ordered his eldest son Crispus to be executed. Allegedly, Fausta, Constantine's wife, framed Crispus in an attempt to have her own sons made emperor. It was not long before Fausta herself was killed on Constantine's orders (apparently by being locked in an overheated bath), perhaps due to her plot being revealed.

330 The new city of **Constantinople** was officially dedicated. Some historical accounts mark 330 CE as the beginning of the "**Byzantine**" (or Eastern Roman) Empire. In reality, though, the Greek-speaking people of the city did not refer to themselves as Byzantines. They considered themselves to be Romans, given that a Roman emperor ruled over them.

335- Chandragupta's son, Samudragupta, ruled and earned a
375 reputation as one of the greatest conquerors in Indian history, contributing to the rise of the **Gupta Empire**. Most of northern India was added to his empire, as well as many areas on the eastern coast.

337- Close to death, Constantine summoned the bishop of Nicomedia
361 to formally baptize him. After his death in 337 CE, his three sons, Constantine II, Constantius II and Constans, took over the Roman Empire and murdered most of their extended family in order to secure control. Of the three brothers, Constantius II would prove to be the most ruthless. By 340 CE, Constantine II was dead and Constantius II and Constans would share the empire between them until 350 CE when a rebel general named Magnentius would overthrow and kill Constans. In 353 CE, after losing in battles against Constantius, Magnentius committed suicide, leaving Constantius as sole ruler of the empire until his death in 361 CE.

375- Under Samudragupta's son, Chandragupta II, India enjoyed
414 her Golden Age. The Gupta Empire attained its greatest glory both in terms of territorial expansion and culture. Chandragupta II's primary achievement was his victory around

the end of the 4th century CE over the Shaka-Kshatrapa dynasty and the annexation of the Gujarat. During his reign, Chandragupta II would control most of northern India from the mouths of the Ganges to the Indus river and from what is now northern Pakistan down to the mouth of the Narmada river. In alliance with the Vakatakas, he also controlled a large part of central India.

376   Around this time, a fierce group of warriors called the **Huns** rapidly surged into territories occupied by numerous Germanic tribes, including the Ostrogoths, Visigoths and Vandals. Although the Hunnic leadership initially came from central Asia, the Hunnic confederation was not a single ethnic group. It was instead made up of a variety of tribes of different origins. Anyone could become a Hun if they fought with the Huns and supported Hunnic leadership. From a very young age, their children were raised as warriors and taught to ride horses and shoot arrows.

Due to the invasion, these Germanic tribes were forced to migrate southward across the Danube and westward across the Rhine, seeking refuge among the Romans within the empire and causing a mass overflow of immigrants settling within its borders. The settlers were severely mistreated, neglected and exploited by the Romans. Many grew restless and eventually snapped, declaring war on them.

378   At the **Battle of Adrianople**, a united group of Germanic tribes, led by a chieftain called Fritigern, defeated a large Roman army (of which approximately two thirds were killed in the battle). The Eastern Roman Emperor Valens had vanished in the battle, presumed dead.

379   Theodosius I succeeded Valens in the east (and would go on to become sole emperor in 392 CE). After determining he could not beat the Germanic tribes in battle, he was forced to sign a peace agreement with them in 381 CE and treat then as equals within the empire.

380   Under Theodosius I and his co-emperors, Christianity (in the form as was agreed in the Council of Nicaea in 325 CE) was declared the state religion of the Roman Empire.

395   The Huns staged their first large-scale attack on the Eastern Roman Empire, raiding provinces and destroying cities. The Romans would soon come to recognise the Huns as a grave threat to the security of their empire.

       When Theodosius I died, the empire was divided between his sons (with Arcadius taking the East and Honorius the West). Theodosius I would be the last emperor to rule over the entire Roman Empire.

400   Attila (later known as **Attila the Hun**) was born around this time. His father Mundzuk, a Hunnic chieftain, died shortly afterwards, leaving Attila and his older brother Bleda to be raised by their uncle Ruga. Around this time, the Huns had crossed the Carpathian mountains and created a vast empire centred in present-day Hungary.

402   King Alaric I of the Visigoths invaded Italy, forcing Honorius to retreat and move his empire's capital to coastal Ravenna in northern Italy.

406   A massive horde of barbarian tribes, which included a mix of Vandals, Alans, Burgundians and Alemanni, crossed the lower Rhine and invaded Gaul. Remaining Roman troops in Britain were moved to Gaul to deal with the invasion.

410   Alaric I's Visigothic armies attacked and plundered Rome (though ordered his men that Christian artefacts and churches would be off limits). It was the first time the city had been sacked in around 800 years. The sacking inspired Saint Augustine, a Christian theologian in North Africa, to write the City of God, which came to the defence of Christianity despite Rome's misfortunes. Alaric I died later in 410 CE.

413   Praetorian Prefect Anthemius, who had taken effective control of the Eastern Roman Empire, had the Theodosian Walls of Constantinople erected. They were named after the young Emperor Theodosius II (then only a boy). For the next thousand years, the Theodosian Walls would help prevent Constantinople from being breached by land.

415-   Chandragupta II's son, Kumaragupta, ruled the Gupta Empire
455   during this period. His reign was characterised by a policy of religious tolerance. Inscriptions registering endowments for the holy places of Buddhism and Jainism, as well as for Hindu gods like Vishnu and Shiva, thrived in all parts of the empire.

434   Attila and his brother Bleda became leaders of the Huns after the death of their uncle Ruga. The brothers began raiding the Eastern Roman Empire. The Romans knew they were no match for the Huns on the battlefield so they kept having to pay them off to avoid humiliation. Attila's accumulated wealth and tribute only made his influence more powerful. The policy of forced bribery began in around the mid 420s when the Huns would send envoys to Constantinople demanding an annual payment of gold or else they would attack. When Attila and Bleda came to power, they doubled their demand, which the Romans agreed to pay. This practice continued up to Attila's death.

438   The Theodosian Code, a culmination of a decade's work, was published. It would form part of the Justinian Code, which would be compiled a century later. Prior to this, Roman law was a chaotic collection of nearly one thousand years of confusing and often contradicting precedent not written down in one place. In 429 CE, Theodosius II had appointed a commission to track down and compile every single law, decree, edict or opinion issued by roman emperors since 312 CE. The intention was to have a single source that could be relied on by jurists and that would define the empire politically, economically, religiously and culturally for years to come.

441	In 439 CE, the Romans shifted their forces to North Africa and Sicily to fend off invasions by the Vandals. With Roman forces stretched, in 441 CE, both the Sasanids and the Huns used the opportunity to attack the Eastern Roman Empire's borders.
443	To prevent further annihilation at the hands of the Huns, the Romans agreed to pay off Attila and Bleda double than what they were paying already. The brothers would temporarily return to their homeland with the riches they had extracted from the Romans.
445	Bleda died (perhaps on Attila's orders) leaving Attila as the sole ruler of the Huns.
447	With Roman indemnities unpaid, Attila once again rode into and attacked the Eastern Roman Empire. Meanwhile, a massive earthquake struck Constantinople, severely damaging the Theodosian Walls. Attila's forces were heading to Constantinople but the city's engineers remarkably managed to rebuild the walls before he arrived. When Attila arrived, he could not breach Constantinople and was forced to withdraw.
450	Theodosius II fell from his horse and died, leaving the throne of the Eastern Roman Empire vacant. Meanwhile, a crisis in the west would give Attila cause to invade the Western Roman Empire. As the story goes, Honoria, the rebellious sister of Western Roman Emperor Valentinian III, was betrothed to a man against her wishes. She asked a messenger to send a note to Attila begging to be rescued from her marriage. The note contained a ring, supposedly to prove the message was from her. But Attila mistook this gesture for a wedding proposal. In return, Attila demanded half of the empire as his dowry. Valentinian refused and thus provided Attila with the necessary pretext for an attack.
451	Attila, crossing the Rhine river, turned towards the Western Roman Empire. He completely destroyed a Burgundian kingdom allied with Rome and captured large parts of Gaul.

However, according to legend, Attila turned away from Paris because a devout Christian woman named Genevieve persuaded the city's inhabitants to pray. The Huns' retreat from Paris was seen as a miracle and Genevieve later became Saint Genevieve, the patron saint of Paris.

452   Attila then turned his attention towards, and invaded, northern Italy. In the chaos of the invasion, many inhabitants of the region moved to coastal lagoons looking for a safer place to live, away from the invading barbarians. One of these settlements would eventually form the city of Venice. The imperial court in Ravenna was forced to retreat to Rome, though Attila had set his sights on the city. However, in another apparent miraculous act, Pope Leo I persuaded Attila not to take Rome and withdraw from Italy which Attila agreed to do (perhaps the real reason was that he knew the poor harvest in Italy would not be able to provide the resources he needed to run Rome).

453   **Attila the Hun died**. There are various accounts explaining the cause of his death, though none are reliable. One story is that he fatally choked whilst drunk at his wedding. Another is that his wife killed him. What is known is that, after his death, the Huns descended into chaos and eventual civil war. By 469 CE, the Hunnic empire had vanished. Christianity traditionally viewed Attila as the epitome of evil (the "Scourge of God") but in other cultures - like in modern day Hungary - he is considered a national hero.

455   Exploiting an imperial struggle within the West, the Vandals arrived at the Italian coast and marched on Rome. When they arrived, they sacked Rome and then left around two weeks later taking the city's wealth with them. The word "vandalism" derives from this event. The Western Roman Empire was a pale comparison of its former self. Britain was gone, North Africa was gone, most of Gaul had been split between barbarian factions and Hispania was being attacked by the Goths.

| 455-467 | Skandagupta, a son and general of Kumaragupta, usurped his father's throne by displacing the legitimate crown prince at the time. Only a few years after Attila's death, the Huns clashed with Skandagupta in which he claimed he was victorious over them. When Skandagupta died in around 467 CE, there was a long war of succession that resulted in Budhagupta coming out on top. Budhagupta is considered the last great ruler of the Gupta dynasty before its fall. |

| 472 | The Visigoths took control of the province of Hispania when they occupied Tarragona. |

| 476 | <u>The Fall of Rome</u> |

A group of barbarian soldiers recruited to the Roman army demanded better pay but their demands were refused. So they complained to their captain, the barbarian warlord Odoacer, who decided to lead a rebellion. He marched on Ravenna and exiled Romulus Augustulus, the then-Western Roman Emperor (and who would incidentally go down in history as the last). Odoacer sent a message to Constantinople proclaiming that he ruled Italy and, with that, a new Kingdom of Italy was established. This event is how some historians mark the **fall of the Western Roman Empire**. There were a number of factors that led to this event including corrupt political systems run by incompetent emperors over the years, significant economic downturns, failure in properly handling the migration of the Germanic tribes, attacks by the Huns and other barbarian armies and internal religious disputes.

The Eastern Roman Empire, by contrast, would continue for another millennium. Perhaps its survival, in contrast to the West, was linked to its strong geographical location, its prosperous capital (Constantinople), having fewer enemies to fight (and relative co-existence with the rival Persian Sasanids) and good trade links with India and China. There was no longer a need to draw a distinction anymore between east and west and the eastern part simply continued as the Roman Empire. Besides being predominantly Greek-speaking, the people within the eastern part referred to and identified themselves as Roman. It was not until many centuries later when historians coined them as "**Byzantine**". The population of the Byzantine Empire was estimated to be around 18 million by the turn of the 6th century CE and, at its height, as large as 26 million around 40 years later.

The fall of Rome would create a power vacuum in the West and, what used to be an empire was now a collection of smaller kingdoms - the first so-called **medieval kingdoms** - ruled by different Germanic tribes. By the turn of the 6th century CE, the Ostrogoths under Theodoric the Great (having overthrown and killed Odoacer in 493 CE) ruled Italy and the territories north of it, the Franks and Burgundians ruled parts of Gaul and the Visigoths occupied most of the Iberian peninsula.

Given the extensive reach of the Roman Empire, the Latin spoken in more distant areas differed to those of scholars or politicians. After the empire collapsed, Latin would, over the centuries, evolve into separate languages. These were known as "Romance" languages (that is, the languages derived from the Romans), which were adopted by the locals. The main Romance languages were French, Italian, Spanish and Portuguese. Gradually, literature of these vernacular languages would emerge and take a life of their own. They differed from the Germanic languages, spoken by the tribes in the north of Europe, and Slavonic languages, spoken mainly in central and eastern Europe. Latin, in its original spoken and written form, did still survive, but predominantly among churchmen and scholars.

Speaking of the church, despite the fall of Rome, its people, without a clear ruler, still recognised the Pope in this power vacuum, solidifying the authority of the papacy which would come to characterise the medieval age. During Christianity's early days, Christians were small groups meeting in private, often to evade persecution. However, over the four centuries that followed, things had changed drastically. Christianity had become a powerful hierarchical institution embedded into Roman society underpinned by paid priests, bishops, archbishops and, at its head, the Pope. It had its own legal system, enforced through courts and jails, it governed important issues such as marriage, and people paid taxes to it. Though the Western Roman Empire collapsed, the institution of the church remained firm and, with it, preserved the teachings of Greece and Rome.

496   The Frankish Kingdom made its conversion to Christianity during the reign of Clovis I, credited as the person who united the Frankish tribes and kingdoms into one Frankish entity. Clovis was himself converted (and later baptized) after he married a Burgundian princess in around 496 CE. The transition to Christianity among the Frankish population was gradual as it would take several generations for the people to completely abandon their pagan traditions. Christianization of other Germanic tribes would follow, usually with missionaries seeking first to convert the nobility who would then impose their new faith on the rest of the general population.

497   Budhagupta died. His successors ruled until 570 CE but the Gupta Empire would decline in power. At the beginning of the 6th century CE, a ruler known as Toramana conquered large parts of northwestern India. He may have controlled as much as the Gujarat, Punjab, Kashmir, Rajasthan and Uttar Pradesh. Though Toramana's dynasty's rule in India was short-lived, it was impactful due to its destruction of the Gupta Empire.

525   A monk called Dionysius Exiguus, when tasked by Pope John I to calculate the dates of Easter for the next hundred years, invented the Anno Domini (AD) system of counting time (the same system adopted by us in the West as the Gregorian calendar and being used to write this timeline, albeit using the terminology "CE" (common era) instead of "AD" and "BCE" (before common era) instead of "BC").

Dionysius' calculations placed the birth of Jesus in the year we recognise as 1AD: 1 Anno Domini (Latin for the "year of the Lord"). His method of dating was not adopted at the time. It would not be until the 8th century when Bede the Venerable, an English monk, popularised the Anno Domini system. Even then, it did not become widespread until the 15th or 16th century. The system was eventually formalised by Pope Gregory XIII in 1582. Dionysius' conclusions have since been challenged and the actual birth of Jesus is debated among historians: there is arguably a window of about 4 to 6 years either side of the Year 1 during which Jesus could have been born. Therefore, we must concede the era we adopt today for counting time has no precise historical event as its starting point.

527   **Justinian** succeeded Justin I to become Eastern Roman (or Byzantine) Emperor.

529-   Justinian arranged for a complete recodification of the law.
534   This led to the publication of the *Corpus Juris Civilis* consisting of the Codex - the codification of Roman law - the Digest - a collection of juristic writings, primarily dating back to the 2nd and 3rd centuries - and the Institutes - a student textbook. These works are hugely influential on the civil law system adopted in Europe today.

535-   Justinian's armies embarked on a series of campaigns to
554   recapture Italy from the Ostrogoths. His general, Belisarius, succeeded in recapturing Italy by 540 CE. However, the Romans' new war with the Sasanids stretched their resources, causing them to lose Italy temporarily. But Justinian's new general Narses recaptured and secured Italy in 554 CE.

537   The magnificent Hagia Sophia in Constantinople was built as a cathedral under Justinian. It was the largest cathedral in the world for about a millennium.

541-   A devastating plague struck the Byzantine Empire, including
542   Constantinople, and spread through to Sasanid Persia, parts of

southern Europe and eventually to China. Justinian himself apparently also caught the disease but would eventually recover. The plague (sometimes referred to as the Plague of Justinian) would reoccur over the next two centuries and, in that period, it is estimated to have killed 20 million people and wiped out more than a third of Constantinople's population.

565 Justinian died of a heart attack. He had added more territories to the empire than any emperor before him except Trajan and Augustus. His nephew Justin II became the first emperor to be crowned in the Hagia Sophia.

569 The Lombards, a Germanic tribe from the Scandinavian region, overran Milan. Within a few years, they would have conquered most of the Italian peninsula, a region still recovering from the devastation inflicted during the recent wars between the Byzantines and the Ostrogoths.

570 **Muhammad, the future Prophet of Islam, was born** in Mecca (in what is today Saudi Arabia). He was a member of the Banu Hashim clan, which was part of the Quraysh - a powerful tribe in Mecca - and grew up to be a caravan merchant. In 595 CE, he married his first wife, Khadijah, the wealthy widow of a merchant. After Khadijah's death, Muhammad married a number of women during his lifetime.

589 In or around this time, the Visigoths in Hispania under Reccared I converted to Christianity.

606- King Harsha of Kanauj ruled over north India. In his long reign,
647 he once more established an empire nearly as great as the Guptas. The empire extended from the Punjab to northern Orissa and from the Himalayas to the banks of the Narmada.

610 The Birth of Islam

According to Muslim tradition, Muhammad was said to have received his first revelation from God, via a visit from the Angel

Gabriel (or Jibril), whilst he was praying in a cave near Mecca. It is believed that a series of revelations followed during Muhammad's lifetime, which were first recorded in writing in the middle of the 7th century to form the Qur'an. At the time Muhammad was receiving messages, the area within the Arabian peninsula contained people of multiple faiths: Jews, Christians, followers of local polytheistic religions and idol worshippers. In fact, the Ka'aba, now one of the most important sites in Islam, was at the time a popular pilgrimage site filled with various idols representing different deities. Mecca's economy depended on the business of these pilgrims. However, Muhammad sought to change all this by preaching the oneness of God and denouncing the worshipping of what he claimed to be false idols. Most of the locals opposed Muhammad but the very few that followed his teachings became the **first followers of Islam**.

620   Under Byzantine Emperor Heraclius, the official language of the Byzantine Empire changed from Latin to Greek. Heraclius would reform the empire on a Greek model and adopt Greek culture.

622   The conservative elite of Mecca - threatened by and opposed to Muhammad's teachings of Islam and his denouncing of traditional polytheistic practices which had been popular in the region - forced Muhammad and his companions to flee Mecca and seek refuge in Medina (then called Yathrib), where he gathered forces. This journey (from Mecca to Medina) is known as the Hegira and marks the first year in the Muslim calendar (which is a lunar calendar of 12 months).

624   Hostility continued between Mecca's Quraysh tribe and Muhammad. At the Battle of Badr, the first large-scale military engagement took place between Muhammad's small army of Muslims and a Quraysh army. Against the odds, the Muslims won the battle.

628   Muhammad, intent on fulfilling his visions of entering Mecca to perform pilgrimage, travelled with his 1,400 plus followers to Mecca. However, threatened by the large Muslim presence, the Quraysh were intent on blocking their arrival. Muhammad therefore took refuge in a nearby place called Hudaibiyah. It was here that the Muslims (led by Muhammad) and the Quraysh entered into a peace treaty (the Treaty of Hudaibiyah) pursuant to which an armistice was agreed between the factions: there would be no fighting for 10 years and Muslims would also be allowed to enter Mecca peacefully from the following year onwards. As a result of the treaty, Muhammad's followers increased significantly.

630   After a tribe allied to the Quraysh attacked a Muslim tribe, the Treaty of Hudaibiyah was deemed abrogated and Muhammad's Muslim army marched on and captured Mecca, taking the city from the Quraysh and turning it into the spiritual centre of the Muslim world. One of Muhammad's first acts in the city was to purge the Ka'aba of its idols. Islam now had its base and would go on to spread at impressive speed throughout the Arabian peninsula.

632   **Muhammad died** of a fever at 62 years of age. By this time, more than half of the Arabian peninsula had been converted to Islam. After Muhammad's death, there was disagreement among his followers regarding his successor (or caliph). Some backed Abu Bakr, the father of one of Muhammad's wives, Aisha. But others backed Ali, Muhammad's cousin and son in law (he was married to Muhammad's daughter, Fatima). Those who followed Shia Islam supported Ali and deemed him as true successor (Shia comes from "Shiat Ali" which is Arabic for "followers of Ali"). Sunni Muslims held that it was Abu Bakr. Approximately 90% of Muslims today are Sunni Muslims.

Abu Bakr established his succession and became the first leader of the **Rashidun Caliphate**. Over the next 30 years, Abu Bakr and his successors of the Rashidun Caliphate conquered numerous territories, including the Levant, Egypt, Syria and

Persia, bringing with them their new religion and the new dominant language of that religion: **Arabic** (which eventually displaced Aramaic as the lingua franca of the Middle East). Egypt's capital was moved to Fustat (later to become part of Cairo). The Muslim armies took advantage of the then-vulnerable Byzantine and Sasanid empires by capturing some of their territories. They captured important cities such as Damascus in 634 CE, Jerusalem in 637 CE and Alexandria in 641 CE, all of which had previously belonged to the Byzantines. The Muslim takeover of Persia led to the eventual collapse and subjugation of the Sasanian Empire in 651 CE.

656   The third Rashidun Caliph was assassinated. Ali, Muhammad's son-in-law, and the original rightful successor according to Shia Muslims, was then chosen to succeed.

661   Upon the conclusion of a civil war between rival Muslim factions, the **Umayyad Caliphate** was established, with its capital at Damascus, and succeeded the Rashidun Caliphate. During their reign, they would continue to expand the borders of the Muslim empire.

711-18   A general of the Umayyad Caliphate named Muhammad bin Qasim conquered most of the Sind province (part of modern-day Pakistan). At the same time, towards the west, having already occupied North Africa, the Umayyad Caliphate's armies crossed the straits of Gibraltar and conquered the Visigoths in Hispania, establishing the Iberian Peninsula as a province, with their capital in Córdoba.

720   Around this time, Spanish Christian forces halted the expansion of the Umayyad Caliphate at the Battle of Covadonga. Their victory tends to be marked as the beginning of a centuries-long process called the "Reconquista" where Spanish Christians constantly warred against the Muslims with the goal of driving them out of Spain.

732   In the Battles of Tours, Charles Martel (known as "The Hammer"), the grandfather of the famous Charlemagne, led his Frankish soldiers against the armies of the Umayyad Caliphate in an attempt to halt their advance into Western Europe. The Muslim army was defeated and was forced to retreat to the Pyrenees and back into Hispania.

750   The Abbasids, descendants of Muhammad's uncle Abbas, located in the east of the Muslim empire, overthrew the Umayyad rulers and established the **Abbasid Caliphate**.

751   Ravenna, the last imperial stronghold of the Byzantines in northern Italy, fell to the Lombards, who now threatened to take over all of Italy. Due to East and West being divided on religious matters, the Pope did not appeal to the Byzantine Emperor for assistance against the Lombards. The Byzantines were themselves too preoccupied fighting off Muslim invasions. Instead, the Pope visited those who had forged the strongest state in the West: the Franks. To win them over, he gave the Frankish ruler Pepin (son of Charles Martel) the title of patrician and anointed him King of the Franks. He then invited Frankish troops into Italy to defend Rome against the Lombards as long as Pepin would promise to return all conquered lands to the Pope. Pepin would fulfil his promise, subdue the Lombards and grant territories to the Pope, bringing into existence the Papal States (the remnants of which still exist today, albeit in a shrunken form, as Vatican City).

756   Abd al-Rahman I, a prince of the Umayyad royal family, had been living as a fugitive in the Iberian Peninsula for six years after the Umayyads were overthrown in 750 CE by the Abbasids. Intent on regaining a position of power, he defeated the existing Muslim rulers of the area who had defied Umayyad rule and united various local fiefdoms into the Emirate of Córdoba (otherwise called Al-Andalus).

762   **The Abbasid Caliphate founded the city of Baghdad**, the new capital of the Muslim world and centre of culture and learning.

The construction of Baghdad ushered in the so-called **Islamic Golden Age**. Arabic would become the language of culture, trade and religion (though Persian retained its status as an important literary language). There were significant developments in medicine, literature, mathematics, chemistry, geography, astronomy and philosophy. For example, the Persian mathematician Al-Khwarizmi is credited as the father of algebra. Muslim mathematicians also made major developments in trigonometry and geometry. Documents written in Sanskrit, Chinese, Persian and Greek - including the works of Plato and Aristotle - were collected and translated into Arabic in order for the Muslims to ascertain knowledge of other cultures and further their own.

768   After Pepin died, his son **Charlemagne** (or Charles the Great) became **King of the Franks**. Soon, Charlemagne would unite most of Western Europe and establish the first Western European empire since Rome: the Carolingian Empire. His empire would stretch from the borders of Spain all the way to France, the Low Countries, Germany and central Italy (the latter of which was captured from the Lombards in 774 CE and Charlemagne subsequently claimed the title "King of the Lombards").

788-   The great Hindu philosopher Shankara lived during this time in
820   India. He renewed and systematised Vedanta philosophy and drew upon the philosophical teachings of the Upanishads.

797   The Byzantine Emperor Constantine VI was removed from his throne by his mother Irene who declared herself Empress. Constantine was apparently blinded so brutally by Irene that he died from his wounds.

800   In 799 CE in Rome, Pope Leo III was beaten up by a mob hired by noblemen who violently opposed him. Smuggled out of the city by some acquaintances, the Pope found that his enemies had accused him of various crimes. Leo appealed to Charlemagne who agreed to visit Rome and testify on his

behalf. As a result, he was then cleared of these charges. Then, when Charlemagne attended Christmas Mass, the Pope ceremoniously placed the imperial crown on his head, proclaiming Charlemagne **Emperor of the Romans**. The Latin church in Rome had refused to recognise the legitimacy of Irene's recent takeover in the East as she was a woman hence, to them, the imperial throne was vacant. The Pope's actions nonetheless caused outrage in Constantinople.

Charlemagne, meanwhile, had effectively struck a deal between himself and the Pope: the king would protect and defend the Pope from his enemies and support the spread of Christianity. The Pope would lend his spiritual power to the king and anoint him emperor of the Romans to show that he was a special servant to God. The relationship between church and king, often turbulent, would play a key role in the struggle for dominance throughout the European medieval ages.

843   Pursuant to the Treaty of Verdun, the Frankish Empire was divided into three territories handed down to each of Charlemagne's three surviving grandsons: Germanic-speaking East Francia (from which the Holy Roman Empire, and eventually Germany, would arise) Middle Francia (consisting of Alsace, Lorraine, Burgundy, the Low Countries and the northern half of Italy) and West Francia (which was essentially modern France). By the 10th century, autonomous stem duchies (Franconia, Bavaria, Swabia, Saxony, and Lorraine) re-emerged in East Francia. Stem duchies were mini kingdoms corresponding to old tribal settlements.

862   According to tradition, around this time, a Viking tribe chieftain named Rurik established a capital at Novgorod (in modern Russia) and his people would call themselves the **Rus**. In 860 CE, the Rus had launched a surprise raid on Constantinople. In 882 CE, the successor to Rurik, Prince Oleg, captured Kiev and established the Kievan Rus.

Slavery played a key role in the economy of the Vikings, including the Viking Rus. Such was the extent of slavery in the land of the Rus that the name of the local people they enslaved - the Slavs - is the origin for the English word "slave". The trading of Slavs was an immensely profitable business throughout the medieval ages. They were kept in Scandinavia, though huge numbers of slaves were trafficked and were prevalent in other places, including the Muslim empire. Of course, the concept of slavery was nothing new: it formed the backbone of ancient Roman, Egyptian, Greek and Babylonian societies among others.

909   The Fatimids, a rival Shia caliphate claiming to be descendants of Fatima, Muhammad's daughter, conquered Raqqada (now in Tunisia) and would establish a state controlling the region of North Africa, independent of the mainstream Sunni states set up in Baghdad and Córdoba.

962   Otto I, the King of East Francia, was crowned Emperor of the Romans by Pope John XII, therefore intertwining the affairs of the individual German-speaking states with those of Italy and the Papacy. After this, whoever became king of this region would effectively become Emperor of the Romans upon being crowned by the Pope.

Later, the title **"Holy Roman Emperor"** would be adopted to reflect this position and East Francia would be referred to as the Holy Roman Empire, which was a loose collection of principalities predominantly covering the area we recognise today as modern Germany as well as other surrounding territories. Unlike West Francia – which would eventually become a unified France – the Holy Roman Empire was not, and would never be, one political unified entity. Its power was more symbolic, though, and it would become very influential in the affairs of Europe. The Holy Roman Emperor would be chosen by a group consisting of archbishops and dukes (called Electors), though it was nearly always a German prince that would be chosen for the title.

969   The Fatimid Caliphate, taking advantage of an economic downturn and famine caused mainly by low Nile floods, conquered Egypt's capital Fustat. It then established **Cairo** as its new capital.

987   Hugh Capet founded the Capetian dynasty after he succeeded the last Carolingian King of West Francia, Louis V, who died childless (thus ending the Carolingian dynasty).

988   Seeking closer ties to the Byzantine Empire, Prince Vladimir the Great of the Kievan Rus adopted, and converted his land to, Christianity. He is venerated today as having brought Eastern Orthodox Christianity to Ukraine and Russia. The conversion led to Byzantine culture and fashion entering the society of the Rus.

1000   Around this time, and around 500 years before Christopher Columbus, Viking explorer Leif Eriksson and his crew were said to have reached and settled in North America (in what is now Newfoundland in Canada). Leif named the site Vinland, due to the grapes or berries growing there. Viking settlement in North America was only short-lived, however.

1002   The Duchy of Bohemia (the predecessor of modern Czechia) was incorporated into the Holy Roman Empire.

1032   The Kingdom of Burgundy was incorporated into the Holy Roman Empire.

1044   The earliest known written formula for gunpowder (sulphur, charcoal and potassium nitrate (or saltpeter)) was published in China.

1054   Amidst rising tension between the Pope in Rome and the Patriarch of Constantinople, the two excommunicated one another, rupturing ties between the churches. This came to be called the **Great Schism**, the result of a power struggle between two powerful Christian institutions. The Byzantines had long considered themselves to be the universal leaders of the church. However, the West rejected that claim and, to them, the supreme spiritual authority was the Pope. As a result of the Great Schism, Christianity would split into what are recognised today as two of the largest denominations: Roman Catholicism and Eastern Orthodoxy.

1055   Tughril Beg of the Seljuk Turks, a group of Turkic people who originated from central Asia (mainly modern Kazakhstan), overran Baghdad and ruled as protector of the Abbasid dynasty. The Seljuks had already been growing in power during the early part of the 11th century CE having conquered mainland Persia.

1071   At the **Battle of Manzikert**, a powerful army of Seljuk Turks heavily defeated a large Byzantine army, resulting in Byzantine Emperor Romanos IV being taken prisoner. The defeat played an important role in undermining Byzantine authority in Anatolia and Armenia, which the Seljuk Turks exploited.

1073   Pope Gregory VII, intent on reforming the church, began what was called the **Investiture Crisis**. The crisis was a conflict between church and state over the ability to install high church officials (bishops and abbots) through ceremonial appointment known as investiture. The secular king or nobles would choose the offices of the church, often given to family members. This meant they kept control over, and influenced, church affairs.

The investiture conflict would be a long drawn out struggle for power that would rage on throughout the 11th and 12th centuries putting the church against the state. Pope Gregory VII vowed to put an end to what he saw as corrupt practices in the church. However, Henry IV - the Holy Roman Emperor at the time - objected to church reform. After Henry IV was excommunicated (that is, expelled from church practice), he begged the Pope for forgiveness and eventually a compromise was reached. The discord between the institutions of church and state, however, would continue over the years, at times culminating in violence.

1095-
1099

The First Crusade

Pope Urban II received a letter from Byzantine Emperor Alexius I Comnenus asking for mercenaries to aid him in his fight against the Seljuk Turks. Urban offered his help, perhaps in an attempt to heal the wounds of the schism of 1054, or possibly seeing an opportunity to further extend the influence of the papacy. He called a council of the church to meet at Clermont: in a speech, he pleaded Western Christendom to stop killing one another and take up arms to defend their eastern allies (the Byzantines). While Alexius wanted mercenaries to defend his capital, Urban would go a step further and send whole armies to invade and capture Jerusalem. The term "Crusade" is slightly misleading because it implies the single movement under the control of one individual. Instead, the campaign consisted of multiple armies setting off at different times slowly making their way to Constantinople where they planned to assemble.

One such army that travelled to Constantinople was ruled by a fanatical preacher called Peter the Hermit who was unable to discipline his followers. Riots broke out along the journey that resulted in Belgrade and various German cities being pillaged and Jews falling victim to targeted attacks. When they reached Constantinople, the armies looted the suburbs. Alexius, keen to maintain order, shipped the troops across the Bosporus and warned Peter not to engage the Turks until more troops would arrive. But Peter ignored the advice and carried on anyway only to be defeated heavily by the Turks.

In the next few months, almost a hundred thousand soldiers would pass through Constantinople led by ambitious nobles keen to use the Crusade as an opportunity to carve out territories as kingdoms for themselves. When groups arrived at Constantinople, they were heavily policed and required to pitch tents in small groups outside the city. Alexius would meet the noble leaders within the city and require them to swear a religious oath: any territories they conquer which had in the first place belonged to the Roman Empire would be returned to the Byzantines.

In 1096, the Crusade properly began, with the majority of the Crusaders hailing from Normandy, France and Flanders. Among them were Hugh of Vermandois, brother of Frankish king Philip I, and Robert of Normandy, son of famous former English king William the Conqueror. In 1097, the Crusaders captured Nicaea and, true to their oath to the emperor, returned it to the Byzantines. In 1098, the Crusaders captured Antioch and Edessa. This time, in breach of their oath, they kept Antioch and Edessa as independent Crusader territories. In 1099, the Crusaders besieged and captured Jerusalem, brutally massacring the inhabitants and sparing no-one. They established their own Kingdom of Jerusalem, ending centuries of Muslim occupation of the city.

1109   The Crusaders established the Country of Tripoli. The new lands conquered by the Crusaders were collectively referred to as Outremer (which literally translates as "overseas").

1119   The Knights Templar was founded to protect the road to Jerusalem for Christian pilgrims.

1139   Portugal entered its first stage of independence when Afonso Henriques was acclaimed King of the Portuguese.

1147-49   The **Second Crusade** began in response to the fall of Edessa in 1144. The Muslim army won and the Crusaders lost Edessa.

1155   Frederick Barbarossa, the great warrior German King, was crowned Holy Roman Emperor.

1162   Around this time, the East Asian steppe was home to scattered Mongol and Turkic pastoral nomadic groups. Among them, the warlord **Timogen** (soon to be called **Genghis Khan**) was born to a Mongol clan.

1171   Military commander Saladin overthrew the Fatimid Caliphate in Egypt, restoring allegiance to the Sunni Abbasid Caliphate and establishing the Ayyubid Sultanate. In 1174, he captured Damascus.

1187   At the Battle of Hattin, Saladin's armies outfought the Crusaders and captured Jerusalem. Pope Urban III was believed to have died of shock upon hearing the news of the defeat. The new Pope, Gregory VIII, immediately preached a new Crusade, warning of the rising power of the Muslims.

1189-   The **Third Crusade** began. At least three kings, Holy Roman
1190   Emperor Frederick Barbarossa, Philip Augustus (or Philip II) – the first French king to call himself the King of France – and Richard I (or Richard the "Lionheart") of England immediately declared themselves ready and willing to fight. Barbarossa, though, died from drowning in 1190 mid-campaign.

1191-   Acre (now in modern Israel) was recaptured by the Crusaders
1192   with the help of Richard I of England. In the Battle of Arsuf, Jaffa (also located in modern Israel) was captured too. The Third Crusade ended with the Treaty of Jaffa, concluded by Richard and Saladin, where Jerusalem remained under Muslim control but permitted Christian pilgrims safe passage to visit the city.

1200   Around this time, the population of Europe had grown to about 60 million. London had a population of 30,000, Paris had 80,000 and certain German towns, like Cologne, were growing to over 30,000. Independent Italian city-states, the eventual birth places of the so-called Renaissance, were on the rise with their own growing populations. By this time, Venice was now a well-established Republic (ruled by a leader known as the Doge) with a prospering economy. The city traded with the Byzantines and were known for their glassmaking and shipbuilding skills. Other notable Italian city-states included Milan, Florence and Genoa (the latter beneficially close to the sea like Venice). The success of these states were arguably attributed to the fact that they were separate, not unified. This meant they were each keen to outdo the other with their own individuality and specialties in art and culture. At times, they would even go to war with one another.

In Northern Europe, the cities of Amsterdam, Bruges and Antwerp were prospering, eventually proving to be key marketplaces for goods bought from and sold to other European states. These cities would become important trading posts for the **Hanseatic League**, a commercial and defensive confederation of merchant guilds and market towns in north western and central Europe.

Meanwhile, the **Incas**, one of the last of the great Andean civilisations, were settling in the Cusco region of South America. Cusco, meaning "navel of the world" in Quechua, would go on to become the capital of the **Inca Empire** (and Quechua is still spoken today by over 6 million people across several South American countries). According to legend, the Inca civilisation was founded when Inti, god of the sun, took pity on the primitiveness of mankind and arranged for his son, Manco Cápac, and daughter, Mama Ocllo to emerge from Lake Titicaca and civilise the people.

The Incas made astronomical observations, determining the solstices and equinoxes, dates on which they celebrated important ceremonies. They had no written language but a system of knots to communicate and count. Popular deities included Inti (explained above), Pachamama, goddess of the earth, and Mama Quilla, goddess of the moon.

1202-
1204

Pope Innocent III, eager to restore Christian dominance in the Middle East, called for a new Crusade (which would become the infamously disastrous **Fourth Crusade** or **Sack of Constantinople**). It was agreed by the Crusaders that Egypt, considered a weak spot but an overall richer prize than Jerusalem, would be a better target for attacking the Muslims. This plan was dictated by Venice which, by hiring its transport to the Crusaders, would itself have much to gain economically from an Egyptian campaign.

Thus, in exchange for large sums of money, the Crusaders contracted with Venice to build a huge fleet to transport thousands of soldiers to Cairo. However, fewer Crusaders arrived in Venice than anticipated meaning the city would not have enough money to cover its shipbuilding costs. The Doge, Enrico Dandolo, effectively held the Crusaders to ransom, persuading them to capture the Hungarian city of Zara on behalf of Venice in order to repay the money owed for the ships. Zara was a Christian city and so Pope Innocent III forbade the invasion. Even some of the Crusaders were not comfortable with doing this. The Doge, however, ignored the Pope, along with the majority of the Crusaders, and nevertheless Zara was besieged, successfully stormed and eventually fell to Venetian rule. When the Pope heard about this, the Venetians and Crusaders were excommunicated.

Then, in 1203, the Crusaders were seemingly convinced by a usurper of the Byzantine Empire, Alexius Angelus, to capture Constantinople and restore him and his father Isaac II to power. The Crusaders sailed to Constantinople, sacked the city and Isaac II and his son were subsequently restored to the throne as planned. However, the victory was short-lived as a riot then broke out in the city and a mob deposed Isaac and Alexius. They were eventually captured and killed. The usurper this time, Alexius V, was crowned the new emperor. In 1204, the Crusaders, perhaps in desperate need of resource to continue their campaign, launched an all-out attack on Constantinople. They breached and burned the city, capturing it and slaughtering its inhabitants. It was stripped of its riches, which were shipped back to western churches.

The Crusaders would never reach Jerusalem. Instead they built a Latin Empire amidst the ruins of Constantinople. Alexius V was eventually captured and executed. 57 years later, the Byzantines would recapture the city and put an end to the Latin Empire. Nevertheless, the sacks of Constantinople would mark the beginning of a decline for the Byzantine Empire over the next two centuries. Latin and Ottoman pressure, coupled with internal disintegration, would prove decisive for the eventual end of Byzantine rule.

Over the next century, there would be several more official crusades (which ended in 1291) and, over centuries to follow, many more unofficial crusades.

1206   Timogen, having risen to power through a combination of intimidation and forging political alliances with various Mongol rulers, united the Mongols and was declared the Great Khan: leader of all the Mongols. Under Timogen (now Genghis Khan), the Mongols overran northern China and the eastern Islamic lands. By 1220, his armies had conquered notable cities such as Samarkand and Bukhara (both now located in modern Uzbekistan).

1223   At this time, the Kievan Rus had disintegrated due to infighting amongst the various princes. The disunited southern princes faced a Mongol raiding group at the Kalka River and were easily defeated.

1227   **Genghis Khan died,** perhaps from illness attributed to a battle injury. Before his death, he had named his third son Ögedei to be his successor. By this time, Genghis Khan's empire stretched from Mongolia all the way to the Caspian Sea. The Mongols are infamous in history for their extreme brutality and the slaughter of millions of people caused by their ruthless pursuit for dominance. On the other hand, the **Mongol Empire** generally tolerated diversity of culture and religion under its rule and introduced a free-flowing and efficient system of trade and communication across Eurasia, which gave way to the spreading of different customs, ideas and cuisines throughout the continent.

1229-
1236
Iltutmish, ruler of territory in northern India with its capital in Delhi, was consecrated as Sultan of Delhi by a representative of the Abbasid Caliphate of Baghdad. He effectively founded the Delhi Sultanate.

1237-
42
A Mongol army, led by Batu Khan — a grandson of Genghis Khan — conquered the territories of the Kievan Rus. They invaded and destroyed most Russian cities including Vladimir, Rostov and Kiev. The city of Novgorod was spared because it submitted to Mongol rule. Parts of Eastern Europe, including Hungary and Bulgaria, were also invaded but further attacks were halted upon the news of Ögedei's death which required Batu and most of his army to return home to partake in the election of the next Mongol leader.

1258
Under the authority of Möngke Khan, the leader of the Mongol Empire and another of Genghis Khan's grandsons, the Mongols besieged and eventually captured Baghdad, wreaking havoc on the city. The subjugation of Baghdad would lead to the collapse of the Abbasid Caliphate. But in 1261, a member of the Abbasid dynasty was installed as the Caliph in Cairo under the rule of the Mamluks.

1261
The Byzantines recaptured Constantinople, restoring their rule over the city and ending the Latin Empire.

1271
Marco Polo from Venice set sail for east Asia with his father and uncle. In 1275, after years of trekking through places like Persia and Samarkand, he eventually reached China where the court of the Mongol leader, Kublai Khan - another grandson of Genghis Khan - resided. Under Khan's command, Polo served as an envoy, fulfilling diplomatic missions on behalf of the empire.

1273
Rudolf Habsburg, the Count of Habsburg, was elected King of

the Germans. Up to this point, the **Habsburg House**, though powerful, was a relatively minor dynasty on the world stage. It took its name from Habsburg Castle, a fortress built in the 1020s in present-day Switzerland.

1278   At the Battle of Marchfield, Rudolf of Habsburg, the newly-elected German king, defeated King Ottokar II of Bohemia and, in the aftermath, secured the Duchy of Austria as a possession. Vienna in Austria would be the headquarters of the Habsburg monarchy right up to the end of the First World War in the 20th century.

1283   A man called Daniil Aleksandrovich founded the **Principality of Moscow**, a puppet state of the Mongol Empire.

1291   Acre, the last remaining Crusader state, fell to the Mamluk Muslims, **ending the Crusades officially**.

1294   Kublai Khan died. By this time, the Mongol Empire covered such a vast area of land (stretching from the Pacific to the Black Sea) that it had effectively divided into four separate sub-empires (or Khanates): the **Golden Horde** in the northwest (to which the principalities of the Kievan Rus paid tribute), the **Chagatai** in central Asia, the **Ilkhanate** in the southwest and the **Yuan** dynasty in the far east (with its capital built on the site of the old city of Zhongdu, where modern Beijing is).

1295   Marco Polo returned to Venice. In around 1296, whilst Venice was warring with Genoa, he was captured and imprisoned by the Genoese. During his time in prison, he began writing *The Travels of Marco Polo* accounting his journeys through Asia. The book was published in 1300.

1296   The great ruler Alauddin became the Sultan of Delhi. During his reign, he repelled numerous invasion attempts by the Mongols. Modeling himself on Alexander the Great (or "Sikander" as he was called in India), he also embarked on several conquests and extended his empire in northern India (including conquering Gujarat in 1298) as well as some of the southern parts of India.

1299   The **Ottoman** dynasty was founded by **Osman I**. Very little is known about his origins and early life. Apparently, his father's tribe, escaping the threat of the Mongols, moved away from central Asia and into Anatolia. He forged an alliance with the Seljuk Turks and was granted control over Söğüt, a town close to the Byzantine border. Upon his father's death, Osman succeeded him as chief (or "Bey") and began conducting raids on nearby territories, expanding the reach of the Ottomans. Osman and his successors would particularly target the territories of a weakening Byzantine Empire.

1300   Historians differ on this topic but the beginning of the period known popularly as the **Renaissance** can be traced to around the 14th century and spanned over several centuries. "Renaissance" means "revival" or "renewal" and harkens back to what was seen as the bright light of classical antiquity. The Italian city-states, like Florence and Venice, were the real heartland of the Renaissance. In these prosperous cities, artists, composers, writers and scholars thrived alongside the commerce that paid for their work. Urban merchants and manufacturers brought in products and ideas from around Africa and Eurasia. Some families, like the very powerful Medici in Florence, achieved immense wealth from banking and investing and used their riches to support Renaissance thinkers and artists in a system called patronage.

1302-   Pope Boniface VIII feuded with Philip IV of France. The Pope,
1309   wanting the church to be independent from the state, protested against the trial of churchmen before Philip's royal courts and the continued use of church funds for state purposes. He issued the Unum sanctam bull, which declared that the Pope had supreme power over everyone, and threatened to excommunicate Philip. Boniface was soon kidnapped and tortured by Philip's men and died shortly after his release. Philip then arranged for the election of a French Pope, Clement

V, and his installation at Avignon (within the French border). The Avignon Papacy lasted until 1378 and, during its existence, developed a reputation for corruption that estranged major parts of western Christendom.

1311   In the English town of Lincoln, construction of **Lincoln Cathedral** was completed. At the time, at 160 metres (or 520 feet), it overtook the Great Pyramid of Giza as the tallest building in the world and held that title until 1549 when its spire collapsed.

1312   The famous West African king, **Mansa Musa I** of the Mali Empire, came to power. He is considered by some to be the richest person that has ever lived, amassing immense wealth through exploiting his kingdom's natural resources of gold and salt. By subjugating cities such as **Timbuktu** - which became a major centre for learning, culture and commerce - he gained control over key trade routes linking the Mediterranean and the West African coast.

1324   Mansa Musa I, a devout Muslim, travelled to Mecca on pilgrimage, accompanied by a huge entourage. Apparently, when he stopped in Cairo, he spent and gave away such a massive amount of gold that it triggered mass inflation, causing the economy in the region to suffer temporarily. When he returned from Mecca, he began to revitalise the cities in his empire. Meanwhile, tales of his vast wealth had spread to Europe.

1328   Charles IV of France, the last surviving son of Philip IV (whose other sons, Louis X and Philip V, had been king previously), died without a male heir, ending the Capetian dynasty. He was succeeded by his cousin Philip of Valois to become Philip VI, the first King of France from the House of Valois. Isabella, the sister of Charles IV, Louis X and Philip V, had previously been married to King Edward II of England whose son, Edward III, claimed he had a right to the French throne. A long war (to last more than a century) would soon break out between England and France.

1336   In the 1330s, the Ilkhanate, with its heavily urbanised population in Persia and the Middle East, was severely ravaged by a great plague (later to be referred to as the Black Death). The Ilkhan and his sons were killed by it. What followed was a rapid disintegration of the Ilkhanate into many small minor kingdoms. In around 1336, in the southwest corner of the Chagatai Khanate, in Transoxiana, **Timur** was born. From a Turko-Mongol background, Timur would later be referred to as **Tamerlane** because, according to legend, he was left permanently injured when shot as a young boy (hence "Timur the Lame" or "Tamerlane").

1337   The **Hundred Years' War** began, lasting until 1453. It consisted of a series of battles fought between the kingdoms of England and France, the two nations wrestling for the right to rule France.

1347   <u>The Black Death</u>

In October, a Genoese trading ship landed at the busy port of Messina in Sicily and docked near other ships. This ship in particular contained rats carrying fleas which in turn carried certain bacteria (which scientists today call Yersinia pestis) that proved to be deadly when transmitted to humans. There were two main forms of plague infection, the cause of which depended on the route of entry: bubonic and pneumonic. The bubonic plague was most common and was caused by the bite of the flea (where the flea would excrete bacteria into the bloodstream). The bacteria would then travel through the lymphatic system to the nearest lymph node, such as in the armpit or groin, where it reproduced, causing the lymph node to swell (giving the term 'bubo'). Other organs would then be infected, causing internal bleeding. Those who caught the bubonic plague were more likely than not to die from it. The pneumonic plague would infect the lungs. Any person with pneumonic plague could transmit the disease via airborne droplets to other humans. Almost everyone who caught the pneumonic plague died from it.

The plague most likely originated in Asia across which it travelled along the Silk Roads. In 1346, it was already sweeping through the Golden Horde by the Black Sea. After reaching Constantinople and the Italian ports in 1347, it then spread rapidly northwards to France and then eventually to Britain. The Middle East and Egypt were also devastated by the plague.

Between 1347 and 1352, the Black Death caused between 20 and 30 million deaths in Europe alone, wiping out over a third of its population. The population of Constantinople shrank to less than 100,000 at one point. People at the time were oblivious to the true cause of the plague. To some, it would have felt like the impending apocalypse. Many also spread rumours that the Jews were behind the outbreak and they were targeted for persecution.

1356   A decree, known as a "golden bull", was promulgated by the then-Holy Roman Emperor Charles IV, a German king. Its purpose was to formalise the election process of the Holy Roman Emperor, place the election of the ruler under the control of the seven Electors and to ensure that the candidate elected by the majority should succeed without dispute. Out of the Electors, three were archbishops and four were secular princes, each from the prominent German states of Bohemia, Saxony, Brandenburg and the Palatinate respectively.

1370   Timur gained effective control of much of the western Chagatai Khanate, establishing the Timurid Empire with Samarkand as its capital. He then married a descendant of Genghis Khan. Over the next thirty years, Timur embarked on a remarkable campaign of military conquests. His military successes saw him conquer land that spans the modern day countries of Iraq (including Baghdad), Iran (including Isfahan), Afghanistan, Pakistan, Azerbaijan, Georgia, Uzbekistan, Turkmenistan,

Tajikistan, Kyrgyzstan, large parts of Turkey and Syria, and the northwestern portion of India (including Delhi). Like the Mongol Empire, the Timurid Empire was notorious for its brutality. It is estimated that Timur's armies killed around 17 million people, which was about 5% of the global population at the time.

1378   When Pope Gregory XI died, the College of Cardinals, pressured by loyal Romans, elected an Italian Pope: Urban VI. The French responded by electing Pope Clement VII in Avignon. This created a schism (known as the Western Schism) causing disunity in the church which, combined with stories of unspiritual indulgences, served to undermine its authority. In 1417, however, a council was called to end the Western Schism resulting in the election by church leaders of a single Pope: Martin V.

1380   The Grand Prince of Moscow, Dmitri Donskoi, defeated the Golden Horde Mongols at the Battle of Kulikovo. Over the next century or so, the grand princes of Moscow continued to consolidate Russian land to expand their territory and increase their power.

1381-   The great Bengali poet Krittibas lived during this time. He was
1461   commissioned by the Bengali Sultanate to translate the epic *Ramayana* into Bengali. The Sultanates of Bengal, together with the Sultanates of other regions, made similarly important contributions to promote the development of regional languages in India.

1398   The Sultanate of Delhi, already on the decline at this point, was finally shattered when the armies of the Timurid Empire swooped down and sacked Delhi. Timur infamously had around 200,000 people killed and took the spoils of Delhi. For 15 years after the raid, Delhi virtually ceased to exist and most of its Hindu population had been exterminated. Gujarat, Malwar and Jaunpur would emerge as Sultanates in their own right. In the west, Lahore, Multan and Sindh would remain under the control of Timur's descendants.

1405   Timur died and his empire would soon collapse with him as his heirs squabbled over control.

1415   The English army under King Henry V defeated the French at the Battle of Agincourt.

1428   English forces had besieged Orleans, one of the last key French strongholds which, if captured, would have meant almost certain victory for the English over the French. A young peasant girl, **Joan of Arc**, allegedly had visions of saints instructing her to lead a French army to victory. She followed through with these revelations and successfully reclaimed Orleans for the French, further repelling the English armies. The tide of the Hundred Years' War had been turned in France's favour.

1429   Charles VII was crowned King of France. The following year, however, the Burgundians captured Joan of Arc and handed her to their English allies. After being found guilty for heresy, she was burned at the stake.

1438   The reign of **Pachacuti** (or Pachacutec) of the Incas began. He was responsible for the initial expansion of Incan territory beyond Cusco. Together with his son, Tupac Yupanqui, he controlled a vast Incan Empire. It is believed that, during Pachacuti's reign, perhaps around 1450, **Machu Picchu** was built in the mountains, 2,430 metres (or 7,970 feet) above sea level. When the Spanish eventually arrived in this part of the world in the following century, such was the secrecy of Machu Picchu that they would never discover it. Its secret would only be revealed to the rest of the world when American explorer Hiram Bingham was led to it in 1911.

1451   A new Sultan, **Mehmet II**, inherited the Ottoman throne at 19 years old. Soon to be known as Mehmet the Conqueror, he would expand Ottoman control in the Balkans. Determined to secure his legacy, he set his sights on capturing Constantinople from the Byzantines.

1452   The Byzantine Emperor Constantine XI received a visit from a young Hungarian named Orban, a specialist in the construction of large cannons. However, Constantine could not afford his high salary nor did he possess the materials necessary for constructing such a large siege cannon. Orban soon left Constantinople to work for Mehmet II, who could afford his services, and design cannons for the Ottomans to destroy city walls.

1452   One of the most renowned figures of the Renaissance, **Leonardo**, was born in **Vinci** in northern Italy (within the territory ruled by the powerful Medici family).

1452   Frederick III from the House of Habsburg was elected Holy Roman Emperor. He was the first member of the Habsburg family to be given the title. This began three centuries of Holy Roman Emperors from this royal family, which would go on to become one of the great ruling dynasties of Europe.

1453   <u>The Fall of Constantinople</u>

On 23 March, Mehmet II and his armies marched to Constantinople. When they arrived at the city's gates, Mehmet demanded immediate surrender. Receiving no reply, he began to attack on 6 April. By 29 May, **Constantinople had fallen to the Ottomans. The Byzantine Empire**, and therefore the eastern part of the Roman Empire, **had finally ended**. Constantine XI's body was never found, though some claim he was beheaded. Up to this point, Constantinople, with its strategic location and seemingly impregnable Theodosian Walls, had survived numerous sieges and attacks over the centuries. But the city walls were no match for the Ottoman cannons.

Once the capital of the Christian world, Constantinople was

now under the hegemony of Muslim rulers. The famous Hagia Sophia, like other churches, was converted into a mosque. Byzantine scholars became refugees and migrated to Western Europe, particularly the prosperous Italian republics, where they brought with them the culture of Greek and Roman civilisation (including vast amounts of literature) that had been preserved under their auspices for all that time. This migration, and the safeguarding of Greek and Latin manuscripts and works, arguably gave the key impetus for the transition from the "dark ages" to the Renaissance (or at least accelerated it).

Despite Muslim domination during the centuries of Ottoman rule, the Greek Orthodox Church still served a very important function in being responsible for the Christian populations. The Patriarch of Constantinople was directly answerable for them to the Sultan.

The fall of Constantinople secured the Ottoman Empire's foothold in the eastern Mediterranean. They already controlled much of south eastern Europe and had established a navy that would patrol the Black Sea, Adriatic Sea and other seas in the region. For other European nations, Ottoman domination meant that land routes to Asia and certain sea routes had become difficult and dangerous. Europe needed to find alternative paths to the Afro-Eurasian trade. This sparked new voyages, particularly from the Iberian Peninsula, and would usher in an **Age of Discovery** - but also untold destruction - of new worlds by Europeans.

1453   The Battle of Castillon effectively **ended the Hundred Years' War** between the English and French, leaving France victorious and England left with only Calais as a territory.

1453   **Johannes Gutenberg** and Johann Fust printed the Bible using Gutenberg's recently-invented **printing press**. In 1454, the first copy of the so-called Gutenberg Bible was displayed at the Frankfurt trade fair. Although printing techniques, including movable type, had been used in China for many centuries, printing in Europe could be carried out more quickly because the Latin alphabet only contained 26 characters.

Before Gutenberg's printing press, most books were copied by professional scribes from other books by hand. As well as being time consuming, expensive and prone to errors, it also meant that books were not easily accessible and so were not a part of most people's lives. That all changed with the printing press. By the 1480s, Venice had become the printing capital of the world: there would be 417 printing presses in the city within 30 years. In the first 50 years since the printing press came to Europe, over 20 million volumes of books were printed. Books could now be available to more people more quickly and ideas could spread more easily. It was a revolution in media.

1458   Mehmet II captured Athens. Most of mainland Greece and the Aegean islands would be under Ottoman control by the end of the 15ᵗʰ century. Cyprus and Crete would remain under the control of Venice until 1571 and 1670 respectively when they too would fall to the Ottomans.

1460   This year marked the death of Infante Dom Henrique. Better known as Prince Henry the Navigator, he was a son of John I (formerly King of Portugal) and Queen Philippa (whose brother was King Henry IV of England). During his lifetime, Dom Henrique (though neither a sailor nor navigator himself) sponsored and encouraged exploration, the study of navigation and the development of new tools to aid that navigation. Indeed, intent on increasing their trading power and attracted by the potential of big gold findings, the Portuguese were sailing southwards, establishing commercial networks on the east coast of Africa. Trading posts were set up in places like Arguin - off the west coast of present-day Mauritania - and São Jorge da Mina - in present-day Elmina in Ghana - such places forming part of the 'Gold Coast' as it became nicknamed.

As the global market began to open up, however, so did the slave trade. It would not be long before these trading posts would be used to ship slaves in large numbers to Europe. It became commonplace for Portuguese explorers to mercilessly raid African villages in newly-discovered lands and force the inhabitants back as captives to be traded for slave labour. Soon, the wealthy plantations in Portugal were filled with African slaves. Dom Henrique's legacy was not only the dawn of the Age of Discovery but also the rise of the African slave trade.

1469 **King Ferdinand II** of the Kingdom **of Aragon** married **Queen Isabella I** of the Kingdom **of Castile**, uniting the leading Christian kingdoms in the Iberian Peninsula. They would be referred to as the Catholic Monarchs. By the mid-13th century, the Emirate of Granada had become the last remaining portion of the peninsula that was Muslim-ruled. All other territories had been reclaimed at some point by Christian forces as part of the Reconquista. By the 15th century, the most prominent among all of the separate Christian kingdoms that made up old Hispania were Castile (occupying the northern and central parts of the Iberian Peninsula), Aragon (making up the northeastern territories) and the Kingdom of Portugal (the far western part). With Aragon and Castile united by marriage, the Catholic Monarchs now set their sights on conquering Granada.

1474 Despite the structure's long history, the **Great Wall of China** as it exists today was constructed around this time under the Ming Dynasty. The Great Wall comprises of a series of walls and fortifications in northern China. Estimates suggest the length totals more than 13,000 miles (or 21,000 kilometres). Its origins trace back to around 220 BCE when Qin Shi Huang, the first emperor of a unified China under the Qin Dynasty, ordered that prior fortifications between different states be removed and a number of existing walls along the northern border be combined into a single system to protect China against attacks from the north.

1475   The artist **Michelangelo** was born in a village called Caprese, near Florence.

1477   At the Battle of Nancy, Charles the Bold, Duke of Burgundy, was defeated and killed by French-backed armies. Charles had no male heirs so the male line of Burgundians ended with him. He did, however, have a daughter called Mary of Burgundy who later that year married **Maximilian**, the son of the Holy Roman Emperor Frederick III (who was the first Habsburg to be crowned such). Whilst France inherited Burgundy, Mary inherited the Low Countries (consisting of present-day Netherlands, Belgium and Luxembourg), which had belonged to the Burgundians. In 1482, Mary of Burgundy died in a riding accident, allowing Maximilian - and thus the Habsburg dynasty to which he belonged - to inherit her territories.

1478   Ferdinand and Isabella launched an Inquisition, with its aim being to rid their kingdoms of any opposition to the Catholic faith and expose heretics.

1480   The Grand Prince of Moscow, Ivan III (or **Ivan the Great**), defeated the armies of the Golden Horde Mongols at the Battle of the Ugra River, bringing an end to Mongol subjugation of the Russian principalities.

1485   **Christopher Columbus**, a Genoese sailor, presented plans to Portuguese King John (or João) II of crossing the Atlantic to get to Asia by sailing west from Europe. However, the King's experts advised against it, perhaps due to the country's focus on continued exploration of the eastern Atlantic. Columbus' younger brother, Bartholomew, appealed to the English and French courts with the same plans and request for sponsorship but he was also rejected.

1485-   The Moscow Kremlin was built around this time.
95

1488   Portuguese sailor Bartolomeu Dias successfully rounded the Cape of Good Hope (the southern tip of Africa), paving the way for sea passages from Europe to Asia.

1492   <u>The Discovery of America</u>

In January, the last remaining Muslim ruler in Iberia, Emir Muhammad XII of Granada of the Nasrid dynasty, surrendered complete control of the Emirate of Granada to Ferdinand and Isabella after losing the last battle of the Granada War. The surrender of Granada to the Catholic Monarchs is considered to be one of the most significant events in Spain's history as it marked the completion of the Reconquista and the unification of all Spanish territories (thereby forging the beginnings of what we recocgnise today as **Spain**).

In March, an edict known as the Alhambra Decree was issued by the Catholic Monarchs ordering the expulsion of practising Jews from the Kingdoms of Castile and Aragon and the relinquishing of their territories and possessions. Jews were given until August to choose between conversion and exile. A considerable number of Muslims were also forced to flee.

In April, in what is known as the "Capitulations of Santa Fe", Christopher Columbus began negotiating with the Catholic Monarchs the conditions of a Spanish-sponsored voyage to Asia by sailing west from Europe. In the terms of the Capitulations, it was stated that, upon his return, Columbus would tell the monarchs - and only the monarchs - what happened during the voyage. Also, Columbus would receive 10% of all revenue generated from the new lands he could claim for the Spanish crown.

In August, Columbus' fleet, consisting of 3 ships - Santa María, Niña and Pinta - left the Andalusian port of Palos de Frontera. They made a stop at the Canary Islands before beginning their trans-Atlantic voyage. On 12 October, Columbus and his crew set foot onto what they believed to be a small island off the East Asian coast. Columbus immediately named the island San Salvador (we now know the island as part of the modern-day Bahamas) and he and his crew met the locals. On 21 October, they set sail for a larger island and reached what is now Cuba. Here, they brutishly captured the inhabitants and kept them as prisoners. In early 1493, Columbus and his companions arrived back in Lisbon and then returned to Castile, bringing with them their captives. Over the next 10 years, Columbus would make three more voyages to the **"New World"**.

The discovery of the New World marked a historical turning point for the fortunes of Europe. As explorers in the name of the Spanish crown ventured further into the New World, Spain would amass vast amounts of wealth from these territorial gains. By the mid-16th century, silver and gold extracted from the mines in the Americas (for example, the mines in Potosí which yielded silver in abundance) were pouring into Spanish ports. Seville in particular grew immensely rich from gold and sliver imports. **Spain had entered its Golden Age** and, for the rest of Europe, a new, previously untapped, market had opened up.

New products were introduced to the Eurasian market like pumpkins, potatoes, maize (or corn), tomatoes and chocolate. In turn, the Europeans introduced horses, sheep and pigs to the Americas for the first time. Central and South America's original inhabitants were the first to farm and smoke tobacco, a product which the Spanish also eagerly brought back with them to share with the rest of the world. Some of the other foods, like potatoes, are believed to have significantly increased the overall calorie intake of Europeans. They were reliable in production and could be dried and stored in large quantities. Higher calorie consumption led to better quality of living, decreased starvation and increased populations. One could argue this all created the appropriate conditions for the eventual ideas, inventions and scientific discoveries that were characteristic of the ages of enlightenment and industrialisation to follow.

But the immense wealth and new foods brought into Europe from the discovery of the Americas came at the highest cost: the lives of the natives. Within a century of European invasion of the Americas, the populations of Native Americans would fall by around 90%, mainly due to being slaughtered, often mercilessly, by the Europeans or because of the diseases (such as measles and small pox) the European invaders brought with them to which the natives were not immune. For those who survived, the children were taught Spanish and the women were forced to marry Spaniards. Churches were erected and local customs were substituted for Christianity. Ruthless Europeanisation of the Americas had begun.

1493   Maximilian succeeded his father Frederick III upon his death to become the next Holy Roman Emperor.

1494   Portugal and Spain signed the Treaty of Tordesillas, which provided a permanent line of demarcation between Portuguese and Spanish discovered lands. The line was drawn 370 leagues west of the Cape Verde islands. Everything to the west of the line would belong to Spain and everything to the east to Portugal.

1494   A 12-year old prince called **Babur** ascended the throne of Fergana (now in Uzbekistan). His mother descended from Genghis Khan and his father was a great-great grandson of Timur. During his lifetime, Babur would go on to establish the Mughal Dynasty in India.

1496   In arguably one of the most significant marriages in European history, Holy Roman Emperor Maximilian I arranged for his son Philip to marry Joanna of Castile, second daughter of Ferdinand II and Isabella I.   Joanna's sister was Catherine of Aragon, who would later become the first of six wives of the infamous English monarch Henry VIII. The marriage of Philip and Joanna forged a strong political alliance between the

Spanish monarchy and the House of Habsburg. It soon also produced a son, Charles, who would go on to become one of the most powerful rulers in Europe, if not the world.

1498   **Vasco da Gama**, a Portuguese explorer, successfully sailed around the tip of Africa and into the Indian Ocean having set off from Lisbon in 1497. His voyage was sponsored by King Manuel I of Portugal who was keen to compete with the Venetians and Ottomans for domination of the eastern trade routes by finding a new passage to India. Da Gama became the first European to reach India by sea arriving at the harbour in Calicut (now in Kerala). When he first arrived in India, he had discovered a highly developed Indian Ocean commercial network with trading posts run by sophisticated Muslim traders. After his discovery, the Portuguese would set up their own trading post - their first in India - controlling the ports and collecting high fees.

The Portuguese swiftly secured control of the Indian Ocean trade route by the turn of the century. Over the course of the following century, they would come to trade with the Mughals (soon-to-be the powerful new rulers of India). To fund its vast empire, the Mughals were dependent on international trade. India had no silver mines and very modest gold mines so it needed precious metals from abroad to create its currency. The Portuguese could provide this. In exchange, they sought after India's spices (black pepper and cinnamon to name a few) which they shipped back home to sell. Portugal's control of the sea trading routes meant it could avoid having to buy goods transported by land from the east. Such goods were charged at higher prices due to their passing through numerous checkpoints and requiring the payment of taxes and duties. Shipping goods by sea, though not without its risks, bypassed these. Portugal could buy the spices directly from India directly at a cheaper price and sell them on the European market for a bigger profit.

1499   Italian explorer **Amerigo Vespucci** began a series of expeditions from Spain to the "New World". Vespucci subsequently made claims that the new lands discovered by Columbus belonged to a whole new continent. Columbus had erroneously believed he had discovered the eastern side of Asia (which is why he called the local inhabitants "Indians"). In 1507, a cartographer called Martin Waldseemüller, inspired by Vespucci's findings, published a world map, the first to show sections of the new continent. He named the new continent after Vespucci: **America**. It was, literally speaking, well and truly put on the map.

1500   The Atlantic Slave Trade

Global trade and colonialism also brought with it slavery, which lasted over three centuries. European conquerors imported millions of Africans to work as slaves - usually under horrendous circumstances - on mines and farms in the Americas. All so they could fuel the insatiable demand from Europeans for commodities and consumer goods back home. The slaves would have been crammed into slave ships in the most cruel and untenable of conditions to be shipped to the Americas. Around 1.5 million are believed to have died along the journey.

The slave trade was by no means unique to the Atlantic and did not begin with the Americas. Over the course of the 15th century, the Portuguese had already been trading captured Africans and shipping them back home. There had also existed a wider international slave market in the Middle East and Asia for centuries prior to this (and the role of the Vikings in slavery has been explained previously).

There are a combination of reasons as to why Africans specifically were picked for the Americas by Europeans. One is that Africa, particularly the West African coast, was better located geographically to facilitate the trade. Another is that, as already mentioned, an established slave network already existed in Africa, a model initiated by the Portuguese and soon followed by the Spanish. It was far easier for Europeans to exploit an existing market. Another is that Africans were already immune to diseases that were prevalent in the Americas (the Europeans by contrast were highly vulnerable to these illnesses). Lastly, so much of the Native American population had been wiped out, dying from either harsh working conditions imposed by their conquerors or the diseases they brought with them from Europe: African slaves were imported to fill the void.

Despite the protests of African rulers, bemoaning the kidnapping of their people, the Europeans carried on. To help them justify slavery and the inhumane treatment of Africans, they often depicted and portrayed them as sub-human, less intelligent or immoral. Unfounded myths of black inferiority would become ingrained in Western culture and would pass from generation to generation.

Before the mid-17th century, the Atlantic slave ships took an annual total of around 7,500 Africans to the western hemisphere. But, beginning in the late 17th century, there was a considerable upsurge in African slavery. By the end of that century, the rush for trade, empire and colonialism was in full swing. Tobacco plantations had been set up in North America and sugar mills were operating in the Caribbean and South America. In the following century, one million slaves worked in the sugar industry and diamond and gold mines of Brazil. Altogether, an estimated 12 million Africans were used in the slave trade: around half this number went to the Caribbean, 40% went to Brazil and 5% to the US.

1500   **Sikhism** had begun at the beginning of the 16th century in the Punjab region of India when **Guru Nanak** began teaching a faith distinct from Hinduism and Islam.

1500   A Portuguese fleet led by navigator Pedro Álvares Cabral landed in what is now Brazil and claimed the territory on behalf of King Manuel I of Portugal.

1501   After several prior attempts to capture Samarkand had failed, Babur was finally driven out of his kingdom by Muhammad Shaybani Khan (another descendant of Genghis Khan) of the Uzbeks.

1503   Leonardo Da Vinci painted the **Mona Lisa** around this time, though the exact year is not known.

1504   After recuperating from his losses and building up an army, Babur crossed the Hindu Kush mountains and captured Kabul.

1504   When Queen Isabella of Castile died, in the absence of any living sons, her daughter Joanna succeeded her (Ferdinand remained King of Aragon). Joanna, though, was declared mentally unstable and in 1506, Philip would be recognised as King of Castile. However, Philip died within 3 months of his reign, leaving behind his son (and Ferdinand's grandson) Charles, only 6 years of age at the time.

1505   A German student at the University of Erfurt named **Martin Luther**, instead of enrolling in law as intended, decided to change path and become a monk (his decision allegedly arose after almost being struck by lightning, an event he saw as divine intervention). Luther soon entered St Augustine's Monastery in Erfurt.

1505   Ivan III (or Ivan the Great), responsible for laying the foundations of a Russian state, died. Under his son and successor, the Grand Prince Vasily III, Moscow continued to grow in size and power.

1510   The Sultan of Bijapur lost Goa in battle to the Portuguese, who would set up a permanent settlement there.

1512   The painting of the **Sistine Chapel** in Rome (now in the Vatican) by Michelangelo was completed.

1513   Juan Ponce de León, a Spanish explorer, discovered Florida in North America.

1516   When Ferdinand of Aragon died, his grandson Charles succeeded him to become **Charles I, the first King of all of Spain**. Charles would go on to rule one of the world's largest empires. From his mother's side, he inherited Spain, territories in Italy and the Spanish territories in the New World. From his father's side, he ruled the Burgundian territories, notably the Low Countries.

1517   <u>The Protestant Reformation</u>

The Reformation is said to have began when Martin Luther published the *Ninety Five Theses* against indulgences on 31 October. He nailed them to the door of a church in Wittenberg (now in Germany).

The historical context leading up to the Reformation is important in order to appreciate its significance. The Church in Rome, or the Roman Catholic Church, was enormously influential on people's lives in Europe. Over the centuries, it had developed into a powerful institution, with the Pope at the head, owning vast amounts of land across Europe. Its courts, religious laws and a huge administration of religious officers imposed the church's domination. As part of this, the parish priest played a major societal role: baptizing, marrying, hearing confessions and providing last rites. All key social services were carried out by the church, such as giving alms to the poor and running orphanages. The church controlled education too. Before the printing press was invented, only the parish priest, able to read and write Latin, would have access to the Bible. Often, the only way a person could learn about the Bible was from what the priest told them.

Martin Luther's Ninety Five Theses denounced indulgences. An indulgence was recognised by the Catholic Church as promised remission from punishments for sin, either for a living person or for the dead believed to be in purgatory. The recipient of an indulgence would need to perform an action to receive it, such as praying or performing good deeds. By the 16th century, it was commonplace for indulgences to be sold for money. It had reached a point where church officials were convincing people to "buy" their salvation through the practice of selling indulgences.

In 1517, the Pope released a special indulgence to raise money to continue building Saint Peter's Basilica in Rome (now in the Vatican). In the northern region of the German states, a friar named Johann Tetzel was pursuing this practice and it was this that led to Martin Luther's accusations of church corruption.

To Luther, salvation was not something that could be bought. He believed in salvation through faith alone. Luther argued that a person's relationship was with God and not with the priest, that Christians can only be saved through the grace of God and that the church's rituals did not have the power to save souls. Luther proclaimed messages such as "sola scriptura" ("only the Bible"), "sola gratia" ("only grace") and "sola fide" ("only faith"). By 1520, Luther was lecturing and openly promoting the doctrine of sola fide. He had written a series of pamphlets explaining his ideals, using the newly-invented printing press to spread his message.

Luther's actions would eventually lead to the church in Western Europe splitting into two major denominations: **Protestantism** and **Catholicism**. European royal families and their populations became divided on this topic, leading to numerous bloody wars being fought over the next few hundred years.

1517   The Ottoman Empire under Selim I conquered Egypt, ending the Mamluk Sultanate.

1519   On behalf of the Spanish monarchy, Spanish explorer (or "conquistador") Hernando Cortéz formally claimed land in what is now part of Mexico. Cortéz and his fellow conquistadors eventually encountered the Aztecs, at the time under the leadership of Montezuma II. After being received peacefully in Tenochtitlán, the Aztec capital, Cortéz and his men deceitfully turned on the Aztecs, massacred them in a frenzy and took Montezuma hostage. Eventually, Montezuma would be killed too. In the ensuing chaos, Cortéz was temporarily forced to flee Tenochtitlán but he eventually returned in 1521 with reinforcements from Cuba, besieging the city, capturing it and then destroying it, **bringing to an end the Aztec Empire**. Cortéz would govern the city on behalf of the Spanish and renamed it Mexico City.

1519   Holy Roman Emperor Maximilian I died. Since his son Philip was dead, he had already arranged for his grandson, Charles I of Spain, to be elected the new emperor. Through flexing considerable financial muscle, Charles secured the election and became **Charles V, Holy Roman Emperor**. Charles at this point ruled over Spain, the Low Countries, the Duchy of Burgundy, the Habsburg lands, certain territories in northern Italy and all of Spain's colonies.

1519   Babur's army besieged the fortress of Bajaur (now in Pakistan) on the north western border of India.

1520   Suleiman I (or **Suleiman the Magnificent**), the only surviving son of Selim I, became the Sultan of the Ottoman Empire. During his reign, he embarked on a series of military conquests which included capturing Belgrade in 1521 (ruled by the Kingdom of Hungary at the time) and doing battle with the Habsburgs and Safavid Persians. He also helped turn the Ottomans into a major naval power.

1521   Pope Leo X excommunicated Martin Luther. At the imperial **Diet of Worms** (an assembly that took place in the German city of Worms), Luther was called to defend himself in front of the new Holy Roman Emperor, Charles V. Luther refused to recant. As a consequence, an edict was issued by Charles V declaring him a heretic. Luther, however, managed to escape arrest, mainly with the help and protection of a number of German princes, including Frederick the Wise (Elector of Saxony) who staged a kidnapping and then hid Luther at Wartburg Castle.

1521   The **Viceroyalty of New Spain** was established with Mexico City as its capital. Its territory would eventually encompass all of central America, parts of North America, a portion of the Caribbean and the Philippines (the latter named after Philip II of Spain). Viceroys (or vice-kings) were responsible for good governance of, and economic administration over, their territories. They were of high social standing, almost without exception Spanish-born, and served fixed terms.

The Spanish conquistadors referred to the small communities of Native Americans as "pueblos". Under Spanish influence, each pueblo would install its own church and thousands of Native Americans would be baptized. European diseases had torn through and wiped out many of the pueblo peoples.

1522   Whilst in hiding, Luther began work on translating the New Testament into German. It was published in 1522, paving the way for ordinary German people to read the Bible. Access to a translated Bible and Luther's teachings created a dedicated following of German princes, eager to wrestle power away from the Pope. From this, **Lutheranism** was established and would go on to become one the main branches of Protestantism.

1522   The survivors of the fleet of Portuguese explorer Ferdinand Magellan, which first set sail in 1519, became the first known humans to circumnavigate the world.

1524- Rallied around Protestantism (though condemned by Luther
1525   himself) German peasants rebelled against their lords in the German-speaking states. Around a hundred thousand people were killed in this rebellion which was eventually suppressed.

1525   The **Duchy of Prussia** was established as the first Lutheran state.

1526   On an Indian battlefield near Panipat, Babur encountered the great army of the Sultan of Delhi, Ibrahim Lodi. During the battle, Lodi was killed along with most of his men. After the battle, Babur occupied Delhi and Agra, usurped the throne of Lodi, and laid the foundation for the eventual rise of **Mughal** rule in India. The word "Mughal" derives from the Arabic and Persian corruption of "Mongol" and it emphasised the Mongol origins of the Timurid dynasty. The economy of the Mughal Empire would flourish, in part, due to the hard currency - in the form of gold and silver from the Americas - flowing in from European merchants to buy India's coveted natural resources.

1527   A mutinous army serving under Charles V, which had not been paid in months, sacked Rome, brutally murdering men, women and children. Charles V seized an opportunity here to exercise control over the Pope and much of the Italy.

1528   A hurricane in the Gulf of Mexico blew a boat of Spanish soldiers onto the coast of Galveston island in what is now Texas. They were the first Europeans to set foot in the western part of North America.

1529   Suleiman the Magnificent besieged the Habsburg capital of Vienna but failed to take the city.

1530   Babur's son Humayun (who fought at the Battle of Panipat) succeeded his father to the throne of Delhi and became the second emperor of the Mughal dynasty. His half-brother inherited Kabul and Lahore (the further northern parts of Babur's empire).

1531   The Schmalkaldic League of Lutheran Princes was officially established by the German states of Hesse and Saxony (within the Holy Roman Empire) as a military and religious alliance to protect Lutherans against potential military aggression by Charles V.

1532   Francisco Pizarro entered what is now Peru with 180 Spanish conquistadores and defeated the Inca Emperor leading to the **downfall of the Inca civilisation**. Pizarro and his men used the deceitful tactics similar to those of Cortéz in Mexico to overcome the Incans. He first arrived in peace and invited the Incan ruler, Atahualpa, to a banquet before turning on him and his people. Eventually, the Spaniards executed Atahualpa.

1533   Ivan IV (better known as **Ivan the Terrible**) became the Grand Prince of Moscow.

1535   The Ottoman army of Suleiman the Magnificent captured Baghdad from the Safavid Persians.

1540   Humayun was driven into exile by the Afghan ruler Sher Shah. He would eventually take refuge in Persia while his infant son Akbar was to be raised in Afghanistan.

1541   With Protestantism on the rise, **John Calvin**, a Protestant reformer, became the spiritual leader of Geneva and established the Republic of Geneva. Calvin would set up a theocratic state there where citizens would be strictly regulated and penalised for 'vices' such as blasphemy, drunkenness, dancing and gambling. Calvinism is recognised as another major branch of Protestantism.

1542   The **Viceroyalty of Peru** was established by the Spaniards. With Lima to become its capital, it would have jurisdiction over Spanish South America.

1543   The work of Polish astronomer **Nicolaus Copernicus**, called *On the Revolutions of the Heavenly Spheres*, was published (the same year in which he died). He developed a heliocentric theory, which determined that the sun, rather than the earth, was at the centre of orbit.

1546   The Schmalkaldic War began with Charles V and his allies fighting the Schmalkaldic League over certain territories within the Holy Roman Empire.

1547   Ivan the Terrible was crowned the first **Tsar of Russia**. "Tsar" is derived from the word "caesar".

1549   **St Mary's Church in Straslund** (now Germany), originally built in the 13th century, at 151 metres (or 495 feet), became the tallest building in the world until surpassed in 1647 when its spire was struck by lightning and collapsed. For a temporary period (between 1569 and 1573), the Cathedral of Saint Peter of Beauvais in France held the title until its tower also collapsed.

1555   Humayun, with Persian support, regained his kingdoms in Punjab, Delhi and Agra and the Mughal Empire was re-established.

1555   The **Peace of Augsburg** was a treaty signed between Charles V and the Schmalkaldic League, ending the Schmalkaldic War. The peace treaty granted Lutheranism official status within the Holy Roman Empire and let each state's princes choose the official religion within the domains they controlled, meaning communities would either be Catholic or Protestant depending on the choosing of their prince.

1556   Humayun died when he accidentally fell down the stairs of his library in Delhi. His son Akbar (later to become known as **Akbar the Great**) succeeded him aged 13. Under Akbar's reign, the Mughal dynasty considerably expanded its empire in India. By the time of his death in 1605, the Mughal Empire stretched as far as Afghanistan in the north, Sindh in the west, Bengal in the east and the Godavari river in the south. A Muslim himself, Akbar allowed for freedom of religion, particularly for Hindus and Jains. He also abolished the 'jizya', the poll tax imposed by Muslim rulers on non-Islamic subjects (it would, however, be re-introduced by later rulers). Along with religious toleration,

Akbar promoted and encouraged the development of art and culture.

1558 **Charles V died** in a monastery he had retired to in the previous year. Before his death, he had divided his empire: he left Spain to his son Philip (who became Philip II of Spain) along with the Low Countries (which today make up the Netherlands, Belgium and Luxembourg) and his Italian territories; and he left the title of Holy Roman Emperor to his younger brother, Ferdinand (who became Ferdinand I).

1565 Spanish colonisation of the Philippines (named after the then-Spanish king) began. 6 years later, Manila was established: it served as a major trading hub connecting Asia to the Americas allowing for goods and silver currency to reach the Pacific without having to pass through Europe.

1568 The **Dutch Revolt** (otherwise known as the Eighty Years' War or Dutch War of Independence) began. It was a rebellion instigated by dissenters within the Spanish Netherlands - correlated to the Low Countries - opposed to Spanish and Catholic rule by Philip II of Spain. Particular causes for discontent were high taxation imposed by the Spanish crown and the persecution of Calvinists. The revolt was led by **William I Prince of Orange** (also known as William the Silent).

1571 At the Battle of Lepanto, the fleet of the Holy League (a Christian alliance between Venice, Spain and the Papal States) defeated the Ottomans, leading to their first major naval defeat since the 15th century.

1572 In what became known as **Saint Bartholomew's Day Massacre**, thousands of Huguenots (French Calvinists) were killed in pro-Catholic riots in France.

1579 The Union of Utrecht was signed, unifying the northern provinces of the Netherlands, until then under Spanish control, in a confederation called the **United Provinces**.

1580 Philip II seized the Portuguese crown, beginning a 60-year period of union between Spain and Portugal.

1581 The United Provinces, effectively the beginnings of the **Dutch Republic**, proclaimed their independence from Spanish rule. William I of Orange became the de facto ruler. The southern provinces of the Netherlands remained part of Spain and the Spanish war with the Dutch continued.

1582 After institution by a papal bull, Pope Gregory XIII formally introduced the **Gregorian calendar**, a reform of the Julian calendar and the system we use today in the West for counting time: the same calendar used to prepare this timeline.

1584 William I of Orange was assassinated under the direction of Philip II of Spain.

1584 Ivan the Terrible died of a stroke. His son Feodor I succeeded him as Tsar.

1585 As part of the ongoing Eighty Years' War, the Spanish captured the city of Antwerp, forcing its Protestant inhabitants to flee. Generally, the religious conflicts in Europe around this time led to upheaval for many Europeans, including Jews from Spain and Portugal and Huguenots from France. Many sought refuge in the United Provinces and places like Amsterdam, known for its religious toleration.

1587 The first English settlement in the New World (known as the "lost colony of Roanoke") was founded by English explorer Walter Raleigh. However, the colony would soon be abandoned.

1588 In what is known as the **Spanish Armada**, a Spanish fleet sailed towards England in an invasion attempt. Philip II of Spain, who had previously been married to Catholic English Queen Mary I (who died in 1558), sought to overthrow Queen Elizabeth I who had since restored England to Protestantism (and who had thrown her support behind the Dutch Revolt). However, a combination of bad weather and disease ended in disaster for the Spanish fleet, which suffered heavy losses and was eventually forced to abandon its plans.

The losses generally inflicted on the Spanish military during the 16th century, combined with heavy war expenditures, unpopularly high taxes, defaults on loans, and their failure to control the influx (and price fluctuations) of gold and silver from the American mines, led to several bankruptcies of the Spanish monarchy by the end of the century. By comparison, the Dutch had a more confident financial system - which some would describe as the first modern economy - that undoubtedly contributed to their eventual success in their revolt against Spanish rule.

1589   The Harmandir Sahib, also known as Darbar Sahib was built. It is a Gurdwara (Sikh temple) located in the city of Amritsar in the Punjab region of India. As the prominent pilgrimage site of Sikhism, it is commonly referred to as the **Golden Temple** in English.

1598   Tsar Feodor I died childless so Ivan IV's advisor Boris Godunov became Tsar. But after his sudden death in 1605, his widow and teenage son were brutally murdered and an imposter, claiming to be Ivan IV's son, seized the throne, though he too was soon murdered. This sparked a period in Russian history known as the **Time of Troubles**, during which the region slid into anarchy and rebels and foreign armies laid waste to Russia's lands. Polish-Lithuanian troops occupied Moscow and Smolensk and Swedish armies occupied Novgorod.

1598   The Edict of Nantes was passed by King Henry IV of France which, despite being a Catholic state, recognised the rights of Huguenots to practise their religion without persecution.

1598   Philip II of Spain died and was succeeded by his son Philip III. Before his death, Philip II had authorised an expedition which led to the founding of a new province in North America called New Mexico (with its capital soon to be placed in what is now Santa Fe). It formed part of the territories belonging to the Viceroyalty of New Spain.

1600   By this time, the world population had risen to over 500 million.

1600   Queen Elizabeth I of England granted a Royal Charter to the **English East India Company,** giving it the exclusive right to trade with merchants in all lands east of the Cape of Good Hope. Via ocean routes, the company's fleet would explore new places from where it could buy goods at a cheap price and sell them on at a profit back in Europe.

1601   Russia suffered a great famine that, over the next two years, would kill two million people (around one third of Russia's population).

1602   The Dutch government (or the United Provinces), keen to do business free from the constraints of Spanish authority, and to displace the Portuguese trading monopoly in East Asia, set out themselves to dominate the intercontinental spice trade. They wanted to get their hands on popular spices, such as clove, nutmeg and cinnamon, to sell for themselves and control the market.

In the decade prior to the beginning of the 17th century, successful trading ventures by well-designed and well-built Dutch commercial ships brought back very high returns for investors. Typically, investors were funding individual ships only for a single voyage. But such investments were high risk because of the dangers of sea travel (harsh weather conditions, disease and piracy to name a few). Therefore, investors began funding several ships at a time so that, if one failed to return, their investment would not be completely written off.

The Dutch government recognised the economic benefits of pooling resources and consolidated all of these investments. It set up the **Dutch East India Company** (the **Vereenigde Oost-Indische Compagnie** or "**VOC**" for short) as an official colonial agency that was granted a monopoly in spice trading with the East Asian market. The VOC issued shares of stock to the general public, making it the world's first formally listed public company. Members of the public could invest in the VOC's success, buying shares in the Company and earning a decent return on their investment. The VOC established an exchange in Amsterdam (underpinning much of what we recognise today as a modern stock exchange) where shares in the Company could be bought and sold. The Dutch government would give the Company significant financial backing as well as the legal power to negotiate treaties, create overseas settlements, uphold its own laws and judiciary and even to wage wars.

1603   The Dutch set up their first permanent trading post in Banten in Indonesia. At first, the VOC's interests were purely commercial. However, in order to fully exploit its economic potential in Indonesia, it fought with the locals and other Europeans. The Company would control affairs in Indonesia for around 200 years until the Dutch state eventually took full control of the region.

1605   Mughal emperor Akbar died from illness. His son Salim took the throne under the name Jahangir. He would go on to marry Nur Jahan of Persian nobility.

1607   **Jamestown** - named after the new King of England James I - a town in the recently founded **Colony of Virginia**, became the first permanent English settlement in the Americas. It was here that, in 1613, the famous Pocahontas was kidnapped by the English and held for ransom. She was converted to Christianity and married John Rolfe, a tobacco grower.

1608   The English East India Company arrived at Surat in India and, within a few years, had established a permanent factory there. Surat was the port used by the textile manufacturers of Gujarat and was the most important centre for overseas trade for the

Mughal Empire. There was high demand in Europe for cotton, silk and spices and the British would have to compete fiercely with the Dutch and Portuguese to manufacture and sell these goods. In 1612, the East India Company fought and won a battle against the Portuguese for control over Surat.

1608   The French founded Quebec City (in where the Canadian province of Quebec is today). In the early 1600s, French traders had established settlements there and at Montreal along the Saint Lawrence River. French Jesuits also travelled to the colony to bring Catholicism to the natives.

1609   **Henry Hudson**, an English explorer hired by the VOC, sailed into what is now New York Bay and found the homeland of the indigenous Lenape people. He was seeking a north eastern passage to the spice markets of Asia but, recognising the natural resources of the area, a land rich with furs, fish and vegetation, he immediately laid claim to the Lenape territory for the VOC.

Native Americans would trade animal pelts with the Europeans for about two centuries. Over this time, companies from Russia, England and Mexico (and soon the new United States) would be locked in fierce competition with each other for the fur trade in the West. They hired mountain men (called trappers) to do the work of capturing the animals.

1612   The Russians defeated Polish-Lithuanian armies at the Battle of Moscow. Today, National Unity Day is celebrated in Russia every 4 November to commemorate the victory over Poland-Lithuania.

1613   **Michael Romanov** was elected by nobles to be crowned **Tsar Michael I of Russia**. The Romanov dynasty would go on to rule Russia for more than 300 years.

1615   Influential Italian astronomer **Galileo Galilei**, originally from Pisa, travelled to Rome to defend himself against the clergy regarding his support for Copernicus' heliocentric theory. He would be condemned by the Catholic Church as a heretic and was forbidden from teaching his theories. Despite the suppression, Galileo's book, *Dialogue Concerning the Two Chief World Systems*, was published in Florence in 1632.

1618   The devotedly Catholic Ferdinand II, new Habsburg King of Bohemia (part of present-day Czechia), sent royal representatives to inform powerful Protestant nobles in Prague that it, along with the rest of Bohemia, would be Catholic territory. In what is referred to as the "Defenestration of Prague", the representatives were literally thrown out of windows by angry Protestants. This act of aggression triggered one of the most brutal wars in history known as the **Thirty Years War**, which was fundamentally a religious war between the Holy Roman Empire and the Protestant states. Various different states in the fracturing Holy Roman Empire were involved as were France, Spain, the Italian states, Sweden, Denmark and England. Mainland Europe fell into chaos and millions would die, not only through slaughter but from starvation.

1619   The first shipment of African slaves arrived in the English colony of Virginia to grow tobacco. The number of African slaves in Virginia would rise quickly, as well as the amount of tobacco grown, turning Virginia into a very prosperous trading outlet for the English that settled there.

1620   A group of Puritans (who were separatists from the Protestant Church of England) were facing religious persecution in England. Some had fled to the Netherlands but faced difficulties settling there. The group, in search of religious freedom, set sail from Plymouth in England on board a ship called the Mayflower. Their intended destination was Virginia but the ship was blown off course and ended up in what is now part of Massachusetts. On board the ship, the Puritans (who came to be known as **Pilgrims**) wrote and signed a constitution which would govern the new settlement. The constitution came to be known as the **Mayflower Compact** and the newly founded land became the colony of **Plymouth**. The journey ended up being fatal for many Pilgrims who did not bring enough provisions for the winter and they froze or starved to death. The tradition of **Thanksgiving** in the US dates back to the celebratory feast put on in November 1621 by those who survived.

1624   The Dutch West India Company sent European traders and settlers to colonise the area that is now the island of Manhattan. It was arguably the best natural deep-water harbour on the Atlantic coast and a prime location for the then-lucrative international fur trade. The European settlers traded goods to the locals for beaver pelts to ship back to the continent. In 1625, the Company established **New Amsterdam** at the southern point of Manhattan, the capital of the colony of New Netherland, which would stretch as far as Fort Orange (today's Albany). Other settlers would create surrounding farms and villages scattered across today's Bronx, Brooklyn, upper Manhattan, Queens, Staten Island and northern New Jersey.

1627   Mughal emperor Jahangir died and **Shah Jahan** ascended the Mughal throne. He matched Babur and Akbar both in military strength and cultural ambition. During his reigh, he would extend the influence of Mughal rule in the south and sponsor some of the beautiful buildings which defined the Mughal period, including the Red Fort in Delhi and Taj Mahal in Agra.

1629   The province of **Carolina**, named after King Charles I of England, was established in North America. Enslaved Native Americans were part of the early workforce in the colony but the English soon turned to importing African captives. By the early 18th century, Carolina would have an African majority and European minority. The official separation by the English crown of the province of Carolina occurred much later in 1729, creating North Carolina and South Carolina.

1633   An English East India Company trading post was established in Bengal.

1639   The Red Fort in Delhi was constructed and would serve as a place of residence for the Mughal imperial family. Also, by this time, the English East India Company had settled in Madras where the local ruler agreed to grant trading concessions, allowing the Company to undercut competition - both foreign and local - and establish a foothold in the region.

1642   Dutch navigator Abel Tasman, employed by the Dutch East India Company to explore the Pacific, discovered an island that would around 200 years later be named after him: Tasmania. In the same year, he became the first European to discover New Zealand (named after the Dutch province of Zealand). The region would not be fully exploited until more than a century later when British explorers arrived.

1643   Louis, the son of Louis XIII of France and Anne of Austria (whose father was Philip III of Spain) became **King Louis XIV** at the age of four years old. During his infancy, Anne of Austria ruled as regent. Louis XIV would become known as the **"Sun King"** due to his perceived divinity and belief that he enlightened others with his grace. France would become Europe's dominant cultural, political and military power in the 17th century under Louis XIV.

1644   Fort Saint George in Madras was founded and became the first English fortress in India.

1647   The **Strasbourg Cathedral** in France, originally constructed in 1439, at 142 metres (or 466 feet), became the tallest building in the world until surpassed in 1874.

1648   The Peace of Westphalia brought an **end to the Thirty Years War**. The treaty also formally **ended the Dutch Revolt** and recognised **the independence of the Netherlands**. Even before the end of the conflict, the Dutch were already making inroads in international trade. Internally, they had expanded their cities and built a complex network of canals connecting the major cities, enhancing trade and communication. In fact, they were living through what is commonly seen as the "**Dutch Golden Age**" which they enjoyed for the remainder of the century. Architecture flourished as did art, giving a platform for the famous Dutch artists of the day, such as Rembrandt, Hals and Vermeer. The Netherlands also became known for its religious tolerance: Jews from the Iberian Peninsula, Huguenots from France, prosperous merchants and economic and religious refugees from the Spanish-controlled parts of the Low Countries all found safety in Amsterdam.

1651 The major European powers with established colonies around the world adopted **mercantilism**, an economic system which was aimed at ensuring the respective European country, fully exploiting its colonies, exported more than it imported in order to stockpile as much gold and silver as possible. In 1651, having invested heavily in its navy, the English government passed the first of a series of Navigation Acts. Via these Acts, England would regulate its global trade networks by obliging its colonies to sell raw materials to it exclusively and by subsequently requiring those colonies to buy, at a higher price, the goods manufactured using those raw materials. In essence, the goal was to 'feed' the economy of the 'mother' country at the expense of the colonies. Also, the Acts required that imports and exports from English colonies had to be on English ships, so colonies could not trade with one another or with foreign ships. High tariffs were also a common feature of mercantilism, discouraging trade with foreign goods and encouraging exchange of goods within the empire.

These policies caused friction between European states, often competing against one another for the same resources. The regulation of the Navigation Acts was arguably one of the key causes behind a series of wars between England and the Netherlands (known as the **Anglo-Dutch Wars**), three of which took place in the 17th century.

At the heart of mercantilism was the idea that, in order for a nation to grow richer, it had to try and produce everything it could - either within its own borders or via its colonies - and reduce to a minimum any reliance on foreign imports. The goal was to achieve total independence of trade and this was to be done through regulation and restriction. This economic philosophy would be challenged in the next century, particularly after the publication of Adam Smith's influential *Wealth of Nations.*

1651   Hooghly was the location of the first English settlement in Lower Bengal. Granted with permission to trade by the Mughals, the English East India Company would eventually set up its own factory there.

1652   South Africa became the first European colony in Africa. The first Dutch immigrants settled at Table Bay. They initially set up a small stopover point for the ships of the VOC, but it soon became the foothold for territorial expansion and colonisation. Eventually, Dutch peasants - called Boers - began to settle in South Africa. From 1658, Robin Island was used as a penal colony (it was where Nelson Mandela would serve most of his prison sentence).

1652   The First Anglo-Dutch War began and lasted two years.

1653   Construction of the famous **Taj Mahal**, commissioned in 1632, was completed. It was 73 metres (or 240 feet) tall and was used to house the tomb of the Emperor Shah Jahan's favourite wife, Mumtaz Mahal.

1658   When Shah Jahan fell seriously ill in 1657, the tension between his sons made an ensuing war of succession inevitable. Overpowering and killing his brothers, **Aurangzeb** ascended to the Mughal throne. Shah Jahan eventually died in 1666. During the five decades of Aurangzeb's reign, the Mughal Empire expanded considerably, particularly in the areas of South India, so much so that it could hardly be ruled any longer.

Aurangzeb spent a lot of money on putting down revolts, which arose frequently during his long reign. Unlike Akbar, who was a patron of the arts, he banned court musicians and poets. He also discriminated against non-Muslims and reinstated the unpopular jizya tax.

1661   Upon the death of his Italian chief minister, Louis XIV decided to rule France by himself, ushering in a period of personal rule and absolute monarchy, which he epitomised through his extravagances. The concept of absolute monarchy was that the monarch would reign supreme with his or her power unchecked by any other body (such as the legislature or judiciary).

1664   The French East India company was founded. Though the French were a late-comer to India, they would quickly establish themselves in the region and were poised to overtake England for control over trade in the Indian subcontinent.

1664   An English fleet sailed into the harbour of New Amsterdam and seized the Dutch colony. They renamed it for King Charles II's brother, James the Duke of York, and "New Amsterdam" became **"New York"**. Most Dutch residents stayed on and adjusted quickly, maintaining their language and customs while their businesses prospered alongside England's trading empire. New York would grow into a thriving port and an important Atlantic trading point. Merchants would ship wheat and flour to Caribbean ports in exchange for sugar, molasses, and rum. They also sent ships across the Atlantic to sell fur, fish and lumber and bring back European goods in return. Like with other colonies in America, enslaved Africans were bought and sold in New York too.

1665   The Second Anglo-Dutch War began. Overall, it ended up being a failure for the English. However, in the peace treaty in 1667 (the Treaty of Breda), English control of New Amsterdam (recently renamed New York) was formally recognised.

1667   After the conclusion of a war between Russia and Poland-Lithuania (which began in 1654), the eastern part of Ukraine, including Kiev, became part of the Russian Empire, while the western part remained part of the empire of Poland-Lithuania.

1668   The English East India Company took possession of Bombay Castle and would go on to build a defensive structure around it.

1672   The Third Anglo-Dutch War broke out and lasted two years.

1674   The French East India Company established a trading centre in Pondicherry in southern India. The French would soon also settle in Chandannagar in West Bengal.

1681   King Charles II of England granted a land charter to English Quaker William Penn and with that the **Colony of Pennsylvania** was established. Penn introduced a policy of religious toleration: many religious groups flocked to the colony, particularly those who were facing persecution in Europe. Immigrants arrived from England, Germany, Ireland, France and elsewhere. Pennsylvania would become one of the most populous of the colonies in North America.

1682   Louis XIV moved his court to the small French village of **Versailles**. He would soon convert the lodge there into one of the most spectacular European palace complexes of its day, acting as a symbol for the king's power and France's greatness. Meanwhile, French explorers would soon colonise new land in North America, which would later be called Louisiana (named after the Sun King himself).

1682   **Peter I** became **Tsar of Russia**. He was credited for expanding the empire and modernising Russia. He was the first Russian ruler to travel abroad, touring Europe and learning the latest developments in science and shipbuilding. As well as reforming the navy, he modernised the army and promoted industry, trade and education in Russia.

1683   In the **Battle of Vienna,** the Polish-Lithuanian king Jan Sobieski joined forces with the Habsburg monarchy and Holy Roman Empire to drive away the invading Ottoman armies. The battle is seen as a turning point in the history of the Ottomans, putting an end to their expansion into Europe. The battle would eventually lead to Habsburg rule being solidified around Austria, Hungary and other Eastern European territories.

1685   Louis XIV saw the presence of Protestants in his realm as undermining his rule. He revoked the Edict of Nantes causing many Huguenots to flee France and migrate to states that would allow them to practise their religion without persecution (such as England, the Netherlands, certain German-speaking states, and the North American colonies).

1686   The English East India Company went to war with Aurangzeb due to disagreements over the payment of local taxes. The war is referred to as Child's War (after Sir Josiah Child and his involvement in it).

1687   The book *Philosophiæ Naturalis Principia Mathematica* (or *The Mathematical Principles of Natural Philosophy*) by **Isaac Newton** was published, setting out Newton's laws of motion among other findings. It described that simple mathematical formulas could explain and predict the movement of objects within the universe.

1690   Child's War ended after Aurangzeb had driven the English out of their factories. The East India Company sent envoys to plea for a pardon. Aurangzeb ordered that they prostrate themselves before him and demanded the Company pay a fine. However, the Company's representatives would soon manage to persuade Aurangzeb to issue a firman: a royal decree that would allow them trade concessions.

1692   The town of Salem in Massachusetts and surrounding areas experienced the infamous Salem witch trials, where trials and executions took place against people accused of witchcraft.

1696   The English East India Company built Fort William on the bank
        of the Hooghly River in Bengal.

1698   By the end of the 17th century, the GDP of the Mughal Empire
        was around a quarter of the world's economy. It was made up
        of a minority Muslim ruling elite vastly outnumbered by Hindus.
        Indian princes had been incorporated into the ruling class,
        though the Mughal elite still retained the highest positions within
        the empire.

        The Mughals instituted and relied upon an effective tax
        collection system that generated the revenue to run its empire.
        Local leaders called Zamindars usually collected the taxes. The
        English East India Company began to bribe Mughal officials
        into giving them 'zamandari' rights (that is, land ownership
        rights and the right to collect taxes) over three villages:
        Kalikata, Gobindapur, and Sutanuti (all three of which would
        comprise present-day **Kolkata** in West Bengal).

        Over the course of the 18th century, the Bengal government
        suffered huge losses in trade whilst the East India Company, by
        contrast, would profit from their exploitation of zamandari
        rights and various trade concessions granted to them. The
        Company also bred corrupt officials who would trade privately
        and avoid paying any tax, enriching themselves in the process.

1699   Between the mid-17th and 19th centuries, there were significant
        developments in agriculture. A so-called 'agricultural
        revolution' occurred due to innovative ways to increase crop
        yield - like crop rotation and land reclamation - combined with
        new developments in ploughing techniques that helped increase
        productivity. Also, the opening up of global trade allowed
        knowledge of agriculture to be shared across different
        continents. The increase in agricultural productivity would allow
        for cities to grow at the rapid rates in which they did during
        the industrial revolution: the cities' people needed feeding and

only efficient agricultural practices could keep up with growing demand.

1700   Charles II of Spain, who suffered from illness his entire life, died childless (apparently due to impotency). The death triggered a major succession crisis that would impact all the major European powers. In 1700, the Spanish Empire consisted of Italy, the southern parts of the Low Countries (referred to as the Spanish Netherlands), the Philippines and a large portion of the Americas. Tension ran high in Europe because acquisition by one nation of all the Spanish territories undivided would have threatened the continent's delicate balance of power.

One of Charles II's sisters, Maria Theresa (at this point deceased) had been married to Louis XIV. Just before Charles' death, it had been stated in his will that his kingdom was to be left to the grandson of Louis XIV and Maria Theresa: Philip, Duke of Anjou. Philip thus became Philip V of Spain. However, Holy Roman Emperor Leopold I, of the Habsburg dynasty, claimed that his son, Archduke Charles, should be the successor to the Spanish throne on the basis that Charles II was a Habsburg by descent. The disagreement eventually plunged Europe and its colonies into global conflict. On one side stood France, Spain and several German principalities. On the other side stood the newly formed Grand Alliance, consisting of England, Scotland, the Netherlands and the Holy Roman Empire. The war, known as the **War of the Spanish Succession**, began in 1701 and would last 13 years.

1701   Elector Frederick III, son of Elector Frederick William (known as the "Great Elector") was crowned Frederick I of the Hohenzollern dynasty and **the first King of Prussia**. During the medieval period, the House of Hohenzollern played a relatively minor role on the world stage. Overtime, though, they would hold two important regions. The first was Brandenburg, which made the Hohenzollern ruler one of the four secular Prince-Electors (those who were responsible for officially electing the Holy Roman Emperor). The second was Prussia, a region located outside the Holy Roman Empire, originally formed as a Crusader state by a group of German knights called the Teutonic Order. Therefore, the Hohenzollern ruler would be called both the Elector of Brandenburg and Duke of Prussia.

During the reign of Frederick William (the "Great Elector"), Brandenburg-Prussia established its own standing army, separate from the imperial army which served the Holy Roman Emperor. During the reign of his son, Frederick, Brandenburg-Prussia would become the Kingdom of Prussia as a result of an agreement between Frederick and Holy Roman Emperor Leopold I during the War of the Spanish Succession. The deal was that Frederick would ally with, and provide an army to, Leopold for the war in exchange for being given the title of King.

1703   Tsar Peter I founded the city of **Saint Petersburg** on the Baltic coast. It was a remarkable achievement though it cost the lives of many thousands of serfs. By this time, Russia had fully incorporated serfdom into its laws, limiting the rights for peasants to move freely from land to land and tying them irrevocably to their landowners who controlled their life and work.

1707   The parliaments of England and Scotland unified to form the **Kingdom of Great Britain**.

1707   Aurangzeb died aged 89. Following his death, revolts from various factions (such as the Rajputs, Marathas and Sikhs) began to spring up around the empire. Aurangzeb's son Bahadur Shah took the throne and, after him, a series of week rulers followed in quick succession presiding over the fragmentation of the Mughal Empire.

1713   The Treaty of Utrecht marked the beginning of the end of the War of the Spanish Succession. Whilst Philip V was formally recognised as the King of Spain, he renounced his claim to the French throne.

1715   **Louis XIV died**. At the time of writing this, his reign of 72 years and 110 days is the longest recorded of any monarch of a sovereign country in European history. Louis XIV's great grandson Louis became King Louis XV aged just 5.

1721   Peter I was given the title Emperor of Russia.

1739   The Shah of Persia, Emperor Nader Shah, launched an invasion on the Mughals, looking to exploit their crumbling empire. In the aftermath of the Battle of Karnal, his army captured the Mughal capital of Delhi.

1739   As part of Philip V's administrative reforms (known as the Bourbon Reforms), a new Viceroyalty of New Granada (the northern part of South America consisting of modern Colombia, Panama, Ecuador and Venezuela) was carved out of the existing Viceroyalty of Peru.

1740   King Frederick I's grandson, also called Frederick, became King Frederick II of Prussia. He would be known as "Frederick the Great" due to his significant military victories and his expansion of Prussia's territories.

Meanwhile, when Holy Roman Emperor Charles VI died, another succession crisis ensued. His daughter Maria Theresa succeeded the Habsburg crown, which sparked controversy due to questions around the legitimacy of royal inheritance by a woman. Questioning the legitimacy issue, and sensing an opportunity to increase Prussia's power, King Frederick II invaded the Austrian province of Silesia. This triggered a full-scale European war between Prussia (allied with France, Spain, Bavaria, Saxony and other states) and the Habsburgs (allied with Great Britain, the Netherlands and Russia among others). The war became known as the **War of the Austrian Succession** and lasted 8 years.

1741   Vitus Bering, a Danish explorer employed by Russia, led the first expedition to chart the coast of Alaska. The Bering Strait, Sea and Island are all named after him.

1748   Montesquieu's *The Spirit Of Laws* was published and was well received outside France, particularly in the British-occupied colonies in North America.

1748   The War of the Austrian Succession came to an end with the Treaty of Aix-la-Chapelle. Maria Theresa was confirmed as Archduchess of Austria and Queen of Hungary, but Prussia retained control of its captured territory, Silesia.

1754   The Treaty of Aix-la-Chapelle arguably caused more problems than it solved. North American territories remained in dispute and, when the French colonists started building forts close to British territory, the British colonial forces, a portion of which was commanded by a young George Washington, sent troops to attack the French colonists. This triggered the **French and Indian War** with each side supported by military units from Britain and France and their respective Native American allies.

1756   Siraj-ud-Daulah inherited the throne of the Nawab of Bengal (the nawab was a ruler subordinate to the Mughal Emperor). When the British refused his demands that Britain stop interfering in the political affairs of his region, pay taxes and cease building fortifications, his army seized Fort William in Calcutta, captured British soldiers and kept them as prisoners. News was sent to British officials in Madras and a fleet sent an expeditionary force under the command of a colonel named Robert Clive.

1756   **The Seven Years' War** began, with the fighting having already escalated since the beginning of the French and Indian War (which had begun two years earlier). The French captured British-owned Menorca before the Prussians invaded Austrian-owned Saxony and the fighting between the European powers spiralled from there.

France allied with Austria, Russia and others to fight against a newly formed alliance of Britain and Prussia (previously enemies). Spain would eventually enter the war in 1762 to fight against the British. With battles fought across mainland Europe, North America, the Caribbean and India, the Seven Years' War was a truly global war (some would say the true first world war).

1757   Robert Clive's armies met Siraj-ud-Daulah and his French allies at Palashi (or 'Plassey') and decisively won the battle. In order to win, Clive had bribed Mir Jafar, the commander-in-chief of the Nawab's army, and promised to make him Nawab of Bengal. Thus, in an act of betrayal, Mir Jafar was able to take a large portion of the Nawab's army away from the battlefield.

The victory at the **Battle of Plassey** was the first major military success of the British East India Company in India. Robert Clive was elevated to Governor of Bengal by his superiors in Madras. Going forward, the Company's primary objective was not necessarily to rule but to expand trade and exploit commercial privileges granted by the local rulers. Its officers sought to use political, economic and diplomatic methods to extend their influence. The Company began a Residency System under which it appointed 'Residents' to manage relations with India's many princely states (the Company's trade interests being the primary focus). Through this system, the Indian princes of their native states would be assured of protection from internal and external aggression through the deployment of the Company's troops. In return, they had to pay for the maintenance of those troops and accept a British Resident in their court. Mir Jafar was made the Nawab of Bengal as promised by the British but, in reality, he was just a puppet ruler.

1758   Governor Robert Clive appointed Warren Hastings as the British Resident in the Bengali capital of Murshidabad.

1759   Referred to as "Annus Mirabilis" in British history, Britain would win major battles over the French in the Caribbean, India, Europe and Canada, turning the tide in the Seven Years' War, and consolidating British sea power.

1760   When Mir Jafar refused to agree to the East India Company's additional demands, he was deposed and replaced by Mir Qasim as the new puppet Nawab of Bengal.

1762   Jean-Jacques Rousseau's *The Social Contract* was published.

1762   During the Seven Years' War, Peter III, who had recently acquired the throne of Russia, switched allegiance to a struggling Prussia saving them from defeat. This move alienated many within Russia, including Peter's wife Catherine who arranged for Peter to be overthrown. He soon died and Catherine took the crown to become Catherine II. She has been referred to as **Catherine the Great** for the revitalisation of Russia under her reign and her contribution to Russia being recognised as one of the leading powers in Europe.

1763   **The Seven Years' War ended** with Britain and its allies victorious. Under the Treaty of Paris, the French were forced to give up most of their territories in North America (including Canada), the Caribbean and parts of northern India. The war effectively brought French control of India to an end, allowing the British more freedom to influence the subcontinent exclusively. The Spanish were also forced to give up Florida to the British.

1764   The new Nawab of Bengal Mir Qasim also grew tired of British influence. In defiance, he formed a coalition with Shuja-ud-Daulah, Nawab of Avadh, and Shah Alam II, the Mughal Emperor. However, their combined forces were defeated by the British in the Battle of Buxar. Mir Qasim fled the battlefield and committed suicide. Mir Jafar was reinstalled as Nawab of Bengal.

1765   Pursuant to the Treaty of Allahabad, signed on the back of the defeat at the Battle of Buxar, Mughal Emperor Shah Alam II granted the British East India Company 'diwani' rights. This meant the Company now had rights to collect tax revenue on behalf of the Emperor directly from the people of the eastern province of Bengal-Bihar-Orissa. In return, the Company would pay an annual tribute to the Emperor. This was a major turning point for the Company because it no longer needed investment from the British government to buy merchandise in India. Instead, it could fund its purchases from the tax revenue received from Bengal: it could become economically self-sufficient.

The Company would use the tax revenue to buy goods in Bengal and the money generated from sales would go to Britain rather than be spent in Bengal, effectively sucking money from India. Corruption was also rampant among the Company's officers, who further plundered Bengal's wealth.

Robert Clive returned to India from England to become Governor of Bengal for a second term. He would eventually leave in 1767, having accumulated a vast amount of wealth for himself personally. During his term, he introduced a dual system of government where civil administration was to be administered by the Nawab of Bengal but revenue collection was to be collected by the East India Company (something the Nawab would have no control over).

1765   The American Revolutionary Movement (1)

One of the catalysts for the American Revolution was the introduction of the Stamp Act by the British government, designed to tax the 13 American colonies. All printed material, including legal documents, newspapers, and even playing cards, had to carry an official stamp and the stamp itself cost money. Britain would use the tax revenue to pay the cost of imperial warfare. Whilst they had emerged victorious from the Seven Years' War, the consequence of it was mounting national debt and they looked to the colonies to raise revenue.

The British tried to justify that the expense incurred in defeating the French and Native Americans in the French and Indian War should be paid by the colonists, which profited from that protection. They also increased military presence on the North American continent and imposed the cost of this on the colonists. From the British perspective, the taxes were reasonable, and the Americans ought not to object to the amount (the colonists were, after all, taxed approximately one shilling for every 26 shillings paid by a homeland Briton). However, it was the principle that was objected to. From the perspective of the American colonists, they did not have the rights of other Englishmen including the right not to be taxed without representation (the popularly-used slogan 'no taxation without representation' was adopted as a motto by a recently-formed revolutionary group called the Sons of Liberty). After increased pressure, the British eventually repealed the Stamp Act in 1766.

1767   The Townsend Act was enacted by British parliament, introducing import duties on various goods (such as paper, glass, lead and tea) imported to the American colonies. This sparked outrage within the American colonies and violent demonstrations erupted. In protest to the Townsend Act, merchants in some colonies entered into non-importation agreements (that is, they banded together and agreed not to import British goods). Eventually, the taxes from the Townsend Act were repealed in 1770. However, the British government retained the import duty on tea as a symbol of parliament's control over the colonies. Out of principle, though, some colonists would just boycott tea whilst others smuggled in cheaper Dutch tea.

1767   In India, the Anglo-Mysore War was fought between the British East India Company and the Sultan of Mysore, Hyder Ali. The Company branch in Madras strongly desired more power over Mysore because it oversaw the profitable trade of the Malabar coast where the Company purchased pepper and cardamom. Hyder Ali won with the assistance of the Nizam of Hyderabad. The Company would go on to fight three more wars with the Kingdom of Mysore.

Generally, the battles in which the British engaged in India were rarely fought on a large scale and were often supplemented with Indian mercenaries at minimal expense to the British taxpayer.

1769   To protect Spanish interests in North America, particularly due to rumours that Russian traders were building outposts along the Pacific coast, a Spanish expedition was sent to, and eventually settled in, the region that is now the US state of **California** where a chain of forts and missions were created. Eventually, 21 Christian missions would be established in the region including San Diego, San Francisco, San Antonio and San Jose.

1769   **Napoleon Bonaparte** was born in Corsica to a relatively modest family of minor Italian nobility. He spoke Corsican and Italian and would not start learning French until he was ten.

1769   The **Great Bengal Famine** began and lasted approximately four years, killing around ten million people. An estimated third of the population in the region stretching from Bihar to Bengal starved to death. The famine was caused by exploitative tax revenue expansion policies of the East India Company which crippled the economic resources of the rural population and sought only to enrich Europeans at their expense.

1769   British explorer **Captain James Cook** and his crew landed in New Zealand. In 1770, he then sailed to the east coast of

Australia. Cook's final voyage ended in tragedy for him when, in 1779, he was killed during a skirmish in Hawaii.

Cook's voyages yielded a wealth of scientific information and charted the Pacific. Where he expected to find a continent, Cook stumbled across only islands. However, his team had managed to chart the whole of the east coast of Australia, which would eventually become New South Wales.

1771   Warren Hastings became Governor of Bengal.

1772   The British government opened an inquiry into the East India Company's alleged corrupt practices in India (which included tax collectors exploiting Indian farmers and numerous Company employees accumulating vast amounts of wealth using Company revenue). Robert Clive was attacked by his political opponents and charged with corruption. After the inquiry, in 1774, Clive died (possibly from committing suicide).

1772   The first of the three so-called "Partitions of Poland" occurred. The last partition took place in 1795. The Poland-Lithuanian Commonwealth would be carved up between Habsburg Austria, Prussia and Russia. Poland would not re-emerge as an independent nation until 1918.

As a result of the partitions, Russia, which up to this point only contained a minority of Jews, inherited a large Jewish population. Catherine decreed that Jews could only live in the so-called Pale of Settlement (a region consisting of Belarus, Lithuania, Moldova, a large portion of Ukraine, and parts of Latvia, Poland, and western Russia) and would be excluded from most other Russian cities.

1773   The American Revolutionary Movement (2)

The East India Company was struggling financially. There were numerous reasons behind its mounting debts but a key cause was the large-scale famine of 1769 which significantly lowered production in the Bengal region. Another key cause was the reduction of tea consumption in North America due to the colonists boycotting British tea - or smuggling cheap Dutch tea into the colonies - which severely undermined the Company's revenue (it is said the Company was left with tons of tea leaves rotting in its warehouses).

British parliament enacted two key pieces of legislation in 1773. The first was the Regulating Act, the principal aim of which was to bring the East India Company in line and overhaul its administration. The Act also brought the presidencies of Madras and Bombay under Bengal's control. It elevated Warren Hastings from Governor to the new title of Governor-General. And a council was set up: it composed of four members sent from London who could advise and, if necessary, out-vote the Governor General. A Supreme Court (the first in India) was established at Fort William to better administer the justice system. The Act also prohibited the servants of the Company from trading privately or accepting bribes.

The second piece of legislation was the Tea Act. The aims of this law were to offload the excess tea in the Company's warehouses and sell that tea to the colonies by undercutting the price of smuggled Dutch tea. The Tea Act allowed the Company to ship its tea directly to the American colonies without having to land in England and the Company was not required to pay an additional tax in England. As a result, the Company could sell the tea at a cheaper price and undercut the price of smuggled tea. Despite this, however, the colonists were still required to pay the same rate of import duties on tea pursuant to the Townsend Act (to recall, the Townsend Act was repealed but not the tea tax).

The lowered price on tea did not have the British-desired effect of pacifying the American colonists. Instead, it had the opposite effect of rousing suspicion and anger against the British. By allowing the Company to sell directly to the colonies, the colonial merchants that would otherwise be part of the enterprise were cut out of the picture. Also, the colonists saw it as an offence that they would be taxed whilst the Company could get away with not having to pay the tea tax in England. In addition, they continued to protest against the principle of the British being able to tax whatever they wanted, in this case tea.

Colonists responded by boycotting tea, intimidating the Company's pro-British agents and gathering in mobs at harbours to deter Company ships from offloading their cargo. In one incident in December, a group of men disguised themselves as Native Americans, boarded three Company ships, stole approximately £15,000 worth of tea and dumped it into the sea. This incident became known as the **Boston Tea Party**.

1774   The British government responded harshly to the Boston Tea Party incident and brought in the Coercive Acts (or what the colonists described as the "Intolerable Acts"), which were a series of repressive measures imposed on the colonists. For example: the Boston Port Act closed the port of Boston until the colonists reimbursed the British government for the damages caused by the incident; the Massachusetts Government Act curtailed self-government in Massachusetts; and the Quartering Act forced colonists to house British soldiers whenever ordered to do so.

Outraged in particular by the curtailment of self-government in Massachusetts, a group of delegates from 12 of the 13 colonies (not Georgia) met in Philadelphia (at the time, the most prominent city) to coordinate the resistance of the Intolerable Acts. Known as the **Continental Congress**, this is considered to be the first ever American government.

1774   A war between Russia and the Ottoman Empire ended with Russia victorious, gaining new lands from the Ottomans and, as a result, allowing the Russian navy access to the Black Sea.

1774   Louis XV died. As his son was already dead, the throne passed to his grandson, who became **Louis XVI** at the age of 19. His wife was **Marie Antoinette**, daughter of Maria Theresa who ruled the Habsburg Empire.

1775   In April, hundreds of British soldiers based in Massachusetts marched from Boston to Concord in order to destroy American military supplies. Local militiamen fought against British troops and the Battles of Lexington and Concord in Massachusetts followed. The infamous "shot heard round the world" refers to the first shot that was fired in the Battle of Concord, marking the beginning of the **American Revolutionary War**. In June, the Continental Congress established a Continental Army with George Washington appointed as its Commander-in-Chief.

In July, the Continental Congress presented to English King George III the Olive Branch Petition, which was a final plea for reconciliation. The petition proposed that it would recocgnise the sovereignty of the King, though expressed discontent for ministerial policy. However, George III ignored the petition - even refusing to read it - and instead issued a Proclamation of Rebellion, branding members of the Continental Congress as rebels and traitors. As Congress saw it, the only way forward from here would be to force independence from the British.

1776   English-born political activist Thomas Paine had published a pamphlet called *Common Sense* advocating independence for the people in the Thirteen Colonies.

1776   The Viceroyalty of Río de la Plata (corresponding to modern Argentina, parts of Chile, Paraguay and Uruguay) was carved out of the Viceroyalty of Peru, which was left with jurisdiction over what is now Peru and parts of Bolivia and Chile.

1776   The Wealth of Nations

The book ***An Inquiry into the Nature and Causes of the Wealth of Nations***, written by Scottish economist and philosopher **Adam**

Smith, was published. Smith introduced a number of tenets which play a major role in today's modern economy. *The Wealth of Nations* is said to have marked the birth of modern capitalism and is considered one of the most important and influential books in recent history.

Smith's theories sought to dismiss the intellectual underpinnings of mercantilism, the prevailing theory at the time. According to the mercantilist system, wealth was assumed to be fixed and finite and the goal of a state was to accumulate (or stockpile) as much gold and silver by exporting the largest possible quantity of products and importing as little as possible. Countries therefore relied on self-sufficiency and restricted trade with rival nations to avoid imports. Of course, colonialism (that is, the exploitation of other countries' resources) helped European nations to achieve this.

Mercantilism did not sit well with the American colonies, which were obliged to buy British goods and were constrained in whom they could trade with. This eventually led to revolution and, against the backdrop of the American Revolutionary War, Smith challenged the contemporary theory of mercantilism (and thus colonialism) in his book, proposing a more radical notion for its time.

He argued that the best way for a nation to grow its wealth was not by attempting to produce everything by itself, as no country could ever thrive in every sector, but by trading freely with others. Countries had natural strengths in particular areas. France, for example, had the right climate for producing wine more cheaply than Scotland which, in theory, could grow grapes in greenhouses, but the extra costs of heating would make Scottish wines far more expensive than French wines. Instead, Scotland would be better off focusing its workforce and capital on producing wool, which it could do in abundance, and then selling the wool to other countries (like France). The wealth of both the buying and selling nation would rise as labour and capital would always be optimally employed and directed to those sectors in which a nation could specialise easily. The government's role, according to Smith, should be to reduce tariffs and then step out of the way to allow free trade to flourish between nations, maximising the wealth of all.

Smith is considered to be the founding father of economic liberalism. From his work, the field of economics grew, advancing the ideas of private property and free markets we are so familiar with today. By the time of Smith's death in 1790, Britain was rapidly industrialising and his theories would resonate in a country (and soon a world) that was changing fast (more on the Industrial Revolution to follow).

1776   American Declaration of Independence

Whilst in the throes of revolution, the American colonists wrote the *Declaration of Independence*, which was ratified on **4 July**. It was drafted by Thomas Jefferson from Virginia, John Adams from Massachusetts, Benjamin Franklin from Pennsylvania, Roger Sherman from Connecticut and Robert Livingstone from New York. A famous passage from it reads as follows: "*We hold these truths to be self evident, that all men are created equal, that they are endowed by their creator with certain unalienable rights, that among these are life, liberty and the pursuit of happiness.*"

In the same month, the British poured more soldiers in to the war, landing them in New York. In August, British forces won the Battle of Brooklyn (also known as the Battle of Long Island) and had driven George Washington's Continental Army out of New York City. For the next seven years, Manhattan would serve as Britain's headquarters in its fight against the American rebels.

Washington's army would fight back, however. On Christmas night, he and his army daringly crossed the icy Delaware River and launched a surprise attack on the British at the **Battle of Trenton** in New Jersey, winning the battle for the Continental Army.

1777   The Articles of Confederation became the first constitution agreed between the Continental Congress consisting of the original 13 states: Connecticut, Delaware, Georgia, Maryland, Massachusetts, New Hampshire, New Jersey, New York, North Carolina, South Carolina, Pennsylvania, Rhode Island and Virginia.

Meanwhile, a victory for the Americans at the **Battle of Saratoga** in October proved to be a pivotal moment in the American Revolutionary War. France then entered the war in support of American independence. In 1778, France formally declared war on Britain. In 1779, Spain joined in on the side of the American and French armies.

1780   The Inca rebel Túpac Amaru II and his wife led a rebellion against Spanish authorities in an attempt to restore the former Incan Empire and liberate the local people in the Andes from increased Spanish demands for labour and taxes. However, in 1781, the Spanish colonial government put down the Inca rebellion and had Túpac and his wife executed.

1780   In what became the Fourth Anglo-Dutch War, the British and the Netherlands went to war over secret Dutch negotiations with the rebelling American colonies. After the end of the war in 1784, the Dutch East India Company was left in financial ruin and would eventually dissolve in 1799.

1781   A combination of George Washington's and his French allies' armies surrounded and defeated the British at the Battle of Yorktown, effectively spelling defeat for the British.

1783   The Treaty of Paris, ratified by the British government and the Congress of the Confederation - the recently-established governing body of the United States of America - formally **ended the American Revolutionary War** and signalled **British formal recognition of the independence of the United States**.

1783   Empress of Russia Catherine the Great annexed the Crimea, nine years after the Crimean Khanate had formally gained independence from the Ottoman Empire.

1784   The East India Company Act (also known as Pitt's India Act or second Regulating Act) intended to address the shortcomings of the 1773 Regulating Act by bringing the East India Company's rule in India under further control of the British government.

1785   Napoleon entered the French army as Second Lieutenant. He would rise up through the ranks of the army, particularly during the tumultuous years of the French Revolution (which was on the horizon).

1787   The Northwest Ordinance was enacted by the Congress of the Confederation, creating new territory northwest of the existing 13 States and setting up a process to allow new states carved from that territory to join the United States. The Ordinance outlawed slavery in the new northwest territory.

1788   The British established New South Wales in Australia as a penal colony where British convicts would arrive as the first settlers.

1788   The US Constitution

On 21 June, the **United States Constitution** went into effect after ratification by 9 of the 13 States. A federal government was established which presided over both national and state affairs. The Constitution also established a separation of powers where the executive, legislative and judicial branches were divided, meaning in theory no branch could be too powerful.

For the legislative branch, the Constitution stipulated that all legislative powers were to be vested in a Congress, consisting of two Houses: a House of Representatives and a Senate. The number of members of the House of Representatives, also called Congressmen, would be proportionate to each State's population and would serve for two years, after which their seats would be up for re-election (voted for directly by popular vote).

The Constitution also incorporated something called the "Three-Fifths Compromise". During the time of the Constitution's ratification, there was a growing anti-slavery (or abolitionist) movement in the northern States. Pennsylvania was the first State to begin the gradual abolition of slavery in 1780 and other northern States followed in due course. By contrast, the economy of the southern States relied heavily on slavery. Therefore, the southern States were keen to include African slaves in the calculation of the population - in order to boost the number of seats in the House of Representatives - whilst the northern States argued that slaves should not be counted, primarily because they could not vote or own property. Hence, a compromise was reached in the Constitution under which every enslaved African American would be counted as three-fifths of a person for taxation and representation purposes. This compromise gave the southern States more electoral power than they would have had if the enslaved population had been ignored entirely but less electoral power than they would have had if the enslaved population was fully counted. The Constitution also had a fugitive slaves clause, which meant that an escaped slave would have to be returned to their master, regardless of whether that slave escaped to a State where slavery was abolished.

The Senate, by contrast to the House of Representatives, would have a fixed two members (called Senators) from each State. Senators would serve six-year terms, though the terms were to be staggered such that a third of the seats would be up for re-election every two years. Senators would be voted by the State legislatures until the 17th Amendment was passed in 1913 establishing direct election of Senators by popular vote.

Meanwhile, on the executive side, the first Presidential election was held in 1788. There were no political parties or election campaigns. The election was uncontested and George Washington won. He would go on to serve two terms, though he declined a third term, setting the precedent that a President would only serve two. Alexander Hamilton became the first Secretary of the Treasury. Advocating a strong federal government, Hamilton created a national banking system that assumed the States' debts.

1789   The French Revolution

France's economy was in crisis. The various wars fought in the 18th century left the nation virtually bankrupt. To compound matters further, there had been years of bad harvest. The price of bread was so high that many could not afford to eat, leaving the countryside full of beggars. Their suffering stood in stark contrast to the lifestyles of rich aristocrats and members of the royal court who continued to live luxuriously while the rest of the country starved. The monarchy and nobility benefitted from tax exemptions while taxes on the poor and middle classes remained high with little to no relief. They were required to pay virtually all of the taxes and foot the bill for France's costly wars. Moreover, the French monarchy's financial and military support to the Americans in their recent war for independence was seen as a hypocrisy: the French government was advocating and fighting for liberty and democracy in North America yet continued with repression and absolutism at home.

At the time, France had a legislative body called the Estates General, which consisted of three Assemblies: the First Estate, representing the nobility, the Second Estate, representing the clergy, and the Third Estate for everyone else. The Estates General traditionally served a mere symbolic function, used by the French monarchy for political communication and applied as a ceremonial façade. Also, it had last convened in 1614. But, in May 1789, due to France's desperate economic condition, Louis XVI convened the Estates General for the first time in over 150 years. France's population had changed considerably since 1614. The non-aristocratic members of the

Third Estate now represented around 96% of the population and yet it could still be outvoted by the other two Estates via the principle of "votes by order" (that is, the collective vote of each Estate would be considered one vote and so the First and Second Estates could out-vote the Third Estate two-to-one). The Third Estate demanded a system of proportionate representation in government: one vote per delegate. The other Estates, keen to hold onto their privileges, opposed this.

On 17 June, the Third Estate declared themselves a National Assembly of the People, making it clear that they would conduct the affairs of the nation with or without the other Estates. On 19 June, the clergy voted to join them. Louis XVI subsequently dismissed the assemblies. On 20 June, the members of the Third Estate found a closed door at the location where the Estates General was being held (the King had denied them entry). So instead they went to the nearby tennis court building. The president of the new National Assembly then read out an oath, famously referred to as the "Tennis Court Oath", vowing "not to separate, and to reassemble wherever circumstances require, until the constitution of the kingdom is established". The Oath was then documented.

On 23 June, the King ordered the National Assembly to disperse. However, the Count of Mirabeau, one of the revolutionaries, famously voiced his refusal in a short impassioned speech. Soon after this event, members of the nobility had joined the National Assembly eventually forcing a reluctant Louis XVI to give in. The National Assembly renamed itself the National Constituent Assembly on 9 July.

Soon, riots overran Paris and on 14 July, insurgents **stormed the Bastille** fortress to seize ammunition. The unrest in the capital, together with rumours of a foreign invasion, led to a great panic in the rural communities. The peasants' anger was vented on feudal estates, which they pillaged and burned in the summer of 1789. Meanwhile, the National Constituent Assembly had become the effective government of France. In

August, they voted to abolish unequal taxation, feudalism and privileges for the nobles and clergy.

On 26 August, the *Declaration of the Rights of Man and Citizen* was adopted. Inspired by the ideas of contemporary enlightenment philosophers, it was a document that vowed to protect property, ensure trial by jury and guarantee free speech and religion. The first Article read: "*Men are born and remain free and equal in rights*". On 5 October, thousands of women marched on Versailles demanding bread. Louis XVI was forced to move to Paris with his wife Marie Antoinette and the rest of their family.

The events in 1789 would only be the beginning of the turbulent years to come, both in France and the rest of Europe. Like the American Revolution, the **French Revolution** was an important historical episode because it challenged the age-old principles of absolutism and consolidated the ideal that a nation is composed of citizens, who have a right to their say regarding how their government should rule. It would be the catalyst for a chain of revolutions that would play out during the 19th century. The road ahead, however, was by no means peaceful and change would not occur overnight. The French Revolution itself was extremely violent and the cause for many injustices (and would continue to be the case in the upcoming years).

Interestingly, the political terminology "left wing" and "right wing" derive from the French Revolution where there were divisions in the National Assembly: the republicans, who wanted to do away entirely with the monarchy sat on the left whilst the nobility, most loyal to monarchy, sat on the right.

1789   **George Washington** was inaugurated as the **1st President in US history**.

1790   **Washington DC,** the new capital of the USA, was founded.

1791   A slave-led uprising erupted in the French colony of Saint-

Domingue, now part of Haiti. At the time, the slaves in the region working on the sugar plantations outnumbered the white settlers by more than ten to one. The bloody fight against French oppression would last 13 years.

As a result of the insurrection, the sugar industry on the colony was wiped out. The refugees from the revolt fled to neighbouring Spanish-occupied Cuba and brought with them their money and know-how, eventually leading to Cuba becoming the world's sugar capital. Despite growing calls to end slavery in its colonies, Spain continued it late into the 19th century, arguing the economy relied on it too heavily to give it up.

1791   Construction of the Brandenburg Gate, now a famous landmark in Berlin, was completed under the reign of King Frederick William II of Prussia.

1791   The National Constituent Assembly dissolved itself after having given France its first constitution. The Legislative Assembly took its place but would only last a year. The Assembly would consist of two radical groups fighting for power: the Girondins and Jacobins. One of the Jacobins, **Maximilien Robespierre**, would rise to prominence. He called for a more republican form of government and the abolition of the monarchy.

1792   In April, the Legislative Assembly declared war on Austria and Prussia in an attempt to spread the revolutionary cause but also out of fear that exiled French nobles were stirring up a counter-revolutionary movement to restore monarchy in France.

On 10 August, King Louis XVI evaded capture by an armed mob and took shelter with the Legislative Assembly. However, he was soon arrested. On 21 September, the members of the newly-created National Convention - which had recently succeeded the Legislative Assembly - met for the first time and agreed to abolish the French monarchy and establish a new French Republic. 22 September 1792 was declared the first day of "Year I" under the new Republic (though this calendar system would be short-lived: it was abandoned in 1805).

1792   The beginnings of the New York Stock Exchange were formed via the Buttonwood Agreement signed by 24 stockbrokers at Wall Street.

In the next 20 years, the population of New York would treble in size (to about 96,000) and would surpass Philadelphia to become the United States' most populous city and busiest seaport.

1793   After a narrow vote to decide his fate, **Louis XVI was executed** via a new killing instrument called the guillotine. **Marie Antoinette was executed** later in the year. Meanwhile, Spain, Portugal, Britain and the Netherlands joined a coalition to fight against France.

The Jacobins soon took control of the National Convention from the Girondins. They committed France to a so-called **Reign of Terror**, via the setting up of the "Committee of Public Safety", which oversaw the execution of thousands of political enemies (often under the orders of Robespierre).

1794   Due to his excessive measures, Robespierre grew increasingly unpopular, particularly among rising rival factions, and there were calls for his arrest. Apparently, he attempted to commit suicide by shooting himself, but only managed to injure his jaw. Nonetheless, he and his allies were arrested and then executed.

1795   New factions in France led to a new government being established called The French Directory.

1796   Spain formed an alliance with France. In doing so, it made itself an enemy of the British, the dominant naval power at the time, which used their navy to impede trade between Spain and its American colonies. Unable to keep their monopoly over the colonies, the Spanish were forced to relax their trade restrictions. Now, the Spanish Americans could trade legally with other colonies, as well as with neutral countries such as the United States.

By the end of the 18th century, approximately one quarter of Latin Americans were mixed race. Many Creoles (those of Spanish descent but who were born in the Americas) began to question Spanish authority. The recently-relaxed trade restrictions introduced by Spain would have further increased the Creoles' desire for self-determination. Thus began the struggle for economic (and eventual political) separation from Spain.

1797   **John Adams** (the first Vice President of the US) became the **2nd US President**. By this time, there were two major political parties: the first were the Federalists, set up by Alexander Hamilton, which were a group of elitists who advocated solid national government, strong economic growth and good trading relations with Britain. The other were the Republicans, set up by Thomas Jefferson, which stood for republicanism, freedom and equality. John Adams was a Federalist, though he would be the only Federalist President in history as his party would soon fall into obscurity.

1798   By this time, Napoleon had made a name for himself as a successful general having evicted Austrian forces from the Italian Peninsula. Britain, however, remained in the war against the French. Napoleon set his sights on invading Egypt, with a view to cutting off Britain's access to India. However, he suffered defeat against the British at the Battle of the Nile, strengthening Britain's control of the Mediterranean.

1798   In India, Lord Richard Wellesley - elder brother of Arthur Wellesley (the Duke of Wellington, famous in Britain for his victory at Waterloo in 1815) - became Governor-General of Bengal. Through wars and economic pressure, Lord Wellesley would oversee the British East India Company becoming the true dominant power over India, ruling large areas of the region with its private armies, exercising military power and controlling administrative functions.

During Lord Wellesley's time in office, he adopted the policy of subsidiary alliances, meaning that Indian rulers were not allowed to enter into any negotiations or make treaties with any other ruler. They were also not allowed to keep an army. They were to be protected by forces maintained by the East India Company and had to pay for that protection. If those rulers failed to make the required payments, part of their territory would be taken away as a penalty.

1799   Napoleon's Egyptian campaign led to the discovery by a French soldier of an artefact known to us as the **Rosetta Stone**. The writing on the stone was a royal decree inscribed in three languages: hieroglyphs (the writing system of ancient Egypt), Demotic (the native Egyptian script used at the time the stone was inscribed), and ancient Greek (the language of the administration - at the point of inscription, the rulers of Egypt descended from the Greco-Macedonian Ptolemaic dynasty). The Rosetta Stone was the key to discovering the language of the ancient Egyptians and their civilisation.

In November, in a coup d'état, Napoleon helped overthrow the unpopular French Directory. He then swiftly established himself as First Consul and, in 1802, he would be made Consul for Life, arguably leading France down the road of a dictatorship.

-    The Industrial Revolution

For 15,000 years of human history up to the point of the **Industrial Revolution**, the vast majority of the population worked on farms to feed themselves and others. They had no running water or electricity, possessed few items of clothing (which had to be hand-washed) and cooked food over a fire. People travelled on horseback, education was a privilege for the few (and not a human right), and time was measured by the patterns of the days and seasons. However, soon this would all change and the pace of this change would be rapid.

By the beginning of the 20th century, the world looked a different place to what it was a hundred years ago. The majority of people were no longer farming but working in shops, transportation, mining, workshops or factories, all organising their working days and hours around timetables. Education for children became more widespread. People were travelling by railway. Some would be wealthy enough to drive cars, own refrigerators, have radios and even fly airplanes.

The Industrial Revolution could be defined as the increase in production of materials arising from the use of machines powered by newly available energy sources. It was not the result of one single invention (like the spinning jenny, power loom or steam engine) or event. Instead, it developed through the collective of people collaborating to make slight incremental changes in productivity over time (a behaviour which was explored in detail in Adam Smith's *Wealth of Nations*). It is generally believed to have started in Britain, perhaps due to the liberalisation of its economy (thanks to the ideas of Smith among others), which allowed for the free exchange of ideas, but also due to the abundance of accessible cheap energy sources available in the ground, particularly coal. Soon, though, industrialisation would spread to Western Europe and the United States. It began taking shape during the mid-18th century with the effects not fully felt until the first few decades of the 19th century. Russia, by comparison to the other European powers, remained economically and socially backward until it began industrialising in the late 19th century.

Industrialisation meant that goods, like textiles and iron, could be produced much more quickly, enabling nations to meet growing demands for products both at home and abroad. Factories would prop up in towns, turning them into major cities. The factories led to an increased demand for workers, which in turn led to a rapidly increasing number of people migrating from rural areas to cities in search of work. To ensure optimum productivity, life in the new factories was dominated by the minutes on the clock: the timetable and the assembly line would become the template for all human activities going forward.

Cotton textiles were one of the first industrially produced products and became a key commodity by the 19th century. Around three quarters of the world's cotton was produced from slave labour in the southern States of the USA, which kept overheads low for America's plantation owners. Increase in cotton production meant that slavery in America increased, and slaves were more harshly treated, in order to keep up with global demand. And the new industries reaped the benefits. Manchester in England, which grew very rich from the cotton industry, would become one of the world's first industrial cities as a result. Cotton textile production too focussed on high efficiency and keeping manufacturing costs as low as possible. Manufacturers were under pressure to make profit and stay in business. One method used to achieve this was to exploit child labour. Without any real recognition for health and safety or human rights, accidents and deaths were frequent and children were often the victims.

Throughout history, there had been a class divide between the aristocrats and peasants. But industrialisation created a new class division: that between the **bourgeoisie** (those who owned factories, corporations, banks and transportation networks) and the **proletariat** (those who worked in the factories and mines for wages: **the working class**). Whilst industrialisation improved economic output, and benefitted the upper and middle classes, those in the working class would be the ones to suffer from poor living conditions. Overcrowded accommodation, poor sanitation, lack of clean water and air pollution were all commonplace, and governments initially did very little to address these problems.

1801   **Thomas Jefferson** of the Republican party (second Vice President of the US) was inaugurated as the **3rd US President**.

1801   Catherine the Great's grandson, Alexander, became **Tsar Alexander I** after his father Peter I was assassinated. By this time, Russia had dropped out of the war against Napoleon. Meanwhile, French victories at the Battles of Marengo and Hohenlinden in the previous year forced the Austrians to seek peace. The ensuing Treaty of Lunéville officially knocked Austria out of the war. Meanwhile, Britain and France made peace pursuant to the Treaty of Amiens, ending the French Revolutionary Wars. However, peace would only be temporary and war would resume again in 1803.

1803   In the landmark decision of *Marbury v Madison* regarding the principle of judicial review, the US Supreme Court decided that it had the power to strike down laws that violated the US Constitution (that is, those laws which were deemed unconstitutional).

1803   Napoleon was eager to sell the French Louisiana territory in North America. His motives to sell may have been that France desperately needed the money to fund the wars against the slaves revolting in Saint-Domingue and potential British retaliation in Europe. President Jefferson bought the Louisiana territory for 15 million US dollars. The purchased territory included a significant portion of land west of the colonies and make up at least 15 of today's States of the US.

The size of the United States practically doubled as a result. Growing numbers of people would migrate to the Mississippi River Valley after the purchase. Some went in search of land and work. Others relocated for social, religious and personal freedoms. Enslaved Africans were brought by force to work in southern cotton plantations, affecting the delicate balance between the slave States and free States.

Meanwhile, Britain had broken its peace with France and declared war. Napoleon gathered a large army as part of his preparations to invade Britain.

1804   Following the Roman example, **Napoleon crowned himself as first Emperor of France** at the Notre-Dame Cathedral. That same year, he brought in the Napoleonic Code, drafted and completed by his appointed panel of jurists. Inspired by the ambitious project of Byzantine Emperor Justinian, the Code standardised the laws of citizenship, family and property across France. However, it was noticeably unfair for women, depriving them of individual rights. For example, a woman guilty of adultery would be treated far more severely than if a man committed the same act. In addition, Napoleon's regime introduced strict censorship and government control of the media in order to enhance his public image.

1804   The Serbian Revolution started a violent struggle for Serbian independence from the Ottoman Empire. As one revolution started, another ended: the slave revolution in Saint Domingue concluded successfully for the rebels, albeit at the expense of heavy casualties on both side. The result of the revolt was the formation of a new independent country in the Caribbean: Haiti.

        Also, by this time, all US States north of Maryland had now abolished slavery.

1804   The **world population** is estimated to have reached **one billion** in this year.

1804-   Shortly after the Louisiana Purchase, President Jefferson
1806   commissioned an expedition to travel westwards through the new Louisiana territory. The purpose was to claim new land for the US and open up a route to the Pacific, particularly before other Europeans could get there. In what became known as the Lewis and Clark Expedition (or Corps of Discovery), Captain Meriwether Lewis and his companion Second Lieutenant William Clark led a group of US army volunteers to carry out this task. The expedition started in Pittsburgh, Pennsylvania in 1804 and travelled west to arrive at the

Pacific Coast in 1805. The group eventually returned home in 1806.

1805   By this time, a new coalition was in full force: Austria, Russia and Sweden had joined Britain in the war against Napoleonic France. Napoleon decided that, to invade Britain, his fleet would need to overpower Britain's navy. However, in October, the British navy crucially defeated a French fleet at Trafalgar, leading to British domination of the seas for the rest of the Napoleonic Wars.

Napoleon's luck changed though when, in November, his forces captured Vienna. Then, in December, Napoleon defeated the armies of the Holy Roman Emperor Francis II and Russian Emperor Tsar Alexander I at the **Battle of Austerlitz**, one of the most decisive battles in his European campaign.

1806   The British seized the Cape Colony from French rule.

Following the Battle of Austerlitz, Francis II abdicated as Holy Roman Emperor and **dissolved the Holy Roman Empire**. Napoleon reorganised the German states within the former empire into the newly established **Confederation of the Rhine**, which became subject to French rule. Meanwhile, to maintain his position as an emperor, Francis reigned over the newly formed Empire of Austria (which was essentially the lands of the Habsburg dynasty) as Francis I.

In the twin battles of Jena and Auerstedt, Napoleon's armies defeated the Prussian armies under King Frederick William III and inflicted heavy casualties. In the aftermath, the French captured Berlin and subjugated the Kingdom of Prussia, bringing it too under French rule.

As a response to the British naval blockade of the French coasts earlier in the year, Napoleon issued the Berlin Decree (known as the Continental System), which brought into effect a large-scale embargo against British trade.

1807   In response to Portugal's refusal to join the Continental System, Napoleon's armies invaded Portugal with the assistance of Spanish king Charles IV. The entire Portuguese royal family and their royal court fled to their South American colony of Brazil.

1808   Napoleon turned against the Spanish monarchy, overthrowing Charles and his son Ferdinand, ending Bourbon rule in Spain. Napoleon then installed his brother, Joseph Bonaparte, as the new King of Spain.

The power struggle in Spain would trigger revolutionary activity in Latin America where the Creoles would fight for autonomy against those loyal to Spanish rule (known as Peninsulars). One person of particular importance to the South American independence movement was Venezuelan-born solider and statesman, **Simón Bolívar** (known today as **El Libertador**). He roused the South American people to rise up against Spanish rule. In the northern part of South America, Bolívar would begin the people's struggle for independence by liberating the region that formed part of the Viceroyalty of New Granada.

1809   **James Madison** of the Republican party was inaugurated as the **4th US President**.

1810   French troops captured Seville and gained control of most of Andalusia. When news of these events arrived in Buenos Aires in South America, this sparked the May Revolution: the Spanish Viceroy was overthrown by Creoles and replaced by an independent government in Buenos Aires. The Viceroyalty of the Río de la Plata dissolved and, in its place, the **United Provinces of the Río de la Plata** (now present-day **Argentina**) was created. The Argentine War of Independence subsequently began, with those loyal to an independent Argentina fighting against those faithful to the Spanish crown.

1811   A military uprising in Asuncion resulted in Paraguay declaring independence from Spanish rule.

1812   **José de San Martín,** having resigned from the Spanish army, set sail for Buenos Aires to join Argentina's revolutionary cause. As well as Bolívar, he would also go on to become an important figure in the South American independence movement.

1812   Napoleon set his sights on invading Russia, particularly after the country's refusal to comply with the Continental System, and gathered an army of up to 650,000 men for the invasion. The Russians refused to engage in battle and instead adopted the tactics of 'scorched earth policy' where they destroyed their resources in the cities and abandoned them before the French arrived, forcing many French soldiers to starve. Finally in September, the two sides engaged at the **Battle of Borodino**, which the French won but suffered heavy casualties in the process. Soon after the battle, the French entered Moscow but it too was left abandoned and burned.

As October arrived, the country grew bitterly cold and Napoleon ordered a retreat. Many of his soldiers were dead, wounded, captured or had deserted. To survive the harsh winter, soldiers were apparently forced to split open animals and crawl inside the carcasses for shelter. Napoleon had expected Tsar Alexander to surrender but he never did. By the end of the year, Napoleon had fully retreated, ending his Russian campaign in disaster. Only a handful of the army that had began the campaign made it back to France alive.

Britain's naval blockade policies sought to restrict the USA from trading with France. To man the blockade, in an action known as "impressment", Britain forced American merchant sailors into its navy. Also, the British were supporting Native Americans in their fight against the attempted western expansion by the US. It was a culmination of these factors that led to the US declaring war on Britain. This war would become known as the **War of 1812**.

1813   Spurred on by Napoleon's recent disastrous Russian campaign, Prussia, Austria, Sweden and a collection of German states joined Russia, Spain, Portugal and Britain to form a new coalition. The French won initial battles against the Prussians and Russians at Lützen and Bautzen. They then won a major battle against the Prussians, Russians and Austrians at Dresden. However, later in the year, at the **Battle of Leipzig** (or the Battle of the Nations) - the largest European battle in history prior to the Great War - a combination of Austrian, Prussian, Russian and Swedish armies defeated Napoleon's armies. Meanwhile, the Spanish and Portuguese, with the support of British forces - led by Arthur Wellesley, the Duke of Wellington - had defeated Joseph Bonaparte and driven French forces out of Spain.

    After only seven years since being formed, the **Confederation of the Rhine was dissolved** by the coalition.

1814   The coalition armies marched on and entered Paris. Soon afterwards, **Napoleon abdicated** and was exiled to the Mediterranean island of Elba. Louis XVIII (Louis XVI's brother) was installed on the French throne, ushering in what is called the Bourbon Restoration.

    With Napoleon's armies defeated, Britain turned its attention to the War of 1812 and captured Washington DC, burning government buildings, including the White House. However, US forces would fight back in subsequent battles.

1815   In the aftermath of Napoleon's defeat, a **Congress in Vienna** was held to discuss the future of Europe and establish a balance of powers to ensure peace would be restored across the continent. The Congress included representatives from Russia, Prussia, Austria, France and Britain and was chaired by Klemens von Metternich, an influential Austrian diplomat. Resulting from the Congress: the new Kingdom of Netherlands was created; Austria regained Venice and northern Italy; Prussia gained the Rhineland among other territories; and

Russia gained portions of Poland. In addition, Russia, Austria and Prussia formed the Holy Alliance to suppress revolutionary movements in Europe that were seen as immoral threats to the legitimacy of Christian monarchy.

Another key outcome of the Congress was - following the recent dissolution of the Confederation of the Rhine - the creation of the **German Confederation**, consisting of 39 German-speaking states (a consolidation of the 300+ states that made up the former Holy Roman Empire). The Confederation, in particular, consisted of territories belonging to Prussia and the Austrian Empire. These two kingdoms would rival one another to be the Confederation's most influential and powerful member. Metternich of Austria dominated the Confederation's affairs up to 1848. However, Prussia was not far behind. During the early 19th century, Prussia was the only German state that could match the power and influence of the Austrian Empire. It was fast becoming comparable in terms of size, population and wealth. Acquisition of the Rhineland gave Prussia access to vast amounts of raw materials such as coal, iron and wood, allowing it to industrialise rapidly during the first half of the century.

There would be growing calls among the German states for unification, which Prussia saw as an opportunity to exert its dominance. Austria saw this as a threat to its own empire and opposed the idea. There were multiple ethnicities within the Austrian borders and, although the German-speakers were a minority, there was a significant percentage in the Austrian Empire which, if they broke away to join a unified Germany led by Prussia, would make the empire smaller and weaker.

In February 1815, Napoleon escaped Elba, returned to France and took control of the country again during a period that came to be known as the Hundred Days Campaign. He gathered an army and confronted the coalition once more. He secured some victories initially but was conclusively defeated by the British, led by the Duke of Wellington, and Prussians at the **Battle of Waterloo**. After his defeat at Waterloo, Napoleon surrendered and was exiled to the island of Saint Helena in the South Atlantic.

Meanwhile, the Treaty of Ghent ended the War of 1812 between Britain and the US, with neither country making any significant territorial gains. However, the war arguably further boosted national sentiment in the US and some Americans described the war as their "second war of independence". During the course of the 19th century, the US would expand significantly. For starters, in the next five years, Indiana, Mississippi, Illinois, Alabama and Maine were all admitted as new States and more would follow.

Also in 1815, **Mount Tambora**, a volcano on the island of Sumbawa (part of modern Indonesia), erupted and killed over 90,000 people. It is the **largest volcanic eruption in recorded history**. Due to the eruption, there were serious consequences for the global climate, leading to harvest failures. 1816 would be described as the "Year without Summer" due to the effects of the eruption.

1816   A representative assembly formally recognised the independence of the United Provinces of the Río de la Plata, recognised today as Argentina.

1817   **James Monroe** of the Republican party was inaugurated as the **5th US President**.

1817   Following an uprising in 1815, Serbia became an independent principality under the Ottoman Empire.

1818   After a daring crossing of the Andes, and victories at the Battle of Chacabuco in 1817 and Maipú in 1818, José San Martín liberated Chile from royalist rule. Chile subsequently declared independence.

1819   The USA purchased Florida from Spain.

1820   The US Congress passed a bill granting Missouri statehood as a slave State - and Maine was carved out of Massachusetts as a free State - under the condition that slavery was to be forever prohibited in any new States north of the 36°30 parallel. The US government was under pressure to maintain the balance and ease tension between free States in the north and slave States in the south, aiming to avoid either group having more power over the other.

1821   After a decline in health, **Napoleon died** in Saint Helena. Decades after his death, his remains were ceremoniously returned to France and placed in a tomb in the heart of Paris.

1821   Following a decisive victory of Simón Bolívar's revolutionary forces against the Spanish monarchy at the Battle of Carabobo, **Gran Colombia**, a collection of recently-freed countries formerly part of the Viceroyalty of New Granada, was established with its capital at Bogotá. Bolívar was elected as its president. Meanwhile, after seizing partial control of Lima, San Martín was made Protector of Peru and **Peru was declared independent**.

        In the same year, after a protracted struggle for independence which began in 1810, the Viceroyalty of New Spain - which covered essentially all of Central America and stretched to parts of North and South America - became the sovereign nation of **Mexico** upon the signing of the Treaty of Córdoba. This ushered in a very brief period of monarchy (which lasted until 1823) called the Mexican Empire.

        After achieving independence, the Mexicans implemented measures to ensure that their lands were well-settled with inhabitants. In the same year, an American named Stephen Austin settled around 300 families and their slaves in the Mexican region of **Texas**. In return for the land, they agreed to convert to Catholicism and swear allegiance to Mexico. But soon, thousands of American squatters (some fugitives and outlaws and others simply in search of better life) were arriving and carving out their own parcels of land without permission, eventually outnumbering the Spanish-speaking "Tejanos". In 1832, Sam Houston, a former Governor of Tennessee, settled in Texas.

1821   Uprisings by Greek rebels began against the Ottoman Turks starting **Greece's war of independence**.

1822   Simón Bolívar and José de San Martín held a private meeting (known as the **Guayaquil Conference**) following which it was agreed that Bolívar would take over the task of completing the liberation of Peru - which he would successfully achieve over the next few years - with San Martín stepping down.

Meanwhile, Portuguese king John VI returned to Portugal after having lived in Brazil during the Napoleonic Wars. However, he left his son Prince Pedro behind to rule Brazil. The native Brazilians saw themselves as culturally different to the Portuguese and had formed a political movement, which resulted in Pedro declaring **Brazil's independence** (he would rule as Brazil's first emperor).

1823   A congress of Central America declared absolute independence from Spain, Mexico and any other foreign nations. The Federal Republic of Central America (consisting of present-day Guatemala, El Salvador, Honduras, Nicaragua and Costa Rica) was formed. However, over the next few decades, a series of civil conflicts would lead (by 1841) to its dissolution and the eventual establishment of the independent countries in central America we are familiar with today.

The Mexican Empire collapsed and, in 1824, the Republic of Mexico was established under a federal constitution. Within decades, its northern territories would soon be engulfed by ruthless US expansionism.

1823   In an address to US Congress, President Monroe sent out a message to European nations warning them that any future attempt to colonise the Americas would be seen as an act of aggression. In return, the US would not meddle in European affairs. This principle of foreign policy would become known as the **Monroe Doctrine**.

1825   In his attempts to liberate as much of Latin America as possible, Simón Bolívar travelled further south and liberated the region referred to by the Spanish as "Upper Peru". It became independent and was renamed **Bolivia** after Bolívar.

1825   **John Quincy Adams** of the Republican party was inaugurated as the **6th US President**.

1825   Alexander I of Russia was succeeded by his brother Nicholas to become **Tsar Nicholas I**.

1827   Joseph Nicéphore Niépce, a French inventor, produced what is considered the **earliest surviving photograph**.

1828   Despite the ambition of Gran Colombia, it was riddled with political sensitivities. Bolívar was not without his enemies and, in 1828, survived an assassination attempt. After this, he retreated to Santa Marta where he died in 1830 while awaiting voluntary exile to Europe.

Despite his attempts to create unity, and with the wars of independence now over, the Latin American regions no longer saw a reason for partnership. Gran Colombia eventually dissolved in 1830 and, the following year, Venezuela and Ecuador were established as independent states alongside New Granada (consisting primarily of Colombia, Panama and other neighbouring states). New Granada would eventually become Colombia in 1863, again comprising mostly of present-day Colombia and Panama.

Meanwhile, after Brazil and Argentina renounced claims to the territory east of the River Plata, Uruguay was established as an independent nation and its constitution was formalised in

1830.

1828   Construction began on the first railroad in the US: the Baltimore and Ohio Railroad. In 1832, New York City would have its first railroad: the New York & Harlem line.

1828-   Russian support for Greece in its struggle for independence led
29   to war between Russia and the Ottoman Empire. Russian victory led to the Treaty of Adrianople which brought further gains in the Black Sea region for Russia. In addition, the Ottomans were required to recognise Greek and Serbian autonomy.

1829   **Andrew Jackson** was sworn in as the **first US President of the Democratic party** (and **7th** overall) after defeating John Quincy Adams in the 1828 presidential election.

1830   The so-called "**Great Game**" had begun between Britain and Russia. The British established a new trade route to the Emirate of Bukhara (correlating to Uzbekistan and Tajikistan). They intended to gain control over the Emirate of Afghanistan and make it a protectorate. The aim was to create a buffer against Russian expansion and prevent them from controlling any ports on the Persian Gulf.

         The Great Game is the name given to the long-term rivalry between Britain - threatened by Russian expansion in central Asia creeping south towards India, the 'jewel' in the crown of the British Empire - and Russia - keen on extending its empire but equally threatened by Britain extending north of India.

1830   President Jackson signed off on the Removal Act, leading to the US government forcibly removing Native Americans from their ancestral lands in the eastern part of the United States to places west of the Mississippi in order to allow for European American settlement in their place. In all, some 90,000 Native Americans were relocated. Thousands of them died on a route they remember as the "**Trail of Tears**".

1830   Another revolution broke out in France. Charles X, who had succeeded his brother Louis XVIII, had introduced strict censorship of the press, compensation for losses suffered by aristocrats in the 1789 revolution and other regressive measures such as the death penalty for stealing church artefacts. Civil unrest broke out and, in the "Three Glorious Days" of July 1830, Charles X abdicated and was replaced by Louis Philippe of the Orleans dynasty, a proponent for the expansion of voting rights in France.

1831   After a revolution in 1830, predominantly in objection to Protestant rule, **Belgium** separated from the Netherlands as an independent state and adopted its own constitution.

1831   Slave abolitionist William Lloyd Garrison began publishing an antislavery newspaper called *The Liberator* in the US, calling for the immediate abolition of slavery. Two years later, he helped found the American Anti-Slavery Society, which would grow significantly in popularity.

1832   After winning complete independence from the Ottomans, the Kingdom of Greece was established.

1833   In the UK, the **Slavery Abolition Act abolished slavery across the British Empire**. After this, millions of Indian and Chinese workers would fill the gap that the slave workers left, often for low wages. They worked on sugar plantations in the Caribbean, farms in the Cape Colony, railways in East Africa and in the army in Kenya.

        Since the British occupation of the Cape Colony, Afrikaners (the Dutch-speaking people who had already settled there (also called Boers)) clashed with their new British rulers. Since many were reliant on slave labour, the abolition law was unwelcome news for them. Many Boers felt compelled to depart their homes to avoid British rule and moved inland, venturing further into Africa.

In the same year, the UK also enacted the Government of India Act where it was decided that the East India Company should cease to be a trading company and become a purely administrative body.

1834   Under the influence of Prussia, the Zollverein, a customs union within the German Confederation, officially started in order to strengthen the economies of the German states and limit trade barriers between them. Austria was not included.

1835   The Texas Revolution began after a decade of political and cultural conflicts between the Mexican government and the growing population of American settlers in Texas.

1835   The British imposed special taxes on Indian salt to enable the sale of its own-imported British salt. The tax raised the price of Indian salt and made it difficult for Indians, especially the poor, to buy the salt they needed. This policy continued throughout the 19th century, during which the British would introduce a series of "salt laws" that made it illegal for Indians to collect, manufacture or sell their own salt.

1836   US Congress passed the controversial "gag rule", which prohibited members of Congress from considering anti-slavery petitions. The rule angered representatives of the northern anti-slavery States.

Meanwhile, at the Battle of San Jacinto, a Texian army led by Sam Houston defeated the Mexicans. Texas was made independent with Houston as president. He was convinced Texas would become a State of the US within a few months. However, he would have to wait almost a decade before this would happen.

1837   **Martin Van Buren** of the Democratic party (former Vice President to Andrew Jackson) became the **8th US President**. Upon taking office, he was required to deal with the issue over the newly independent Texas. Its congress called for union with the United States. However, Van Buren refused this, probably because he feared it would disrupt the balance of power too much in favour of the southern slave States and further anger the northern States.

1839-
42

The Opium Wars

From the 1700s, Britain, as well as other European rivals, traded with China for luxury goods such as porcelain, silk and tea. But the Chinese generally did not take an interest in European-manufactured products. They were only interested in one form of payment: silver bullion. Whilst the Europeans had their colonies, and thus access to a cheap supply of silver, this deal worked well for them. However, the international silver market would diminish due to the numerous conflicts fought over the past century, particularly those where colonists fought to be independent from their colonisers.

Britain too was impacted and struggled with obtaining the amount of silver needed to trade with China without damaging its own economy. At the same time, British demand for luxurious goods, especially tea, was increasing significantly, meaning it was heavily reliant on trade with China to meet its demands at home. In the late 18th century, the British East India Company looked to an alternative form of payment to the Chinese: opium. With its control over India secured, the East India Company could, with unfettered restriction, order that the poppy plant be grown on Indian soil (predominantly in the Bengal region) and ship the resulting opium to China.

The Chinese government at first tolerated the opium trade because it benefitted its economy. However, opium addiction in China soon became a widespread societal problem. The effects of opium produced in India were much stronger than the medicinal type the Chinese were traditionally used to. The Qing Emperor banned opium in China at the end of the 18th century, meaning that cultivation of it, as well as trading it with the British, was illegal. Those in breach of the ban were punished harshly. The East India Company, though, ignored the ban and continued to illegally smuggle opium into China. The British merchants used an island off the coast of China - called Lintin (or Lingding) Island - to continue to smuggle the drugs and Chinese opium buyers risked their lives to buy it.

The Chinese government started to become more hostile to foreign merchants and the East India Company withdrew in 1834. In response to this, the British government itself intervened and appointed three superintendents of trade to oversee the British opium business in China, ignorant to its illegality. Soon, they were provocatively approaching Chinese shores to protect the trade. In response, the Chinese government arrested the Chinese who were involved and executed some of them.

The war between China and Britain began when, in 1839, a group of drunken British sailors destroyed property and killed a Chinese peasant. The government wanted to make an example out of one of the sailors by punishing him in accordance with Chinese laws. Whilst the British government agreed to compensate the dead peasant's family, it did not agree to its sailors being subject to Chinese law. The Chinese saw this as an affront and halted trade with the British. Troops were marched into Macau and laid siege on the Canton factories. Chinese war junks were used to block the British merchants. The British then opened fire on one of the junks. This led to the Battle of Kowloon, which resulted in a stalemate. The so-called **First Opium War** continued until it ended in 1842 after the superior British navy took control of Shanghai. The Treaty of Nanking was signed which forced China to pay a large indemnity in silver. The treaty also required the reopening of trade - including the opium trade - and that **Hong Kong was ceded to Britain in perpetuity**.

1839- The **First Anglo-Afghan War** took place, one of the first major
42 conflicts arising from the so-called "Great Game". Such was the paranoia of the British that the Russians would expand into

central Asia and threaten India that they decided to orchestrate a regime change in Afghanistan. They intended to overthrow the ruler Dost Muhammad and replace him with a pro-British ruler, Shah Shuja. The war, however, was a complete disaster for the British who saw almost their entire army wiped out during their treacherous retreat to India. Only one British army officer apparently returned without being killed or captured. Dost Muhammad was eventually reinstalled.

1841   **William Henry Harrison** of the Whig Party became the **9th US President** but died after only 32 days in power, making him the first president to die in office and the shortest-serving in US history. Then-Vice President **John Tyler** stepped in to become **10th US President.**

1843   Around a thousand emigrants made their way to Oregon, land to the northwest of the US that the Americans were seeking to claim ahead of the British. Thousands more would follow in the next few years.

1845   **James Knox Polk** of the Democratic Party was inaugurated as the **11th US President** after winning a narrow election in the previous year. An ambitious expansionist, he annexed Texas to the United States and granted it statehood. Sam Houston was named its first Senator.

By the mid-1840s, thousands of American settlers had filed through the Sierra Nevada mountains and down into California's Sacramento valley. The Mexican army in northern California requested from Mexico City additional soldiers to keep the Americans out.

1845-   The First Anglo-Sikh War was fought between the Sikh Empire,
1846   which asserted sovereignty over Kashmir, and the East India Company. In the aftermath of the war, the Company sold the Kashmir Valley to the prince of Jammu, Gulab Singh. Under Singh, the Kashmir Valley became part of the state of Jammu and Kashmir.

1845-
52

The potato crop failed in Ireland. This was a catastrophe due to Ireland's heavy reliance on the potato as a source of food. It caused the **Great Famine in Ireland** where about a million people died and a further million were forced to emigrate (many to the US) in search for a better life. The sheer volume of deaths and emigration during this time lowered Ireland's population so much that it is said to still be recovering to this day. To add to the hardship, as Ireland was a colony of Britain, despite the famine, much of its produce continued to be exported to feed Britain.

1846

When Mexico refused to sell the provinces of New Mexico and California to the US, President Polk used a border skirmish along the Rio Grande to persuade Congress to declare war on Mexico. The war became known as the **Mexican-American War**.

The US and Great Britain signed the Oregon Treaty to settle the territory dispute between the two nations in the Northwest Pacific, a dispute which Polk had threatened with war unless Britain gave up its claim. The Oregon Treaty set the US and British North American border at the 49th parallel. The territory encompassed an area that included the current states of Oregon, Washington and Idaho, as well as parts of Wyoming and Montana.

Meanwhile, around 10,000 Latter-Day Saints (a minority American Christian denomination) began leaving their homes to travel West to a location which they believed was the perfect home for them and where they could avoid persecution for their beliefs. Under their leader, Brigham Young, they settled in the valley of the Great Salt Lake (now in Utah) starting in 1847. They were better known as the **Mormons** after their scripture, the Book of Mormons, which claimed that, among other things, Jesus Christ had preached in America shortly after his resurrection.

1848   ***The Communist Manifesto***, written by **Karl Marx** and **Friedrich Engels**, was published in London. It defined in print ideas of socialism and class struggles that had been developing at the time. It predicted that the proletariat - the working class - would rise up in revolt against the bourgeoisie (the latter seen to be commoditising the former). The true impact of the Manifesto would not be felt until a hundred years later when communism would spread in certain areas of the world and lead to the Cold War.

In the meantime, resulting from a combination of continuous harvest failures, a rise in food prices, poor economies, job losses, anti-monarchy sentiment, and the spread of liberalist, socialist and nationalist ideals, **revolutions swept across mainland Europe**. They started in January in Sicily before spreading to mainland Italy. By the end of the year, France, the Austrian Empire, Denmark, Hungary, the Italian and German states and elsewhere in Europe were engulfed in one the greatest revolutions the continent had seen.

The demands of the revolutionaries in Europe centred around the creation of constitutionally-directed and democratic government structures and an end to oppression of peasants. Despite these demands, however, nearly all of the revolts were put down quickly and the 1848 revolutions would lead to very little political change. Some lasted a little longer. It took until 1849, for example, for the Hungarian Revolution to be put down by an Austro-Russian alliance.

In the Austrian Habsburg Empire, a rise in nationalism was the key theme behind the rebellions. The empire, with its capital at Vienna, at the time ruled a diverse range of ethnic groups including Germans, Hungarians, Czechs, Poles, Serbs, Croats and Italians all of whom strived for more autonomy. As a result of the revolutions within the Austrian Empire, the very unpopular Klemens von Metternich was forced to resign and flee. Also, Emperor of Austria Ferdinand I abdicated and was replaced by his nephew Francis Joseph. When Metternich and Ferdinand resigned, though, nothing much changed politically due to lack of agreement between the different classes (namely, the aristocracy, middle class, workers and peasants) wanting different things. The disunity among the classes allowed the rebellions to be put down by the Austrian monarchy.

In the Italian states, the subjugated peoples took up arms against their Austrian rulers. Charles Albert, King of Sardinia, declared war on Austria, marking the start of the first **Italian War of Independence**. At this time, most Italians would not have even called themselves Italian. They were Sicilian, Genoese, Venetian, Veronese, Sardinian etc. But there was growing nationalist sentiment over the 19th century which would eventually take the Italians down the road to a unified Italy. The first war of independence, though, was unsuccessful and the Italians would have to wait a little longer to achieve it.

In France, Louis Philippe was forced to abdicate and a new (albeit short-lived) French Republic was established with Louis Napoleon Bonaparte, nephew of 'the' Napoleon, elected as its President. The new Republic abolished slavery in all French colonies.

In the German states, King Frederick William IV of Prussia was forced to call a new German Parliament in Frankfurt to discuss government reform based on liberalism and democracy, draw up a German constitution and attempt German unification. However, these attempts, and the parliament itself, were short-lived and ultimately failed. Frederick William was offered the crown of a unified German empire but refused it, apparently remarking he would "not accept a crown from the gutter" as it was not offered by the German states' princes.

The turmoil of the revolutions and poor economies forced many Europeans to flee mainland Europe and emigrate to the USA, UK and Australia. Many migrants were drawn to America by demands for labour, the promise for land and democratic ideals. Lots of them settled along the East Coast but others travelled into the mid-West, which were already home to the natives. New York, in particular, received a vast number of immigrants, consisting of Irish, German and Scandinavian people among others. Jewish arrivals would make up a large Jewish community in New York.

1848   The Treaty of Guadalupe Hidalgo ended the Mexican-American War and forced Mexico to give up the northern territories of Alta California and Santa Fe de Nuevo México to the United States. Mexico also gave up claims to Texas and accepted the Rio Grande as its northern border with the US.

Meanwhile, in a place called Sutter's Mill in Coloma in California, a man called James W. Marshall stumbled across gold whilst walking along the banks of the American River to check on the progress of the mill's construction. Before the discovery, California was predominantly populated with Native Americans and Mexicans. After this, however, in what would be called the **California Gold Rush**, people from around the world very quickly flocked to California. Chinese peasants, Mexican farmers, European migrants as well as fellow Americans all arrived in search of riches. Around half a billion dollars worth of gold would be found over the next decade. Successive gold rushes occurred in the western part of North America throughout the second half of the 19th century: places such as Fraser Canyon, the Cariboo District and other parts of British Columbia, Nevada, the Rocky Mountains in Colorado, Idaho, Montana, eastern Oregon, western New Mexico Territory and along the lower Colorado River.

The effects of European immigration in new US territories like California were catastrophic for the Native American people and their population rapidly diminished over the course of the 19th century. They were segregated, discriminated against, subjected to horrific treatment and often killed. Native American deaths were also caused by European immigration indirectly. For example, they caught European diseases like cholera. Many starved too: the locals had traditionally relied on hunting game to eat but that game had been driven away and displaced due to the gold mines.

1848-
1849

In India, the British army won the Second Anglo-Sikh War, subjugating the Sikh Empire and annexing the Punjab.

1849

Zachary Taylor (of the Whig Party) was inaugurated as the **12th US President**. In the same year, tens of thousands of people - who would come to be known as the "Forty-Niners" - began their perilous journeys to the mining regions of California in search of fortune. The population of San Francisco, in particular, exploded over the next few days due to this influx of people.

1849

Charles Albert was forced to abdicate and was replaced by his son Victor Emmanuel II who became King of Sardinia.

1850

California was granted statehood and was declared a free State as part of the Compromise of 1850, which was legislation designed to ease tensions between slave States and free States. As part of the compromise, US citizens were obliged to turn fugitive slaves to the authorities, making it easier for slave-owners to recover runaway slaves.

Due to the attraction of gold mining, the population of San Francisco had rapidly grown to about 35,000, making it one of the first major cities in the American West. California now had more immigrants than any other part of the United States.

1850

Zachary Taylor died from an illness and so then-Vice President **Millard Fillmore** succeeded him to become the **13th US President**.

1851

The first major railway opened in Russia after construction of the St. Petersburg-to-Moscow railroad was completed. Due to the harsh working conditions, thousands of serfs lost their lives during construction.

1851   Louis Napoleon Bonaparte staged a coup d'état resulting in a new French Empire. Napoleon was crowned **Emperor Napoleon III**.

1852   Harriet Beecher Stowe's popular anti-slavery novel, *Uncle Tom's Cabin*, was published. Within a year, more than 1.5 million books were in print worldwide.

1852   Lord Dalhousie, the Governor-General of India at the time, introduced the "Doctrine of Lapse" which stated that if an Indian ruler would die without a natural heir, ownership of his territory would be assigned to the British.

1853   **Franklin Pierce** of the Democratic Party, a staunch supporter of the Southern position on slavery, was inaugurated as the **14th US President.**

1853   The **Crimean War** began. By this time, the Ottoman Empire (labelled as the "sick man of Europe") was weakening, having lost various territories - such as Greece - in recent decades. The British feared that the Russians would further exploit the vulnerability of the Ottomans and continue their expansion around the Black Sea, therefore threatening Britain's passage to India.   Emperor Napoleon III of France, keen to restore France's greatness on the world stage, also opposed Russia's expansionist policy.

The incident that triggered the Crimean War centred around access rights of Christian minorities in the Holy Land (correlating to modern Israel and Palestine among other places) which was then a part of the Ottoman Empire. The French promoted the rights of Roman Catholics, while Russia promoted those of the Eastern Orthodox Church. Tension increased when Orthodox and Catholic monks clashed in Bethlehem. Tsar Nicholas I blamed the Turks for the deaths of Orthodox monks. He demanded a Russian protectorate over all 12 million Orthodox Christians in the Ottoman Empire, with control of the Orthodox

Church's hierarchy. When the Turks refused, the Tsar sent his armies into the Danubian principalities. At the ensuing Battle of Sinop, the Russians destroyed a Turkish fleet. Public opinion in France and Britain showed outrage at Russia and, in alliance with the Ottomans, their respective governments found the perfect pretext to wage war against the Russians.

1854   US Congress passed the **Kansas-Nebraska Act**, which created two new territories, Kansas and Nebraska. It proposed to hold a special election that would leave the issue of slavery to be self-determined by the settlers, effectively repealing the 1820 Missouri Compromise.

For more than half a century, members of Congress had been continually quarrelling over whether new territories would be free States or slave States, each time working out a delicate compromise to restore balance in the legislature. The Kansas-Nebraska Act was another attempt at a compromise. In reality, though, it only intensified the issue. On election day, over 5,000 pro-slavery armed men (called "Border Ruffians") flooded into Kansas from Missouri to try and influence the vote: they seized polling places and cast fraudulent votes. They also introduced legislation that made it a crime to criticise slavery. Their anti-slavery opponents (called "Free Soilers") countered the Border Ruffians with their own election and drew up a constitution that outlawed slavery (albeit barring black settlers).

Kansas was left with two conflicting governments and violence broke out between the two factions (the name "**Bleeding Kansas**" was given to the episode). The new **Republican party** (the political party as it is officially recognised today), devoted to halting the expansion of slavery, was formed as a result of the incident.

1854-   The **Siege of Sevastopol** in the Crimean War lasted a year
55   and resulted in victory for the British, French and Ottomans. In 1855, Tsar Nicholas I died and was succeeded by his eldest son Alexander who became Tsar Alexander II.

1856   As violence escalated in Kansas, it found its way into Congress too. When a Massachusetts State Senator called Charles Sumner gave his "*Crime Against Kansas*" speech, a South Carolina Congressman called Preston Brooks beat him half to death with a cane on the Senate floor.

1856   The Treaty of Paris ended the Crimean War: the defeated Russians were forced to respect the integrity of the Ottoman Empire and were prohibited from military access to the Black Sea, curtailing their influence in the region. A key factor during the war was that Austria refused to come to Russia's aid, ending their Holy Alliance.

Russia's humiliation in the Crimean War exposed the nation's underdevelopment both economically and militarily. Unlike the other European powers, Russia had not yet industrialised and did not have the necessary infrastructure to compete with them. Russian factories were not producing the type of weapons or machinery to match other nations and the railway system was inadequate. Upon inheriting the throne, Tsar Alexander II knew that major reforms were required.

1856   A Second Opium War took place leading to a British victory once again.

1857   **James Buchanan** of the Democratic Party was inaugurated as the **15th US President**. In the previous year, his party defeated the newly-formed pro-abolitionist Republican Party. Meanwhile, in a landmark decision from the infamous *Dred Scott* case, the US Supreme Court refused to recognise the freedom of a slave, Dred Scott, even though he had lived for many years on free soil. It was held that all African Americans, whether they were free or slaves, were not US citizens and not eligible to bring a claim in the federal courts. The decision outraged abolitionists.

1857   The **Indian Rebellion of 1857** had its roots in Indian resentment towards British rule, which had been building up over a long period. The specific trigger for the revolt, however, related to the requirements for loading the Enfield P53 Rifle imposed on Indian sepoys (soldiers hired by, and who fought for, the British East India Company). To load the rifle, it required that the user bite the paper cartridge open to release the powder. The paper cartridges came pre-greased. The grease used was said to have a combination of beef and pork fat. Consuming the beef would have been offensive to Hindus, and consuming the pork would have offended Muslims.

At the time, there were over 300,000 sepoys in the army, compared to around 50,000 British troops. 85 soldiers in an army garrison at Meerut refused to take the cartridges. The culprits were sentenced to imprisonment and were put in chains by British officers to humiliate them. A mutiny then broke out and the sepoys marched on Delhi, temporarily occupying it between May and September. Lucknow was besieged until November and Kanpur was also captured. The mutineers had the support of Bahadur Shah, the Mughal Emperor at the time. The British, with the help of the Sikhs (who were resentful of the Mughals who persecuted them) eventually recaptured Delhi and Lucknow and put down the mutiny. The most violent atrocities were committed on both sides. Hundreds of thousands of Indian soldiers, citizens and villagers were killed at the hands of the British and many more would have died from famine and disease. Bahadur Shah, the **last Mughal Emperor**, was arrested and exiled.

1858   A peace treaty was signed, ending the Indian Rebellion of 1857. The British passed the Government of India Act, which nationalised the East India Company and transferred power of India over to the British Crown. The ruling entity became known as the **British Raj**: India was now under the direct rule of Britain. The Governor-General of India acquired a new title: Viceroy of India.

1858   The **French invasion of Indochina**, present-day Vietnam, Cambodia and Laos, began with an attack on the ancient Vietnamese port of Da Nang under the orders of Napoleon III.

1859   A **Second War of Italian Independence** began when France allied with the Italian Kingdom of Sardinia and captured territories from the Austrian Empire.

1859   American businessman Edwin (or Colonel) Drake became the **first American to successfully drill for oil** when, using a driller, he struck oil at Titusville, Pennsylvania. Oil was already a known substance before this time. In fact, the ancient Chinese, Egyptian and Babylonian civilisations had been using oil for various purposes. Also, prior to this time, kerosene (which is refined from crude oil) served as effective inexpensive oil for lighting lamps. It was a cheap alternative to whale oil (the price of which was increasing due to whales almost being driven to extinction). In addition, other oil wells had existed prior to 1859. However, this year is traditionally marked as the birth of the modern oil industry due to the economic boom that would follow from Drake's discovery.

1860   Italian general Giuseppe Garibaldi and his forces conquered south of Italy (including Sicily) and then moved north to unify the rest of Italy.

1860   The recently-formed Republican Party nominated **Abraham Lincoln** as its leader. Later that year, exploiting major fractures within the rival Democratic Party, **Lincoln won the presidential election** with only 40% of the popular vote.

At this time, there were 33 States which made up the United States. A 34th - Kansas - was about to join as a free State. Lincoln won zero votes in 10 States, all southern States, in which effigies of him were burnt in strong protest. To the southerners, the election of Lincoln threatened the institution of slavery which their economies were so reliant on. Out of fear of being overrun by abolitionist policies, the legislature of South Carolina made the first move and called to consider seceding from the Union. In December, it did exactly that. Soon after this, a group of federal soldiers stationed in Charleston (a major city of South Carolina) withdrew to a sea fort called Fort Sumter, edging the US closer to civil war.

1861   In January, Mississippi seceded from the Union. The next day, Florida seceded. Then Alabama, Georgia, Louisiana and Texas followed. In February, a Democrat politician called Jefferson Davis stood on the steps of the Alabama statehouse at Montgomery and took the oath of office as President of the Confederate States of America. A Confederate Constitution was drawn up that was almost identical to the United States Constitution. In March, **Abraham Lincoln** was inaugurated as the **16th US President**.

In April, Confederate troops fired upon the Union garrison at Fort Sumter and captured it in a bloodless victory. The **US Civil War** had begun. The population of the northern States far outnumbered those in the south (including its slaves). Nevertheless, the Civil War would be brutally contested. In July, the **First Battle of Manassas** (the **First Bull Run**) took place in Virginia, which the Confederate army won.

1861   In what became known as the **Emancipation of the Serfs**, Tsar Alexander II abolished serfdom in Russia. Peasants could now be legally free of their landlords. They could now own property, buy land and trade with others. In reality, however, the emancipation did very little for the ex-serfs. In fact, landowners arguably benefitted more: they received generous sums of compensation from the government for the land they had to give up. Also, landowners were entitled to choose which land holdings to give up. By contrast, ex-serfs were left with undesirable plots that yielded little profit and were forced to pay high taxes (known as redemption tax) for the land they acquired, often forcing them to sell all their crop with very little to survive on for themselves. Despite this, the Emancipation of the Serfs would be Russia's first step toward modernisation and expansion of its economy.

1861 **Italy united** under one ruler when **Victor Emmanuel II**, with the support of Garibaldi, was crowned King of Italy. However, Rome was still occupied by the French due to Napoleon's support of the Pope. The Italians did not want to risk war with the French by interfering in Rome.

1861 **Rabindranath Tagore** was born in Calcutta. He would go on to become a successful writer, poet and musician in his native Bengal. With the translations of some of his poems, he would become increasingly popular in the West and one of the key voices of India's spiritual heritage. For India, especially for Bengal, he would be a key ambassador to the rest of the world. He would go on to win the Nobel Prize in Literature in 1913.

1861 Frederick William IV of Prussia died following a series of strokes. He was succeeded by his brother **Wilhelm I**.

1862 The highly influential statesman, **Otto van Bismarck**, was appointed by Wilhelm I as Minister President of Prussia. Intent on achieving German unification with Prussia at the helm, he famously stated in a speech that unification should not look to Prussia's liberalism (like it did in 1848) but its military and industrial strength: *"Not through speeches and majority decisions will the great questions of the day be decided - that was the great mistake of 1848 and 1849 - but by iron and blood"*.

1862 In June, US Congress, then controlled by the Republican party, forbade the army to return slaves to their masters (essentially reversing the Supreme Court's decision in the recent *Dred Scott* case). In July, Lincoln called a Cabinet meeting and decided that he would emancipate the slaves. In August, the **Second Bull Run** (or **Second Battle of Manassas**) took place. Again, the Confederate army won. September saw the **Battle of Antietam**, which proved to be the bloodiest day in US history: around 22,000 people died. It ended in stalemate, though the Unionists claimed victory. Five days later, Lincoln issued his

Emancipation Proclamation pursuant to which, on 1 January 1863, slaves in the rebellion states would be declared free. In December, the Battle of Fredericksburg took place which the Confederate army won.

1863   On 1 January, the **Emancipation Proclamation took effect, freeing the slaves in the Confederate States**. Between the 1st and 3rd July the **Battle of Gettysburg** in Pennsylvania took place leading to a Union victory and creating a turning point in the US Civil War. Also in July, the Confederate stronghold of Vicksburg on the Mississippi River had fallen.

1863   After realising the economic potential of oil production, American businessman **John Davison Rockefeller** and his business partner entered the oil industry by investing in the building of an oil refinery in Cleveland, Ohio.

1864   Union general William Tecumseh Sherman captured Atlanta. This helped Lincoln with his presidential re-election campaign which he won later that year.

1864   Bismarck persuaded Austria to ally with Prussia in a war against Denmark to determine the contested rule of Schleswig and Holstein. Their victory meant Prussia acquired Schleswig and Austria received Holstein.

1865   The Emancipation Proclamation of 1863 had limited effect: it only freed enslaved people within the Confederacy, not within the United States. It was primarily a military strategy to help turn the tide in the Civil War. But Lincoln knew that, in order for the abolition of slavery to be universal and permanent in law, the US Constitution needed to be amended.

In January, the House of Representatives voted in favour (albeit only just) of the **13th Amendment** to the Constitution, **abolishing slavery in the US**. The result of 119 to 56 narrowly exceeded the two-thirds majority required to pass the vote. In April, the **US Civil War came to a close** when Confederate general Robert Edward Lee surrendered officially at Appomattox Court House in Virginia. The total number of people who died in the US Civil War is estimated to be between 650 and 750 thousand.

Whilst African Americans were now "free" in the legal sense, their struggle for freedom and acceptance in society would only continue. Firstly, 1865 marked the birth of the white supremacist group, Ku Klux Klan - originally a group of Confederate veterans - which would go on to intimidate, attack, murder and lynch black people well into the 20th century. Secondly, major political events would quickly unfold to the detriment of African Americans. Initially, things were looking positive when Union general Sherman and the Secretary of War, Edward Stanton, met with twenty leaders of the local black community to arrange plans for their resettlement on land. Shortly after the meeting, Sherman's "*Field Order 15*" promised to carve out 40-acre plots to former slaves in South Carolina, Georgia and Florida. The day before his second inauguration, President Lincoln signed a bill to make the plan official. However, just five days after General Lee's surrender, Lincoln, whilst attending a play in Washington DC, **was assassinated by a slavery advocate and white supremacist called John Wilkes Booth.**

Following the assassination, **Andrew Johnson**, the Vice President at the time, was sworn in as the **17th US President**. In a U-turn, the new President revoked Sherman's *Field Order 15* and declared that African Americans be evicted from that land temporarily granted to them and such land was to be returned to the former (white) owners. In addition, Johnson stifled laws attempting to protect blacks and discouraged efforts to grant them citizenship. He was lenient towards former Confederate States, which soon installed all-white governments and enacted "black codes" designed to limit the freedom of ex-slaves as much as possible.

The former owners had their land returned but not their former free labour force. What replaced slavery, however, was something fairly similar: sharecropping. This meant that ex-slaves still worked the land but would receive a share of the crop that was produced. The vast majority of ex-slaves had no choice but to accept unfavourable labour contracts or else risk destitution. Many, through their desperate circumstances, would be caught up in the criminal justice system. Freed slaves were convicted, very often unfairly and discriminatorily, for not carrying out their sharecropping commitments or for other petty crimes.

In other respects, the Civil War proved very beneficial for northern cities, New York in particular. The war helped to catapult the city's factories and banks to become major players in the US economy. Wall Street bankers loaned the government tens of millions of dollars to fight the Confederacy and profited as a result. Wall Street also allowed financiers to make fortunes on the New York Stock Exchange, trading railroad and industrial stocks and bonds. Within 15 years, New York would also become the nation's largest producer of manufactured goods. The city would display its wealth with its retail centres, mansions, museums and opera houses.

1866   Despite President Johnson's veto of the bill, US Congress managed to pass the **Civil Rights Act**. It affirmed that all US citizens were to be given equal protection under the law, regardless of race or colour. This would be the first of several "**Reconstruction**" laws passed over the next decade, the purpose of which were to integrate black Americans into the United States.

1866   Bismarck accused Austria of stirring up trouble in Prussian-held Schleswig. So Prussian troops marched into Austria-led Holstein and occupied it. Austria declared war on Prussia, starting the **Austro-Prussian War**. Within seven weeks, Austria was defeated by the superior Prussian army. **The Treaty of Prague dissolved the German Confederation** and Prussia soon created the **North German Confederation** to include all northern German states (Prussia standing out as the most influential) and with Austria excluded. The southern German states outside the Confederation were tied to Prussia by military alliances.

In addition, a **Third Italian War of Independence** resulted in another defeat for the Austrians who ceded Venice to Italy. On the verge of collapse, the Austrians agreed on a dual monarchy with Hungary to form **Austria-Hungary** in 1867.

1867   US Secretary of State William Seward negotiated on behalf of the US the purchase of the territory of Alaska from the Russian Empire (still recovering from their defeat in the Crimean War) for just over 7 million US dollars. To the Russians, the Americans were the preferred buyer over Britain, their imperial rival.

1868   On 10 October, Carlos Manuel de Céspedes, a Cuban sugar plantation owner, freed his slaves to raise an army and called on all Cubans to rebel against Spanish rule, thus beginning the first **Cuban War of Independence**. In order to contain the rebels, the Spanish authority divided Cuba into the wealthy Spanish-friendly west - which included Havana - and the east where the rebels were based. The 10th of October is a national holiday in Cuba to commemorate the start of Cuba's struggle for freedom.

1868   **President Johnson became the first US president to be impeached**. However, in his impeachment trial, his opponents failed to obtain the votes needed to convict him. To impeach a President is to formerly accuse them of wrongdoing. When a President is impeached by the House of Representatives, the Senate conducts a vote on whether to convict him. If the Senate votes to convict, then he is removed from office.

Meanwhile, civil rights and equal protection for all US citizens became embedded into the US Constitution after the adoption of the **14th Amendment**.

1869   Former Civil War General **Ulysses S Grant** (of the Republican Party) was inaugurated as the **18th US President**. In this year, construction of the first transcontinental railroad was completed. The railroad connected the existing eastern US rail network at Iowa with the Pacific Coast at San Francisco Bay. To the Native Americans, the railroad was catastrophic. It drove away the free-roaming buffalo, which they so heavily relied on for their livelihood. US citizens were even encouraged by the government to hunt buffalo in order to starve the natives into submission.

After the Civil War, there was an increased demand for beef, which had been used up by the soldiers during the war. To meet the demand, and with the introduction of railroads, men in the West would lead cattle trails to the closest railroad so the cattle could be loaded onto freight cars and taken to eastern markets. In less than two decades, millions of cows and steers were herded in this way. The men who brought cattle to the railroads were referred to as "**cowboys**". They were a mixed group of former Confederate cavalrymen and immigrants who had only recently learned to ride. There were Indian and African-American cowboys and also Mexican vaqueros, whose ancestors had introduced cattle to the West centuries earlier. The term "cowboy" has been used in popular Western culture ever since.

In the same year, the **15th Amendment** was approved by Congress: a citizen's right to vote could not be denied based on race, colour or whether that person was formerly a slave.

1869   Leo Tolstoy's *War and Peace* was published.

1869   **Mohandas Karamchand Gandhi** was born in Porbandar, a princely state (now part of Gujarat).

1869   After a decade of construction, the **Suez Canal** was finally completed by the Suez Canal Company, the majority of which was owned by French investors. The remaining shares were owned by the Egyptian government, then under the rule of the Ottomans (themselves heavily influenced by Britain). The British government was at first opposed to the project but eventually caught on to its significant benefits: the canal, a waterway connecting the Red Sea with the Mediterranean Sea, could considerably shorten sea journeys between Asia and Europe, allowing goods to be traded faster. In 1875, the British bought Egypt's shares in the Suez Canal Company.

1870   John D. Rockefeller became the first oil baron when he formed **Standard Oil Company**. By the end of the century, Standard Oil had almost monopolised all aspects of America's lucrative oil business, including its refining, production, transportation and marketing.

1870   Using his powers in media, manipulation and diplomacy, Otto van Bismarck provoked Napoleon III into declaring war on Prussia (referred to as the **Franco-Prussian War**). The French were swiftly defeated by the Prussians and Napoleon III was captured and imprisoned. As a result of the loss, France was declared a republic again and the North German Confederation acquired the region of Alsace-Lorraine. French troops also withdrew from Rome, allowing for the newly unified Italy to capture the city and unite the peninsula fully. This soured relations between Italy and the Papacy, the latter of which had now lost its independence.

1871   **Germany became a nation for the first time** in history when a **unified German Empire** was proclaimed at a ceremony in the Palace of Versailles in France. **Wilhelm I** became Emperor (or **Kaiser**) and **Bismarck** was elevated to the position of Empire's **Chancellor**. The southern German states of Bavaria, Baden and Württemberg were soon incorporated. Eager to compete on the world stage, the newly unified country continued its rapid industrialisation programme and invested further into its already impressive military. In many ways the German Empire was in essence a Prussian empire: though all men had a vote in the Reichstag, both the legislative and executive arms of the government remained under heavy Prussian influence. Prussian dominance was also symbolic: its capital **Berlin became the capital** of the new Germany.

1874   Carlos Manuel de Céspedes was killed by Spanish troops in battle.

1874   With the British Raj having assumed full control of India's affairs, the British government **dissolved the East India Company**. To symbolise Britain's colonial rule over India, Queen Victoria adopted the title "Empress of India" two years later.

1874   Renovations were finished on the **Church of Saint Nicholas in Amsterdam** (originally constructed in 1189) making it surpass Strasbourg Cathedral as the tallest building in the world (albeit only for two years). It is 147 metres (or 482 feet) high.

1876   **Alexander Graham Bell**, a Scottish-born American inventor, received a US patent for the **telephone,** which used electricity to transmit sound.

1876   **The Battle of the Little Bighorn** took place. By 1870, most Native American tribes had been forced into reservations. Inspired by tribe leaders like Sitting Bull and Chief Gall, the Natives in the Great Plains of North America continued stubbornly to hold out against US expansion. The battle (also known as **Custer's Last Stand** - though there was no real evidence to show any heroics on the part of Lieutenant Colonel Custer) was one of the greatest Native American victories of the Plains Wars. But it proved only to be a pyrrhic victory for the Natives. In the aftermath, the US government continued to apply pressure towards confining the Natives to reservations.

1876   After renovations, **Rouen Cathedral in Normandy** became the tallest building in the world at 151 metres (495 feet), though it would only hold this title for four years.

1877   **Rutherford B Hayes** of the Republican Party became the **19th US President**. The election of Hayes all but ended the so-called Reconstruction Movement in the US. The last federal troops were withdrawn from the southern States, allowing white Democrats to regain full control over them. Over the next decade, the governments in the South introduced the notorious "**Jim Crow**" laws, designed to discriminate African Americans in all aspects of society and enforce racial segregation. Whilst blacks could not be denied the vote pursuant to the 15th Amendment, the South found other ways to prevent them from voting. Literacy tests and the poll tax were brought in as prerequisites. Through centuries of subjugation, exclusion and discrimination, the vast majority of the African American community were poor and illiterate. They stood no chance in meeting these measures.

Legal segregation would be adopted in schools, housing, marriages and many other aspects of daily life. Blacks were forbidden from eating in the same restaurants as whites, or sleeping in white hotels or buying in white stores. Furthermore, southern States had adopted a system of "hiring out" black prisoners - already significantly overrepresented in jails after the Civil War - for cotton picking, working in mines and building railroads among other labour. By the turn of the century, almost all of the hired out convicts in states like Georgia, Alabama and Mississippi were black. Thousands of African Americans migrated from the South to open spaces in the American West and other areas to try and escape the ordeal.

Meanwhile, the US was going through significant industrial change. It had all the resources necessary for an industrial boom: iron, coal, oil, and plenty of grain. Manufacturing and agriculture were the key drivers of industrialisation for them. America's population would grow massively in the run up to the end of the century.

1877   **Thomas Edison**, American inventor and businessman, filed for a patent on his invention, the **phonograph**: the first workable machine to record and play back audio.

1878   The Russians had recently defeated the Ottomans in war and the resulting Treaty of San Stefano was enforced on them. The terms of the treaty, favourable to the Russians, unsettled Britain and Austria-Hungary, which felt so threatened by Russia's gains that further war between the nations, and a potential repeat of the Crimean War, became a real possibility.

To broker peace terms, Otto von Bismarck convened the **Congress of Berlin**, the result of which averted war, at least for the time being. As part of the revised peace terms, independence was granted to Romania, Serbia, Montenegro and Bulgaria. Britain's interests were satisfied as Russia was denied the means to extend its naval power. Austria-Hungary's interests were also satisfied as it was given administrative control over Bosnia and Herzegovina, albeit the provinces remained under the ownership of the Ottomans. Tension in the Balkans, however, would remain as Austria-Hungary would continue to try and exert its influence over the region. The following year, **Germany and Austria-Hungary established a defensive alliance**, primarily to defend each other against Russia which, as a result of the revised peace treaty in Berlin, was left humiliated. The Ottoman Empire too was left further weakened from the treaty.

Notwithstanding the Congress of Berlin, the Great Game between Britain and Russia continued. Not long after, the **Second Anglo-Afghan War** took place when British troops invaded Afghanistan. In one of the most significant battles in Afghan history, the Afghans famously defeated the British at the **Battle of Maiwand**, killing around a thousand British soldiers. Britain won the war overall in 1880. However, their army withdrew when the Afghans agreed not to let Russia threaten India.

1878   A peace agreement was signed between Spain and Cuba

ending their first attempt at independence. Cuba was granted concessions but remained a Spanish colony. During the war, a revolutionary called José Martí had been sentenced to imprisonment. After the war, he was exiled to the US. There, he would raise an army to try and once again free Cuba from Spanish occupation.

1879 **Edison** filed a patent for his newly invented **light bulb**. Although light bulbs had been produced prior to Edison, his was the first that was commercially viable as a product to be sold to consumers.

1880 After construction was complete, **Cologne Cathedral** in Germany became the tallest building in the world at 157 metres (516 feet). It would hold the record for world's tallest building until 1890, but only until 1884 for world's tallest structure.

1880 German physicist **Heinrich Rudolf Hertz** proved by experimentation the existence of **electromagnetic waves**, formulated as a theory by Scottish physicist James Clerk Maxwell over a decade earlier.

1881 By this time, Russia controlled most of the western part of the region in central Asia known as Turkestan, which today covers modern-day Kazakhstan, Turkmenistan, Uzbekistan, Tajikistan and Kyrgyzstan.

In March, **Tsar Alexander II was assassinated** by a bomb orchestrated by the People's Will, a revolutionary faction intent on ridding Russia of autocratic rule and forcing political reform. However, autocracy would continue in Russia, at least for the time being, as Alexander's son immediately inherited the throne as **Tsar Alexander III**. The assassination of Alexander II triggered anti-Jewish sentiment within the Russian Empire as Jews were scapegoated for the attack. Many murderous race riots (known as pogroms) started, particularly in places like Warsaw and Kiev. These continued over the next few decades and, as a result, around two million Jews would flee from the Russian Empire, most of them bound for the USA or Britain.

1881   **James A Garfield** of the Republican Party became the **20th US President** but only lasted just over 6 months before he was **assassinated**. His Vice President, **Chester A Arthur**, succeeded him as the **21st US President**.

1882   A secret defensive alliance, known as the **Triple Alliance**, was formed between Germany, Austria-Hungary and Italy.

1883   Construction of the **Brooklyn Bridge** was completed. At the time, it was the world's longest suspension bridge spanning 1,595 feet (or 486 metres). Its 276-foot (or 84-metre) high towers were Brooklyn and Manhattan's tallest structures at the time.

1883   **Krakatoa,** a volcano in Indonesia, exploded with the force of thousands of atomic bombs. The explosion was apparently so loud it was heard more than 3,000 kilometres away in Australia. Massive amounts of ash and rock spewed into the air, raining down on the surrounding islands and littering the sea with pumice rocks. The collapsing volcano created a tsunami that damaged hundreds of coastal towns and villages on surrounding islands. When the dust cleared, Krakatoa had disappeared, leaving a massive sea-filled crater.

1884   Construction of the **Washington Monument** originally began in 1848 but was put on hold due to the US Civil War. When its construction was finally completed in 1884, it became the world's tallest structure at 169 metres (or 555 feet). It would hold this title for 5 years after which the Eiffel Tower would claim it.

1884   Bismarck called a conference in Berlin with the European powers, including Austria-Hungary, Belgium, France and Britain, to agree a plan for carving up Africa between them. At the time of the conference, 80% of the continent continued to be ruled by local tribes. However, the Berlin Conference led to the so-called "**Scramble for Africa**": European states drew up boundaries, which did not at all reflect or give careful thought to the indigenous cultures and regions that lived there. Instead, the partitioning would have the effect of dividing close-knit tribes whilst also forcing enemy tribes together, sowing the seeds of the conflicts that would plague Africa in the following century.

King Leopold II of Belgium, making his case in the conference for territory in Africa, promised a humanitarian mission that would enhance the lives of Africans, including building schools and hospitals. The European powers agreed to grant him over two million square kilometres in the Congo Basin, a territory he called the Congo Free State (now the Democratic Republic of Congo). However, instead of improving the lives of inhabitants, Belgian officials did the exact opposite. The region, exploited for its rubber production, was filled with mines and plantations and the locals were forced to work under brutal conditions. If quotas were not met, villagers had their limbs cut off and many, including children, were killed or maimed. The operation cost the lives of around ten million people. The atrocities would continue until 1908 when Leopold relinquished his absolutist rule over the Congo Free State, which was subsequently annexed to Belgium as a colony, and reforms were made.

1885   **Grover Cleveland** of the Democratic Party was inaugurated as the **22nd US President**.

1885   German engineer **Karl Friedrich Benz** built what some consider to be the world's first true automobile. The following year, he patented it as the "Benz Patent-Motorwagen".

1885   The **Indian National Congress** was founded. Its aim was to strive for a greater share in government for educated Indians and to create a platform for civic and political dialogue between themselves and the British Raj. Though the Indian National Congress began its first few decades as being fairly moderate in its approach, continued repressive British measures eventually gave rise to more extremist views within the party.

1886   The **Statue of Liberty** (originally called "Liberty Enlightening the World") on Bedloe's Island (renamed Liberty Island in 1956) was completed and dedicated as a gift by the French to the Americans. It was designed by Parisian sculptor Frédéric Auguste Bartholdi and its steel framework was built by Gustave Eiffel. It is 93 metres (or 305 feet) from ground level to torch (a few metres shorter than Big Ben in London). In an era when about three quarters of all European immigrants landed in New York, the statue became a symbol of the city as a gateway to America as well as a mark of Franco-American friendship and freedom. By this time, the population of New York was around 1.5 million, making it the third most populous city after London (just under 4 million) and Paris (around 2.5 million).

Meanwhile, the population of Los Angeles was growing rapidly in the late 1880s upon the introduction of the railroad. In the space of two and a half years, 60 towns had popped up in the area and the Mexican-American heart of Los Angeles was surrounded. By this time, generally, the American West was not a matter of cowboys, Indians, mountain men and explorers but a land largely urban and industrial, with aspects similar to those that made up the industrialised east.

1886   Slavery was finally abolished in Cuba by Spain.

1887   The Ulyanov family, a group of radicals, planned to assassinate Tsar Alexander III. Alexander (or 'Sasha') Ulyanov was the master bomb-maker. However, the plot was discovered and he was hanged. His younger brother Vladimir (better known to us as **Lenin**) would go on to continue exercising revolutionary politics in Russia.

It was not until the 1890s that Russia began to industrialise on a large scale, increasing its iron productivity at a rapid pace, which in turn led to the formation of a recognised working class.

The new heavy industries were particularly concentrated in St. Petersburg and Moscow. Though they expanded quickly, the cities were not prepared for this rapid urban growth. Living conditions were destitute and workers did long hours for low pay. All of this fuelled the revolutionary activity which Lenin became increasingly a part of.

1887   In the US, the **Dawes Act** came into force with the purpose of dividing the communal land of Native Americans. It would have a devastating impact on the Native American population. The Act provided for each head of a tribe to be given 160 acres of farmland. All the remaining tribal lands were left as surplus for whites and other European immigrants to settle. Before the Dawes Act, around 140 million acres remained in Indian hands. Within 20 years, two thirds of that land would be removed from them.

By the 1890s, many of the immigrants who arrived in the US came from southern and eastern Europe, particularly Italy and the Russian and Austro-Hungarian empires, all in search of better lives, escaping destitution or (especially the case with Jews) religious persecution.

1887   German immigrant **Emile Berliner**, working in Washington DC, patented the **gramophone**, the first device to record sound on a **flat disk** (Edison's previous phonograph relied on a cylinder).

1888   Kaiser Wilhelm I died and his son Frederick succeeded him to become the new German Emperor, Frederick III. However, he died of cancer later that year and was succeeded by his son, Wilhelm, who became **Kaiser Wilhelm II**. Frederick III was married to Queen Victoria of England's eldest child, Princess Victoria. This made Kaiser Wilhelm II one of Queen Victoria's many (42) grandchildren.

1889   **Benjamin Harrison** of the Republican Party became the **23rd US President**. He was a grandson of former President William Henry Harrison.

1889   On 22 April, around a hundred thousand settlers surrounded the Oklahoma district on the southern plains where two million acres of Native American territory were being opened up for settlement. At precisely noon the official land rush, known as the **Oklahoma Land Rush**, began. By the end of the day, all acres had been claimed. In the years that followed there would be more land rushes throughout the American West.

1889   Construction of the **Eiffel Tower** (designed by the company of the engineer Gustave Eiffel) in Paris was completed. At 324 metres (or 1,063 feet) from ground to tip, it surpassed the Washington Monument to become the tallest human-made structure in the world, a title it held for 41 years until the Chrysler Building in New York City was finished in 1930.

1890   The **Ulm Minster** in Baden-Württemberg in Germany became the tallest building in the world at 162 metres (530 feet), a title it would hold for four years. At the time of writing, it is the tallest church in the world.

1891   After emigrating to the US in 1884, Serbian inventor **Nikola Tesla**, building on the previous works of Heinrich Hertz, invented the induction coil (or Tesla coil), a device essential to sending and receiving radio waves and something the US Patent Office would later say Guglielmo Marconi relied on for his work in inventing the radio.

1891   Concerned by the growing power of Germany, **Russia and France entered into an alliance**. Both countries agreed that they would attack Germany if it mobilised its army.

        In Russia, construction began on the Trans-Siberian Railway (the Moscow-Vladivostok line), which would take 25 years to build. With a length of 9,289 kilometres (or 5,772 miles), it is the longest railway line in the world.

1893   **Grover Cleveland** of the Democratic Party returned to become the **24ᵗʰ US President**. He is the only president in American history to serve two non-consecutive terms in office.

1893 New Zealand became the first self-governing colony in the world in which all **women were given the right to vote** in parliamentary elections (though they would not be permitted to stand for election themselves until 1919).

1893 Having been called to the bar in 1891 after legal training at the Inner Temple in London, **Gandhi** moved to South Africa to practise law. There, he both witnessed and suffered harassment and discrimination from the white elite. Despite this, he would go on to emerge as a key advocate of the rights of the Indian minority. Apartheid was not yet a legal concept in South Africa but it was very much in practice in society. It was in South Africa where Gandhi would first adopt non-violent resistance measures (which came to be known as "satyagraha") in a campaign for civil rights of minorities. Gandhi returned to India in 1915 by which time he adopted the title **Mahatma** (which is Sanskrit for "great soul").

Swami Vivekananda, a renowned Bengali spiritual leader and key proponent of the Hindu philosophies of Vedanta and Yoga, gave an inspirational speech at the World Parliament of Religions in Chicago, introducing Hinduism to the world. His works and teachings built on those of his guru Ramakrishna who had passed away seven years earlier. Following his return to India in 1897, he rallied Indians to get behind the Indian nationalist movement.

1894 **Philadelphia City Hall** became the tallest building in the world at 167 metres (548 feet) until surpassed in 1908.

1894 **Tsar Alexander III** died after suffering from ill health. His son Nicholas inherited the Russian throne as **Tsar Nicholas II**. Soon afterwards, he married a German princess, and granddaughter of Queen Victoria of England, who became Tsarina Alexandra. At Nicholas' coronation in 1896, disaster struck when a crowd congregated to receive coronation gifts resulting in a crush: over a thousand people died and another thousand were injured.

1895   José Martí and his generals landed in eastern Cuba to join forces with other veteran soldiers from the previous war with Spain. Martí was killed at the very first battle against the Spaniards. The Cuban revolution, however, would continue.

1896   Utah was admitted to the United States as the 45th State. The Mormons, persecuted by the government for practising polygamy, felt that the only way to survive as a people was for their territory to become a State. One of the conditions, however, for granting Utah statehood was that a ban on polygamy be written into the State constitution.

1896   Italian inventor **Guglielmo Marconi,** who had been conducting his own experiments on radio waves (or "Hertzian waves"), patented the electro-magnetic system of radio wave communications, **the world's first patent in wireless telegraphy.** He demonstrated his works to the British government by sending and receiving Morse code-based radio signals in England at distances spanning nearly four miles. Unlike the established telegraph network, Marconi's invention was 'wire-less', the first apparatus for long distance communication, and could be heard by anyone with a radio receiver.

1896   In the US Supreme Court case of *Plessy v Ferguson*, it was ruled that segregation in public facilities was not racist so long as each segregated area was equal in quality. The principle of "separate but equal" allowed the infamous Jim Crow laws to continue to fester in the southern States.

1897   After being arrested for his engagement in Marxist politics, Vladimir Lenin was exiled to Siberia for three years.

1897   **William McKinley** of the Republican Party was inaugurated as the **25th US President**. He was under pressure from the American press to free Cuba from foreign occupation. In their fight against Cuba, the Spanish were adopting ruthless tactics, killing hundreds of thousands of Cuban people. The Cuban revolutionaries sent pictures of Spanish atrocities to the New York newspaper industry (dominated by Joseph Pulitzer's *New York World* and William Randolph Hearst's competing *New York Journal*), which were sympathetic to the Cuban cause. However, President McKinley was reluctant to drag America into war. Instead he attempted peaceful negotiations with Spain.

1897   In the face of growing antisemitism and at a time when nationalism was popular opinion, **Zionism** was established as a political organisation under the leadership of Austro-Hungarian Jewish activist **Theodor Herzl** when he founded the **World Zionist Organization**. Zionism was a movement for the re-establishment of a Jewish nation in their ancient homeland. The homeland in question was based in a region of the Middle East called **Palestine**. The Ottoman Empire at the time ruled over this region where the vast majority of the population was Muslim, a minority was Christian and a smaller minority was Jewish. In Jerusalem, though, the religions were closer to being equally divided.

1898   Manhattan was consolidated with Brooklyn, the Bronx, Queens and Staten Island to make the five-borough city of Greater New York. Overnight, the population of New York City essentially doubled, making it the world's second largest metropolis.

In the same year, Hawaii was annexed as an official territory of the United States.

1898   The American navy sent a modern warship called the USS Maine to Havana, its mission being to protect US property in Cuba. However, in February, the ship unexpectedly exploded. Though the cause of the explosion was unknown, the incident further riled the American public which demanded justice from Spain. President McKinley finally caved to public pressure and **declared war on Spain**. To bolster the US army, volunteer units were called up. The most famous of these were the so-called "Rough Riders" commanded by soon-to-be American President Theodore Roosevelt. Though popularised by American propaganda, their contribution to the war was probably minimal.

The Americans defeated the Spanish in the same year, creating a significant turning point in Spanish history. In the ensuing peace treaty, Spain was forced to give up Cuba, Puerto Rico, Guam and the Philippines. **Spain had virtually lost its empire**. Cuba had not, however, won full independence and instead became an American protectorate.

1900   By the turn of the 20th century, the world population had surpassed 1.5 billion. By the end of the century, it would quadruple to 6 billion.

1901   **President McKinley was assassinated** by an anarchist. **Theodore Roosevelt**, the Vice President at the time, succeeded him as the **26th US President**. Currently, he is so far the youngest ever to take office, aged 42.

Meeting a promise made by the Americans prior to the Spanish War, Cuba would become independent. But by this time, American companies had taken control of a large portion of Cuba's economy and effectively treated the island like a colony in all but name. Sugar represented the vast majority of all Cuba's exports with most of it going to the US. Under Cuba's new constitution, Cubans were allowed to vote for the first time and Tomás Estrada Palma was elected as the first Cuban president, though he allowed his government to remain subject to American influence.

In exchange for withdrawing its troops from the island, the US demanded some guarantees, which were written into the so-called **Platt Amendment to the Cuban Constitution**. The main purposes of the Platt Amendment were to protect American property in Cuba, allow for American intervention if necessary and establish US military bases within the country. Among other locations, the Americans chose **Guantanamo Bay** in the far southeast. The perpetual lease of Guantanamo Bay to the US began in 1903 and continues to this day.

1901   The Americans encountered the most enormous oil gusher seen in the world at **Spindletop Hill** in Texas, leading to a boom in the oil industry and spawning companies such as Gulf Oil and Texaco. With breakthroughs like this, oil would soon emerge as the preferred energy source. Increasing reliance on automobiles, ships and other transportation were the key drivers for the rise in demand for oil. Coal, the core of the industrial revolution in the previous century, had now been eclipsed as the coveted resource.

1903   After purchasing interests in the Isthmus of Panama from France, the US, keen to build a canal in the region, attempted to sign a treaty with Colombia for building rights (the canal zone at the time was Colombian territory). In the late 19th century, the French had previously attempted, but failed for various reasons, to build the canal. When the Colombians refused to sign the treaty, the US switched allegiance to the Panamanian independence cause. When Panama had successfully separated from Colombia and won its independence with American support, it signed a treaty with the US, granting them rights to build their canal and control it.

1903   American inventors, Wilbur and Orville Wright - better known as the **Wright Brothers - successfully achieved the first airplane flight**.

1904   The Japanese made a surprise attack on the Russian navy at Port Arthur in Manchuria (presently north-eastern China) and declared war on Russia.

1904   Known as the **Entente Cordiale**, France and Britain formed an alliance, the purpose of which, among other things, was to protect one another from the growing military threat posed by Germany.

1905   On 22 January, the **1905 Revolution in Russia** began. Tens of thousands of protesters marched to the Winter Palace in Saint Petersburg demanding better rights for workers and more political freedom. However, government troops opened fire on the crowd, killing hundreds of protesters. This date came to be known as **Bloody Sunday**. After this, strikes began to erupt elsewhere, in cities like Moscow and Warsaw.

Along with civil unrest at home, morale was extremely low in the Russian military. Between February and March, the Russian and Japanese armies fought in the Battle of Mukden, resulting in a heavy defeat for the Russians. In June, there was a mutiny on board the Russian battleship, **Potemkin**. In September, Russia and Japan signed the Treaty of Portsmouth, brokered by President Roosevelt, ending their war.

Later that year, in response to the revolution, Tsar Nicholas II reluctantly issued the so-called **October Manifesto**, whereby an elected parliament called the **Duma** was set up and other civil liberties - such as freedom of speech and press - were granted. The rebellions ceased as a result of the manifesto, which was widely accepted by the moderates. However, the Marxist revolutionaries did not believe the reforms went far enough. Indeed, the Tsar still retained certain autocratic powers. In particular, even though no law could be passed without the Duma's assent, the Tsar could still veto any law.

By this period, the Marxist movement in Russia consisted of two main factions: the **Bolsheviks**, the majority group led by Lenin which desired revolution; and the **Mensheviks**, the minority that wished to work with reformers and introduce change gradually. Soon after the October Manifesto was issued, at a Bolshevik conference, Lenin met for the first time a Georgian named

Ioseb Dzhugashvili, later to be known as **Joseph Stalin**.

Meanwhile, Nicholas II and his wife Alexandra met a mysterious man called **Rasputin** who apparently helped cure their sick son. Rasputin's introduction to the Romanov family, and presence in their royal court, brought great scandal due to claims about his mystical healing powers. Many also felt threatened by his alleged political influence over the Tsar and some suspected that he was having an affair with Alexandra. He was eventually murdered in 1916.

1905   The Bengal province in India was partitioned by Viceroy Lord Curzon, creating East Bengal and Assam (consisting mainly of Muslims) as a separate province - with its capital at Dhaka - and West Bengal, Bihar and Orissa as another. Hindus were outraged as they saw the divide as an attempt to undermine their influence. Also, the annexing of West Bengal to Bihar and Orissa reduced Bengali-speakers to a minority. Even though the British claimed that the division was purely for administrative reasons, the arguable real purpose was to create a communal gulf between Hindus and Muslims and strike at the territorial roots of the nationalist and intellectual elite of Bengal. It has been referred to by many as the **"divide and rule"** tactic adopted by the British in order to ensure their dominance would not be threatened by a united India.

1906   Britain launched its new battleship, the HMS Dreadnought, prompting Kaiser Wilhelm II to fund an increased rate of naval construction in Germany. A fierce **naval arms race** began between the nations, an arguably key contributing factor to the First World War soon to unfold. Generally, as well as forging alliances, European nations were building armies and stockpiling weapons out of fear of attack by one another and to prepare in case a large-scale war might break out.

1906   Thousands of American soldiers invaded Cuba, with the legal right to do so under the Platt Amendment. Whilst there was internal strife in Cuba that arguably justified American intervention, some would argue their real motive was to protect the sugar industry in which the US was heavily invested.

1906   The **Muslim League** in India was founded with the purpose of preventing the emergence of a parliamentary political system which could lead to a permanent domination of the Hindu majority over the Muslim minority.

1907   Leo Baekeland, a Belgian-born American living in New York, produced a moldable, hard synthetic he called "Bakelite", which was the **first plastic.**

1907   Britain and Russia entered into an alliance, meaning that France, Russia and Britain were all allies with one another via various intertwining treaties. This alliance is referred to as the **Triple Entente.**

The alliance also signified a conclusion to the Great Game, the intense rivalry between Britain and Russia which dictated their foreign policy for much of the 19th century. The British agreed to recognise Russia's sphere of influence over northern Persia while the Russians agreed to the same in respect of Britain's influence over southern Persia, the region being of strategic importance to both nations. Russia also agreed to keep out of Afghanistan, relieving any pressure on British India. British foreign policy was dictated on the premise that it was more disadvantageous to have bad relations with France and Russia - particularly due to tensions in Persia - than with Germany.

1908   Austria-Hungary decided to annex the dual provinces of Bosnia and Herzegovina, disrupting the delicate balance of power in the Balkan region. The decision enraged nationalists within the region, as well as neighbouring Serbia which had its own ambitions to annex the provinces (home to many Serbs). The event which triggered the First World War in 1914 was caused by the actions of a group of Serbian nationalists who opposed this annexation.

1908   A British businessman called William Knox D'Arcy struck oil in Persia, marking the **first significant discovery of oil in the Middle East**. It had long been known through geological research that there were oil deposits in the region: in previous decades, efforts had been made, and concessions granted, to foreigners to extract oil from Persia. However, these failed for various reasons: cultural barriers, local corruption, lack of funds, difficult working conditions and hostilities held by Persian officials towards the foreigners who meddled were all contributing factors. Undeterred, D'Arcy maintained interest and was granted wide privileges by the Shah of Persia, including the right to explore for, obtain and sell any oil found throughout the region for 60 years (with certain northern provinces excluded to placate Russia). In exchange, the Persian regime would receive £20,000 and 16% of the profits. Little was expected from Knox D'Arcy's venture, and indeed it came very close to collapse, but his team eventually did hit oil against all the odds.

The discovery in 1908 led to the incorporation of the Anglo-Persian Oil Company (the same company which eventually became British Petroleum in 1954, recognised today as BP). D'Arcy was appointed as a director of the company.

At the recommendation of Winston Churchill - then the First Lord of the British Admiralty - who saw the major benefits in switching the Royal Navy's energy source from coal to oil, the British government purchased a majority (51%) shareholding in the company in 1914 to ensure sufficient oil for the navy leading up to First World War. Indeed, during the War, ships, airplanes, trucks and the newly-invented tanks would be powered by and heavily reliant on oil, allowing them to move faster than the enemy.

1908   After a renovation, the **Singer Building** in New York City became the tallest building in the world. Measured to the roof, it was 187 metres (or 614 feet). The Eiffel Tower, though (almost twice the height of the Singer Building), kept its title as world's tallest structure.

1909 **William Howard Taft** of the Republican Party was inaugurated as the **27th US President.**

1909 **The Metropolitan Life Tower** in New York City overtook the Singer Building to become the tallest building in the world at 213 metres (or 698 feet).

1911 The 1905 Partition of Bengal was reversed: Bengal was amalgamated and Bihar and Orissa formed a new province. This time, however, the Bengali Muslims were now the ones angered by the decision.

1912 On 12 April, British cruise ship **RMS Titanic** set sail from Southampton in England to begin its maiden voyage. Its destination was New York. However, in the late evening of 14 April, it hit an iceberg in the North Atlantic and sank in the early hours of the following morning. Out of the approximate 2,220 passengers and crew onboard, over 1,500 died and 705 survived.

1913 **Woodrow Wilson** of the Democratic Party was inaugurated as the **28th US President.**

1913 American businessman **Henry Ford**, intent on making affordable automobiles available to the masses, revolutionised the industry when he installed the first moving assembly line for the mass production of his car, the Model T. The amount of time it took to build the car was reduced from 12 hours to just 2.5, which increased supply whilst decreasing the cost of production.

1913 The **Woolworth Building** in New York City became the tallest building in the world at 241 metres (or 792 feet) until surpassed in 1930.

1914 The First World War

On 28 June, during a visit to Sarajevo in Bosnia, the heir to the Austro-Hungarian throne **Arch Duke Franz Ferdinand and his wife Archduchess Sophie were assassinated** by a young Bosnian Serb nationalist called Gavrilo Princip. He and his accomplices were seeking to free Bosnia and Herzegovina from Austro-Hungary so they could unite with neighbouring Serbia.

The assassination sparked an international crisis the following month: Austria-Hungary issued an ultimatum to the Serbian government, suspected of being behind the assassination, demanding that they adhere to harsh terms. They were intentionally harsh in order for the Austro-Hungarians, backed by Germany, to justify grounds for war if the terms were not agreed. When Serbia refused some of these terms, Austria-Hungary found its justification and declared war on Serbia. Germany then declared war on Russia when Russian troops started to mobilise against Austria-Hungary in support of Serbia. Anticipating that the French would honour their alliance with Russia, Germany declared war on France too.

Germany looked to implement its so-called "**Schlieffen Plan**", a strategy devised by military commander Count Alfred von Schlieffen about a decade earlier due to the threat posed by the Franco-Russian alliance. The plan was to bypass the heavily fortified French border, march through neutral Belgium and Luxembourg, swiftly defeat the French forces and then turn back to face Russian troops, who the Germans anticipated would be slow to mobilise. The German army subsequently invaded Belgium as per their plan. Britain, which had previously agreed to protect Belgian neutrality, issued an ultimatum to Germany. The Germans refused to leave Belgium and thus Britain declared war on Germany. The war that followed came to be known as the **Great War** (later the **First World War**).

It only took a month after the war began for the Schlieffen Plan to fail: German advances in France were checked by French and British forces. Soon there was a stalemate. Both sides' armies then dug into trenches, creating a **Western Front,** which would set the scene - a horrific scene - for most of the Great War. Later in 1914, the Ottomans entered the war on the side of the Germans and Austro-Hungarians, primarily to counter the threat posed by Russia.

1915 The First Lord of the British Admiralty Winston Churchill proposed a plan to launch a naval attack on the Dardanelles, Europe's south-eastern coast, to knock the Ottomans out of the War and open a supply line to Russia. The plan, however, ended in disaster when Allied forces suffered losses going into the Dardanelles Strait. The Allies then decided on an infantry invasion and landed at **Gallipoli.** However, this too ended in disaster when the Ottomans repelled them, forcing an eventual evacuation. Around 50,000 Allied soldiers died and that number included a significant portion of men from Australia and New Zealand.

After the failure of the Gallipoli campaign, Britain decided on throwing its support behind the Arabs in their local struggle for independence against the Ottomans. In a series of letter exchanges, British representatives struck a deal with a leading figure in the Arab region, Hussein bin Ali, Sharif of Mecca, whereby Britain would guarantee Arab independence in the region, and grant land to the Arabs, in exchange for their helping the Allies defeat the Ottomans.

1915 marked the beginning of systematic mass murder by the Ottoman government of Armenian people (who were claimed to be assisting the enemy during the War). The atrocities ranged from mass arrests, mass executions, looting of villages, pillaging and rape as well as death marches in the desert. The **Armenian Genocide** carried on for around five more years and over one million Armenians are said to have died.

1916 Several significant battles of the Great War were fought in this year. Firstly, the **Battle of Verdun** was fought between Germany and France. It was the longest battle of the First

World War that lasted almost the entirety of the year. Despite French victory at the end of the year, the losses on both sides were enormous: there were approximately 980,000 casualties.

Secondly, the **Battle of Jutland** was fought between the German and British navies. It was the largest sea engagement of the First World War and is considered the last great naval battle in history. The first 18 months of the war had seen no major action between the German and British fleets. Aside from a few small engagements, daily routines on board ship were uninterrupted. Yet, prior to the war, both Germany and Britain had been competing with one another on shipbuilding and both nations hoped for a decisive fleet encounter that would decide the balance of power at sea. When their respective fleets finally met at Jutland, within a day, the Germans lost over 2,500 men and the British over 6,000. Despite the heavy losses, the British fleet remained in control of the North Sea.

Thirdly, there was the **Brusilov Offensive** launched by the Russians against the Austro-Hungarians and their allies. It was one of the most successful military operations of the Great War but came at a tremendous human and economic loss to the Russians who were unable to launch another offensive for the remainder of the War. The Austro-Hungarians and their allies suffered about 1.5 million casualties and the Russians suffered up to a million.

Fourthly, the **Battle of the Somme** was fought between the Allies and the Germans on the Western Front. There was a grand plan to launch an all-out assault on the Germans by bombarding them with artillery and then walking over the German line. But the Germans, more resilient than anticipated, survived the bombardment and defended their position. On 1 July, the British army suffered around 57,000 casualties and 19,000 deaths in just one day. The battle, which introduced the tank for the first time, would rage on for 140 days with little territorial gain for the Allies. Over one million men were wounded or killed over the course of the battle.

Meanwhile, anticipating the eventual defeat and collapse of the Ottoman Empire by the end of the Great War, a British diplomat called Mark Sykes and his French counterpart, François-Georges Picot, made a secret agreement recognised today as the **Sykes-Picot Agreement**. It formulated a plan for the carve up of Ottoman-ruled Arab lands, allowing for France and Britain to exercise administrative control and influence over certain territories in the Middle East. Under the agreement, France would obtain Syria and Lebanon whilst Britain would get the region correlating to today's Iraq, Palestine and Jordan. Both countries had strategic and economic interests in the region, especially because of the oil it produced (or could potentially produce in future). In addition, control in the region meant that Britain could secure its western passage to India.

The Sykes-Picot Agreement was made in secret although Russia was privy to the deal at the time. The Bolsheviks - who seized power in Russia a year later - would eventually expose the deal to the public and cause outrage, particularly in the Arab community. The agreement was contradictory to the promise made by the British to Sharif of Mecca Hussein bin Ali in 1915 which guaranteed Arab independence after the War. It also contradicted assurances given by the British and French publicly that they were not fighting for their self-interests but for the rights of the local people to have their independence. However, securing the oil reserves in the region, no matter the cost, was of paramount importance to the Europeans, even if it meant overpromising.

1916   Annie Besant, an Irish socialist, helped establish the Indian Home Rule League on a similar framework to the version in Ireland where a similar independence movement was taking shape. Joining the cause was young political activist **Jawaharlal Nehru**.

1916   In the midst of the Great War in Europe, and revolution occurring in Mexico, President Woodrow Wilson won the US presidential vote, securing re-election for a second term. A major part of the Democrats' successful campaign was the slogan "*He Kept Us Out of War*", alluding to Wilson's policy of non-intervention in foreign wars and the American public's reluctance to be dragged into conflict with either Germany or Mexico.

1917   Britain imported most of its food, and also shipped large quantities of oil, from the USA. The Germans knew this and believed that destroying Britain's merchant shipping line might starve the country to surrender. The only way for this to be effective would be to sink all ships going to British ports, including ships carrying Americans, something that could risk pulling the US into war (despite the Americans insisting on neutrality). The Germans nonetheless took this risk.

The final straw for the US occurred in January when German foreign minister Arthur Zimmerman sent a telegram (the infamous "Zimmerman Telegram") to Mexico, inviting them to join the war as Germany's ally against the Americans. In return, the Germans would finance Mexico's war and help them recover the territories of Texas, New Mexico, and Arizona. The British intercepted the message and presented it to the US embassy in the UK. From there it made its way to President Wilson before reaching the public, among which the cries for war grew louder. The US were now sufficiently antagonised to join the Great War on the side of the Allies, which they did in April.

Meanwhile, the Great War had put intolerable strains on Russia. Economic mismanagement and government corruption led to rising prices and food shortages. In what became known as the **February Revolution,** there were violent demonstrations in Petrograd, (renamed in 1914 from Saint Petersburg to sound less German). Even some of the troops who were ordered to disperse the crowds joined in with the protesters. The February Revolution forced **Tsar Nicholas II to abdicate** in March, ending the Romanov dynasty. A power vacuum was created in Russia with two major factions fighting for control in Petrograd. The first was the Russian Provisional Government formed by the Duma. The second was the Petrograd Soviet, a worker's council.

Between July and November, the **Battle of Passchendaele** took place between Allied and German troops where the Allies attempted to capture Ypres and Flanders in Belgium. The already appalling conditions were made even worse due to the heaviest rainfall in the area in 30 years. Men and horses were said to have drowned in the shell holes. Though the Allies did make advances, the offensive was heavily criticised due to the enormous cost in human lives compared to the seemingly little gain it brought them.

At the beginning of November, British Foreign Secretary Arthur Balfour, in an attempt to keep Jewish supporters on side, wrote a letter to leading Zionist Lord Rothschild stating support for the establishment of a national home for the Jewish people in Palestine. The letter made its way to the press and has since become known as the **Balfour Declaration**. British government representatives had once again overpromised: the Declaration was contradictory to the Sykes-Picot Agreement in 1916 as well as the promise made by the British in 1915 to Hussein bin Ali of independent rule over a unified Arab region (including Palestine).

Just as the Balfour Declaration was made public, Russia's **October Revolution**, led by Lenin's Bolsheviks, had begun. It took place in November but the Russians were still following the old Julian calendar (hence the revolution being in 'October' under the old calendar. Similarly, the February Revolution technically took place in March). Bolshevik Red Guards stormed the Winter Palace where the Provisional Government met and arrested its members. The Bolsheviks now had effective control of Russia with Lenin as their leader. They attacked political opponents, seized businesses and property without compensating owners, assaulted church priests, and ruled with a brutal secret police force. Soon after the October Revolution, **Russia collapsed into a bitter five year-long civil war,** fought between the Red Army, led by prominent Marxist revolutionary Leon Trotsky, and the White Army, those opposed to communist rule.

1918   The new Bolshevik government in Russia agreed to an end to the war with Germany when it signed the **Treaty of Brest-Litovsk**. As a result of the treaty, Russia ceded significant portions of its territory, which would lead to the independence of Finland, Estonia, Latvia, Lithuania, Belarus, Georgia and Ukraine. With Russia out of the Great War, the German military decided they must act quickly before American troops arrived so they launched an offensive (known as the **Ludendorff Offensive**). However, the Allies launched their own counter offensive - known as the **Hundred Days Offensive** - to push the Germans back. The **Battle of Amiens,** the opening phase of the Hundred Days Offensive, saw Britain swiftly gain significant territory and would eventually take the Allies to the end of the War. Meanwhile in Russia, **Tsar Nicholas II, the Tsarina and their five children were executed by the Red Army**.

In November, **Kaiser Wilhelm II was forced to abdicate** after a remorseless offensive of British, French and fresh American troops. With the military in disarray, the Germans agreed to surrender (Hitler would later refer to the German politicians who signed the armistice as the "November criminals" to feed Nazi propaganda). **On 11 November at 11am - the 11th hour of the 11th day of the 11th month - the Great War officially ended**. Approximately 20 million people were killed overall, half that number from fighting and the other half from disease and starvation. Due to insurmountable debts from the billions of dollars spent on the war effort, Europe's economies were in tatters.

Meanwhile, the Allied-backed Arab Revolt led to the **defeat of the Ottoman Empire**, which all but ended one of the longest lasting and richest empires in world history. British and French troops now occupied that region of the Middle East which had been left war-torn and in a state of famine, and their respective governments began to carve up the region's territories between them (as had been agreed during the War).

Just before the Great War ended, the **Austro-Hungarian Empire was dismembered**, resulting in Austria, Hungary, Poland, and Czechoslovakia being created. Also, a national state of Slovenes, Croats and Serbs was formed, encompassing Bosnia and Herzegovina and most of Croatia and Slovenia. Soon it would merge with Serbia and, in 1929, be renamed **Yugoslavia**.

1918 was also the year of the so-called **Spanish Flu**, an influenza pandemic caused by the H1N1 virus that infected an estimated 500 million people (one third of the world population at the time) and killed between approximately 50 and 100 million people. The success of the virus' spread was helped by the movement of troops during the Great War and the confined spaces the fighting created.

The source of the flu is unknown (despite being given the name "Spanish Flu" due to an inaccurate assertion that it originated in Spain). Spain remained neutral during the Great War so its media were the only ones reporting the truth about the flu's devastating impact. By contrast, the countries at war had enforced strict censorship of the media, suppressing any news about the virus to keep up morale. Those reading about the pandemic were only receiving accounts from Spain, thus assuming it originated there.

1919   After long negotiations between the victorious nations at the Paris Peace Conference, the **Treaty of Versailles** was signed with harsh terms imposed on the Germans. They were forced to accept full responsibility of the war, give up all overseas territories and some of their internal land, demilitarise the

Rhineland, reduce their army and navy, cease having an air force, and pay billions of dollars in reparations so great that they were practically un-repayable.

A new assembly was elected by the German people to draw up a new constitution. The assembly met in Weimar and the new republic established came to be known as the **Weimar Republic**. As part of the constitution, the president - elected by all citizens every seven years - could suspend basic human rights and use force to preserve public safety and order. The government would be in the hands of the chancellor, chosen by the president. The chancellor would also be required to have the support of the majority in the Reichstag (the elected legislature) to remain in power. For the duration of the Weimar Republic, the Reichstag would never be dominated by a majority party and instead was ruled by coalitions. In his eventual rise to power, Hitler would exploit this party division within the Reichstag to his own party's advantage.

1919   The Great War had put a considerable strain on India's economy. Prices had drastically risen and the negative effects were felt fully by the urban population and poor communities. More than a million Indians had participated in the War and many of them returned to India as demobilised soldiers. To compound matters, the British government introduced the Rowlatt Acts, which extended the emergency measures of repression against revolutionary activity already put in place by Britain to keep order during wartime. The legislation was mockingly summarised as *"no trial, no lawyer, no appeal"*. It infuriated Gandhi, who was loyal to the British cause during the Great War in the hope Britain would repay India for its loyalty. With no sign of this happening, Gandhi adopted satyagraha and called for a "hartal": the closing of shops and stopping of all business.

Shortly after the passage of the Rowlatt Acts came protests in India. In particular, an unauthorised meeting of Indians took place in an open space called the Jallianwalla Bagh, in the

Punjab city of Amritsar. This was a square surrounded by walls that prevented the crowd from dispersing. Colonel Dyer, a British army officer, ordered his soldiers to fire on the crowd leaving at least 400 dead - including women and children. The official British report on the event tried to cover up the army's wrongdoings.

Gandhi soon outlined the main features of his non-cooperation campaign. British textiles were boycotted (Gandhi encouraged Indians to wear khadi (homespun cloth) instead of British-made textiles) as well as British schools, universities and law courts. All honours and titles bestowed by the British on Indians were rejected. Soon after the Jallianwalla Bagh Massacre, Indian writer Rabindranath Tagore renounced his British knighthood previously awarded to him in 1915 by English King George V.

1919   After decades of a growing temperance movement in the US aiming to take action against the abuses of alcohol, the **18ᵗʰ Amendment** was ratified. Shortly after this, the **Volstead Act** was enacted. The manufacture, sale or transportation of intoxicating liquors in the US would be made illegal in one year's time.

1920   Charles Ponzi, an Italian con artist living in the US, was arrested after defrauding thousands of people with his financial schemes. His scheme, where he would pay off existing investors with money he took from later investors, has since been called a "Ponzi" scheme.

1920   On the back of the Paris Peace Conference, the **League of Nations** was formed. Its purpose was to keep world peace by resolving international disputes. There were 42 founding members and that number would grow to 58 by the 1930s. Though the origins of the League trace back to President Wilson, and his proposed principles of peace known as the "Fourteen Points", US Congress - keen on post-war isolationism - refused to allow America to join it and it never did.

Among other policies, the League adopted a mandate system, whereby former German and Ottoman territories would be administered by League members until ready to be self-governed. The mandated territories were divided into classes depending on their readiness for self-rule.

At a conference in **San Remo** in Italy, following the terms of the Sykes-Picot Agreement in 1916, the Allied nations agreed that mandates would be put in place for Syria, Mesopotamia (now Iraq) and Palestine. The French would receive the mandate in Syria (which included Lebanon) and the British would receive the mandate in Palestine and Mesopotamia. It was unclear, however, what was really meant by "mandate" and how much control League members would actually have over their mandated territories. The Arabs in particular were skeptical: in reality, the mandates were not much more than colonies, allowing the French and British to exercise the influence they needed for their own economic and strategic self-interests, especially when it came to the control of the oil reserves and pipelines.

Following through with the Balfour Declaration of 1917, the British began to allow for the settlement of Jews in Palestine. Over the next twenty years, the Jewish population in Palestine increased by around 300,000. Jews were willing to pay large sums of money to Arab landowners and absentee landlords to acquire land there for their communities to settle. Life became increasingly tough for Arab farmers (or "fellaheen" in Arabic) who had traditionally cultivated the land. Many were evicted as a result of the acquisitions. By the beginning of the Second World War, Jews made up around one third of the population in Palestine. Tensions mounted up in the region, with many Arabs feeling resentment at being dispossessed, and often boiled over into violent confrontations between Jews and local Arabs.

1920 Prohibition of the manufacture and sale of alcohol in the USA took effect. However, this did not stop illegal saloons (or "speakeasies") propping up in the major cities like New York and Chicago to circumvent the law. American tourists also visited Cuba where alcohol businesses (like the local family-owned Barcadi rum company) prospered as a result.

Meanwhile, after almost a century-long struggle for women's suffrage in America, US Congress passed the **19th Amendment**, which made it illegal to deny a citizen the vote based on their sex.

1920   The 1920s in the US have commonly been referred to as the **Roaring Twenties**, a decade associated with great economic prosperity experienced by some Americans (mainly those in the cities). Many of the major American cities were thriving. New York, in particular, which prospered during the First World War by supplying arms, supplies and credit to the Allies, massively grew in population. As its boroughs built outwards to cater for the growth in numbers, Manhattan built upwards and New York became the great skyscraper city, surpassing its rival Chicago. By the mid-twenties, it had replaced London as the world's most populous city.

New industries - like electronics, chemicals and aviation - created new jobs for Americans. Productivity increased, particularly in the automobile industry which had embraced the assembly line method credited to Henry Ford. By the end of the decade, the automobile companies in the US gradually consolidated into the "Big Three" we know today: Ford, Chrysler and General Motors. America led the way in terms of making available the consumer luxuries that many of us are so used to today. Ordinary working Americans could now afford cars. And many could afford other life-enhancing products like toasters, vacuum cleaners, radios, washing machines and refrigerators, increasing time for leisurely activities such as sport and entertainment. The American film industry, which had moved out to Hollywood before the First World War, had become the biggest in the world by the mid-twenties.

The twenties also saw the continued migration of African Americans from South to North in search of better lives. Many moved to popular northern cities like Chicago, Detroit and New York. Harlem in particular (predominantly white at the beginning of 1910) would grow to become the nation's largest urban black community. The radio (which eventually became commonplace in millions of American households) spread the new jazz music scene, with its roots in African American culture, and became synonymous with the decade (the period also often referred to as the Jazz Age).

1921   **Warren G. Harding** of the Republican Party succeeded Woodrow Wilson to become the **29th US President**.

1921   Military commander Reza Khan staged a coup d'état in Persia with the assistance of the British, who were keen to exercise further influence in the region (and on Reza Khan himself) in order to protect India and continually secure profits from their Anglo-Persian Oil Company. By around this time, the Company - in which the British government held a majority share - was responsible for almost half of Persia's revenues. Anti-western sentiment was prevalent in the region, where the people were seeing oil profits being sucked out of their country, to the benefit of a foreign-backed company, and with little to no reward for themselves.

1921   In one of the biggest race massacres in US history, a white mob stormed and attacked Greenwood, a thriving black neighbourhood in Tulsa, Oklahoma, often referred to as the 'Black Wall Street'. In the aftermath of the chaos (today known as the **Tulsa Race Massacre**), around 300 black residents were left dead and the Greenwood district was completely destroyed.

1921   Following a revolt in the previous year, Britain created the **Kingdom of Iraq** to allow for greater autonomy in the region (albeit the British retained their influence and a degree of military control). Faisal, a son of Sharif of Mecca Hussein bin

Ali (orchestrator of the Arab Revolt), was crowned as King Faisal I of Iraq following an English-style coronation.

1922   After a successful uprising led by Mustafa Kemal Atatürk, the already-disintegrated **Ottoman Empire officially ended** when the title of Ottoman Sultanate was abolished by the newly-established Turkish government. The following year, the Republic of Turkey was created. Its capital was moved to **Ankara** and the city of Constantinople was renamed **Istanbul**.

1922   The Russian civil war reached its conclusion, with the Red Army on top, and a new **Soviet Union** was established: the **Union of Soviet Socialist Republics** (or **USSR** for short). Communists now had control of Russia.

1922   Exploiting economic turmoil in Italy, **Benito Mussolini's** nationalist right-wing party - the **Fascists** - marched on Rome, leading to King Victor Emmanuel III to ask him to form a government. Mussolini would go on to rule Italy as a dictator. "Fascist" derives from the Latin word "fasces" which translates in English as "bundle of sticks", the symbol of authority during Roman times.

1922   Gandhi was arrested by the British and tried for sedition, resulting in a sentence of up to six years' imprisonment. However, he was released from prison two years later due to his failing health.

1923   President Harding died of ill health. He was succeeded by then-Vice President **Calvin Coolidge** who became the **30th US President**.

1923   Due to the pressures of having to keep up with war reparations imposed by the Versailles Treaty, the Weimar government in Germany resorted to printing a lot of paper notes to exchange with foreign currency. This had the effect of devaluing the German mark and led to hyperinflation in the German economy. Things got so bad that, by the end of the year, it took one trillion marks to buy one US dollar. It got to the point that it cost more to print a note than the note was worth, making it effectively meaningless.

In and amongst the economic turmoil, army veteran **Adolf Hitler**, the leader of the recently established National Socialist German Workers' (or "**Nazi**") Party, attempted an armed coup in Munich against the Weimar Republic. But the so-called "Beer Hall Putsch" (named accordingly as the attempt took place in a beer hall) failed. Hitler was arrested and handed a lenient prison sentence. During his time in prison, Hitler wrote his book *Mein Kampf*, expressing his antisemitic views and ideologies of racial purity. Within a few decades, they would be put into practice. Hitler's persecution and mass extermination of millions of Jews, Soviets, Romani, Poles and homosexuals among others would be instigated during the Second World War.

1924   A plan was agreed by a commission, headed up by a US financier called Charles Dawes, to help Germany repay its war reparations. The so-called "Dawes Plan" included loans of large sums of money granted by the US to Germany.

1924   Upon Lenin's death, **Joseph Stalin** moved against his political opponents to become the Communist Party's supreme leader. He ruled as a feared dictator, exercising totalitarian control over the USSR's economy and society. Political opponents were frequently arrested, sent to labour camps (or "gulags") or executed.

1925   After the events of 1921, Reza Khan emerged successful and was declared Shah, establishing a new Pahlavi dynasty in Persia. Reza Shah would embark on a series of significant reforms - which included certain freedoms for women and major improvements in education, healthcare and infrastructure - and aimed to turn Persia into a modern, secular, westernized society.

1926   Scottish-born inventor **John Logie Baird** demonstrated a
        television system that could broadcast live moving images. Two
        years later, he sent the first television transmission across the
        Atlantic from London to New York and also showcased the
        world's first colour transmission. Over the decades, particularly
        after the Second World War, television broadcasting would
        become much more widespread. Initially, the way it worked
        was broadcast networks would send electromagnetic signals
        carrying TV programmes exclusively over the airwaves. The
        networks constructed tall towers that broadcast audio-visual
        signals through the air to surrounding areas. Viewers used
        antennas fixed on rooftops, or attached to their television sets,
        to receive the signals.

1927   Aviator Charles Lindbergh became an instant celebrity by
        successfully flying solo from New York to Paris without
        stopping.

1927   The **world population** is estimated to have reached **two
        billion** in this year.

1928   The first true antibiotic, **penicillin**, a bacteria-destroying
        mould, was discovered accidentally by scientist **Alexander
        Fleming**, leading to a breakthrough in modern medicine.

1929   **Herbert Hoover** of the Republican Party was inaugurated as
        the **31ˢᵗ US President**. However, soon after coming to office, he
        would have to face one of the biggest economic crises of the
        century when **the US stock market crashed**. Billons of dollars
        were lost and economic depression swept across the world.

        Although the causes are complex and the subject of debate
        among economic historians, a credit boom is usually one of the
        key factors attributed to the so-called **Wall Street Crash**.
        Investors were borrowing most of the money needed to buy
        shares (sometimes almost as much as 90% of the share price).
        In addition, a speculative bubble had formed: share prices
        increased sharply over the decade, though prices were often

not based on true economic value and were instead dictated by over exuberance in the market. The more share prices increased, the more investors borrowed to buy them. By October 1929, share prices had spiralled so much that they were hugely overvalued. The excesses in the market soon caught up. When companies posted disappointing results, investors considered it the right time to cash in on their profits. Prices in shares then began to fall sharply due to panic selling.

What followed was an economic depression now referred to as the **Great Depression**. Again, its causes are complex. Whilst the stock market crash was one cause, the banking system and an agricultural recession also contributed. The 1920s saw a rapid growth in borrowing for the reasons given above. The American banking system was underpinned by many small to medium sized firms, which meant there were thousands of banks across the country. The effect of this was some were prone to going bankrupt, particularly if there was a run on deposits. Indeed, many banks did collapse, taking with them the life savings of millions of Americans. This led to a knock-on effect where there was general lack of confidence in the market, meaning reduced lending and consumer spending. Prices dropped and businesses had to cut costs (or go insolvent altogether) and make workers redundant, creating mass unemployment.

Alongside the precarious banking system, there was an agricultural recession. Farmers prospered during the Great War when the US government granted them subsidies (they were awarded grants to fund their income and keep prices low for buyers). When subsidies ended, however, production did not diminish, largely due to mechanised farming practices which made food production more efficient. There was surplus food but the demand was not there to meet it. When the depression hit, people were too poor to buy. Therefore, crop prices fell and many farmers fell into debt and went out of business.

The Great Depression was felt globally, too. The US

government loaned considerable amounts of money to Europe, particularly France and Britain, to help rebuild their economies after the war. Germany had also turned to the US to help repay its war reparations (via the Dawes Plan of 1924). When America suffered the depression, it called in its loans and dragged Europe with it into economic decline. The US government exacerbated the recession by raising tariffs to their highest ever (the Hawley Smoot Tariffs). This led to European countries responding with high tariffs of their own and world trade reduced considerably as a result.

1929   On 14 February, in what came to be known as the "Saint Valentine's Day Massacre", seven men in the gang of George "Buggs" Moran were lined up against a wall by people pretending to be police officers and shot to death. Nobody knows who was behind it but Brooklyn-born **Al "Scarface" Capone**, Moran's archrival, was the prime suspect. The case was never solved. The Massacre epitomised the violence that dominated the streets of Chicago, which was the scene of turf warfare between mobster gangs competing for the "bootlegging" business (the illegal sale of alcohol).

1929   The independent state of **Vatican City** came into existence by the Lateran Treaty between the Holy See (that is, the throne of the Bishop of Rome) and Italy. Mussolini struck a deal with the Pope whereby it was agreed that the Papacy acknowledged Italy's existence, and would remain neutral in politics and wars, in exchange for receiving from Italy the Vatican as independent territory.

1930   Gandhi organised a march (known as the **Salt March**) where he and his followers set out from his ashram in Ahmedabad and travelled to Dandi (now in Gujarat). The march lasted 24 days and spanned 240 miles. To protest against Britain's salt laws and break their salt monopoly in India, at the end of the march, salt was collected from the sea in an act of symbolic defiance. After Gandhi collected the salt, many others up and down India followed suit, risking arrest.

A year later, the British government in India (represented by Viceroy Lord Irwin) and Gandhi concluded a pact: civil disobedience was suspended, Irwin released most, but not all, political prisoners and permitted production of salt for individual home consumption. No further concessions were made by Lord Irwin. In particular, land confiscated by landlords from peasants was not recoverable. Nehru saw the pact as a betrayal to the peasants who had been loyal to the cause of Congress and who would continue to be exploited by landowners.

1930   **40 Wall Street** (now known as the Trump Building) became the tallest building (though not structure) in the world at 283 metres (or 928 feet). However, it was overtaken in the same year by the **Chrysler Building,** which, in turn, became the tallest building and structure in the world at 319 metres (or 1,046 feet) and 77 floors.

1931   Al Capone was sentenced to 11 years' imprisonment for income tax evasion.

1931   After construction had completed, the **Empire State Building** became the world's tallest building and structure at 381 metres (or 1,250 feet) and 102 floors. Its title of world's tallest building would last until 1970. Its title of world's tallest structure would last until 1954 when the Griffin Television Tower Oklahoma (or KWTV Mast) overtook it. From the 1950s onwards, various television masts would overtake the KWTV Mast for the title until the Burj Khalifa in Dubai would surpass all of these and claim the title of world's tallest structure (and building) in 2009.

1931   Striving for conquest in China, Japanese forces invaded Manchuria and created a puppet state called Manchukuo. Japan was universally condemned by the League of Nations. It's government's response was to walk out of the League.

1931   A left-wing government in Spain came to power, determined
        to get rid of the centuries-old Spanish monarchy. The king was
        forced into exile and a republic was declared.

1932   Exploiting the economic hardship suffered by the German
        people as a result of the Great Depression, and taking
        advantage of internal political divide, the Nazi Party began
        to grow in power. Hitler scapegoated the Jews and Bolsheviks
        for the country's problems and promised the people a stronger
        Germany. The Nazis had a powerful militia group, the
        "stormtroopers" (or SA), which would accompany Nazi rallies
        and intimidate opponents. In 1932, after an election, the Nazi
        party gained a considerable number of seats in the Reichstag,
        though not enough to form a government on its own and Hitler
        refused to join a coalition unless he were made chancellor.

1932   In India, British Prime Minister Ramsay MacDonald granted
        separate electorates to Sikhs, Europeans, Buddhists and other
        minorities, including the Dalits (the lower Hindu caste members).
        This so-called "Communal Award" was considered controversial
        and fervently opposed by Gandhi who believed it was
        introduced by the British to create social discord among Indians.
        Gandhi objected to a constitution that enshrined rights or
        representations based on communal divisions, because he
        feared that it would not bring Indians together but separate
        them, perpetuate their status and divert the attention from
        India's struggle to end colonial rule. Gandhi, again imprisoned,
        declared an open fast until death. A compromise pact was
        eventually signed due to the public outcry.

1932   American aviator Amelia Earhart repeated Charles
        Lindbergh's feat from five years earlier and became the first
        woman to fly solo across the Atlantic, starting her flight in
        Canada and landing in Northern Ireland.

1932   The Kingdom of Iraq achieved independence and ceased to be
        a British mandate. However, that independence would be
        conditional on Britain retaining its military bases in the region

and continued exploitation of its oil resources.

1933   Rahmat Ali, an activist calling for an autonomous Muslim state in north western India, coined the name "Pakistan" using it as an acronym to refer to the names of five northern regions of British India: Punjab, Afghania, Kashmir, Sindh, and Baluchistan.

1933   **Franklin Delano Roosevelt** of the Democratic Party was inaugurated as the **32nd US President**. His administration helped implement the "New Deal", which was a series of programmes, public work projects, financial reforms and regulations to help lift America out of the Great Depression.

At the end of the year, prohibition in the US came to an end after the 18th Amendment was repealed by the **21st Amendment**.

1933   The King of the newly established and unified Kingdom of Saudi Arabia granted the US company Standard Oil exclusive rights to explore and search for, drill, extract, manufacture and transport petroleum in the country's eastern province.

1933   As a result of falling sugar prices, the Great Depression, and dictatorial behavior by the Cuban President Gerardo Machado, various sects of Cuban society, including university students, took to the streets to protest. Machado deployed his army and police force against them, declared martial law and arrested the demonstrators. Eventually, however, military men accompanied the rebels and Machado was forced to flee the country. His generals now ruled over Cuba and the demonstrations continued. **Fulgencio Batista**, an influential sergeant, called on the soldiers in his barracks to rebel. He then took control of the armed forces and appointed a leading demonstrator, Ramón Grau, to be the new President of Cuba.

Grau's government undertook a vast reform programme in Cuba. In 100 days, he established numerous socialist reforms, which included an increased minimum wage, the eight-hour work day and also a requirement that half the workforce of any industry be Cuban citizens. The reforms worried American property owners and companies. The US had already sent an ambassador, Sumner Welles, to influence matters relating to Cuban leadership. In secret talks with Batista, Welles successfully convinced him to switch sides to the Americans and remove Grau from power.

1933   President Hindenburg of the Weimar Republic appointed **Hitler as chancellor**. Within a month, the Reichstag building was set on fire. Hitler blamed his Communist opponents and used the opportunity to win himself emergency dictatorial powers, which he swiftly used to ban all other political parties, effectively creating totalitarian rule in Germany. He also pulled Germany out of the League of Nations.

1934   Batista forced Grau to resign. He annulled most of Grau's reforms and installed a series of new presidents. The person with the actual power, though, was American-backed Batista. To bolster good relations between the Americans and Cubans, most of the Platt Amendment provisions were repealed. Despite the repeal, however, American influence on Cuban politics, via Batista, would continue.

1934   When President Hindenburg died, Hitler declared himself head of state and adopted the title of **Führer**. Looking to reverse the terms imposed on Germany in the Treaty of Versailles, he began spending extravagantly on a military rearmament programme. He also began to rebuild Germany's economy and ordered for a public works programme, which included the construction of the new "autobahn" (or motorway).

1935   Reza Shah changed the name "Persia" to "**Iran**".

1935   Mussolini's imperial ambitions prompted Italian forces to invade Abyssinia (now Ethiopia). He was keen to add the territory to his Italian colonies of Eritrea and Italia Somaliland. Emperor Haile Salassie appealed to the League of Nations for help but their interference could do very little.

1935 In open defiance against the terms of the Versailles Treaty, Hitler reoccupied the Saarland on the French border and unveiled his new German air force: the Luftwaffe. The League of Nations could do nothing. Later that year, he brought into force the **Nuremberg Laws**, which deprived Jews and other 'non-Aryans' of their citizenship and forbade them from marrying or having sexual relations with 'Aryan' Germans.

1936 The Japanese government signed a pact with Hitler, the purpose of which was to guard against the USSR were it to move on China. In continued defiance against the Versailles Treaty, Hitler sent his troops into the previously demilitarised Rhineland territory. In the same year, despite growing concerns about Hitler's racist policies and talks of boycotts, Berlin went ahead and hosted the Olympic Games in which 49 countries attended.

1936 The left-wing "Popular Front" won the Spanish election. Spanish commander **General Francisco Franco**, who opposed the new government, conspired with other army officers to overthrow them. A violent civil war soon erupted and would last for three years. During the **Spanish Civil War**, Franco's nationalist army would receive support of planes, tanks and weaponry supplied by Germany and Italy.

1936 Palestinian Arabs, opposed to continued Jewish immigration in Palestine, led a revolt against the British. With the help of Jewish militias, the British brutally suppressed the revolt. In 1939, the British government issued a proposal that would curtail Jewish immigration to Palestine and called for the establishment of a joint Jewish and Arab state in Palestine within ten years, a proposition that did not seem to please any side. Despite the restrictions imposed by the British, Jews continued to immigrate illegally to Palestine, particularly those who were under pressure to flee the systematic persecution (and soon extermination) in Nazi-occupied territories. This would continue over the course of the Second World War.

1937   As part of the Spanish Civil War, the Basque town of Guernica was virtually obliterated by a bombing raid conducted by the German Luftwaffe in support of General Franco's army. Over 1,600 civilians were believed to have perished.

1937   The Japanese provoked an incident with Chinese troops and invaded. By the end of the year, the Japanese army had overrun much of northern China. Nanking, the Chinese capital at the time, was captured and Canton was overrun the following year. Hundreds of thousands of civilians were massacred by the Japanese army. China had previously appealed to the League of Nations, which could do little to help.

1938   Spanish nationalist forces led by Franco surrounded the Republicans in Barcelona. Soon the rest of Catalonia would fall and the Spanish Civil War was all but over.

1938   Hitler bullied the Austrian chancellor into agreeing a unification of Austria and Germany. He subsequently marched his troops into Austria unopposed - and even to cheering crowds - successfully achieving the intended annexation (or "Anschluss" in German). He then turned his attention to newly-created Czechoslovakia, which contained communities of Germans that Hitler claimed belonged to Germany. France and Britain signed a treaty allowing Hitler to have the Sudetenland region of Czechoslovakia provided that he agreed to have no more territorial ambitions. British Prime Minister Neville Chamberlain infamously referred to the treaty as "peace for our time", mistakenly believing at the time that his government had tempered Hitler's ambitions without resorting to war.

Within Germany, Nazi Minister of Propaganda Joseph Goebbels gave the signal for organised attacks on Jewish shops, businesses and synagogues. This event which took place in November became known as "Kristallnacht" (meaning

"Crystal Night", named after the shards of glass left from smashed windows of Jewish-owned property). For the first time, Jews were being targeted and sent to concentration camps. Laws were brought in which arbitrarily removed property from Jews, kept them away from public spaces and expelled Jewish children from school.

1938   The partnership between the Saudi government and Standard Oil, known as the Arabian American Oil Company (or ARAMCO), discovered oil in huge quantities. A year earlier, oil was discovered in Kuwait by the US-British Kuwait Oil Company and, in 1940, oil would be found in Qatar too.

1939   Madrid fell to General Franco's forces, bringing an **end to the Spanish Civil War**.

1939   Germany invaded the rest of Czechoslovakia. Hitler then upped his demands for Gdańsk (or Danzig - Polish territory that would connect East Prussia with the rest of Germany). This time, Britain and France issued an ultimatum.

Stalin's Soviet Union - after failed alliance negotiations with Britain and France - signed a **Non-Aggression Pact** with Hitler's Germany in which it was agreed Poland would be split between the two nations and Stalin could invade Estonia, Latvia and Lithuania. After the invasion of Czechoslovakia by the Germans, Mussolini's Italy invaded Albania. **Germany then invaded Poland on 1 September**. Britain and France declared war on Germany two days later. This has traditionally been marked as the **beginning of the Second World War**.

1939   Since 1933, German physicist **Albert Einstein** had been living in the US. Because of his Jewish background and the ascendancy of the Nazis, he did not return to Germany. He finally became an American citizen in 1940. Just before the outbreak of the Second World War, Einstein wrote to President Roosevelt informing him of the possibility of creating a nuclear chain reaction in a large mass of uranium, that would allow for the construction of a new type of destructive bomb.

Einstein's letter advised Roosevelt that the Americans should accelerate research in this field and warned that the Germans were looking into this already. The Germans were doing just that, relying on a team of researchers of their own, which included Nobel Prize-winning physicist Werner Heisenberg (though his research would end up being unsuccessful). The Soviets and the Japanese were too administering their own research to develop such a bomb.

1939   Viceroy Lord Linlithgow signed up to India's participation in the Second World War without consulting the Indian Congress politicians about it. Despite Gandhi's opposition to participating in the War, over 2.5 million Indians volunteered regardless and joined the British military to fight on various fronts for the Allied forces.

1939   Just before the beginning of the Second World War, the Nazis implemented plans to forcibly resettle the Jewish population in ghettos in Poland. Eventually, these plans would turn into systemised slavery and mass murder. At first, Jews were rounded up and shot but Nazi leaders soon devised a more efficient killing method: Jews placed in concentration camps were gassed to death and then their bodies were burned. In one of the worst atrocities in human history, an estimated six million Jews died in the **Holocaust** with over one million of that number believed to be children. Jews were not the only target for genocide at the hands of the Nazi regime: other groups of victims included Soviets, Poles, Romani, homosexuals and the disabled.

Though the Nazis tried to conceal their operation, various reports of the mass killings would find their way to the Allies during the course of the War. Despite the knowledge (or at the very least, suspicions) held by Allied governments, the Holocaust was not made public and immediate action was not taken to stop it. So the atrocities continued until the end of the War when either the Nazis had abandoned the camps or Allied troops had liberated them.

1940   Following Nazi "Blitzkrieg" tactics, French and British troops were swiftly pushed out of Western Europe, leaving it under German occupation. France then surrendered leaving Britain to stand alone against the threat of Germany. Despite devastating bombing raids, which lasted nine months and killed around 43,000 British civilians, Britain would hold strong and successfully repel a German invasion.

1940   Germany's ally Japan, pursuing conquest of China, sought to block the transport of war materials through French Indochina (correlating to modern Vietnam, Laos and Cambodia) and so invaded it.

1940   Fulgencio Batista was elected President of Cuba. He brought in a new constitution which established numerous social reforms. Most importantly, the constitution removed the right for the US to intervene in Cuban affairs. Nonetheless, after Pearl Harbor (see below), Cuba would enter the Second World War with the Americans and support their troops by providing a supply base. During the 1940s, Batista allowed the American mafia - including the menacing Charles "Lucky" Luciano from New York - to prosper in Cuba. The money the gangs obtained illicitly in the US was laundered in Cuba and invested in hotels and casinos (which in turn attracted American tourism) all with minimal interference from the Cuban government.

1941   In a crucial turning point in the Second World War, Hitler planned and executed his great gamble: the German assault on Russia (codenamed **Operation Barbarossa**, named after the 12th century German Holy Roman Emperor), turning the Soviet Union into an enemy and exposing Germany to a war on two fronts. With the Non-Aggression Pact of 1939 broken, the USSR joined the Allies in the fight against the Nazis.

1941   British forces invaded Iran. They were soon joined by troops of the Soviet Union. Britain was fearful that the region might fall into German hands and the Allies accused Reza Shah of harbouring friendly ties with the Nazis. Iran was strategically important to Britain, both due to the oil produced by the Anglo-Persian Oil Company and also because it served as a base for the Allies to ship weapons and resources to the Soviets. Reza Shah was soon forced to abdicate. His son, **Mohammad Reza Pahlavi** (whom the British and Americans eyed up as a key ally) replaced him as Shah. The invasion sparked outrage among the Iranian people, angry at being caught up in the affairs of European warfare. Influenced by the West, the Shah would set out on a programme to help modernise Iran. His reforms, though, would upset those keen to uphold the Islamic traditions practised in the region.

1941   President Roosevelt decided to launch a top-secret scientific military and industrial programme under the code name "**Manhattan Project**". The bulk of the work would be carried out in the Los Alamos Laboratory in New Mexico, headed up by physicist **Robert Oppenheimer** . Billions of dollars went into the project, the purpose of which was to develop an **atomic bomb**.

1941   In another crucial turning point in the War, Japanese aircraft attacked the US Pacific Fleet at **Pearl Harbor** in Hawaii without warning, killing over 2,000 Americans. The US, reluctant to intervene at the beginning, entered the Second World War in response to the attack.

1942   Following Gandhi's "*Quit India*" speech, the Indian National Congress ratified the Quit India Resolution, which began a non-violent movement on a mass scale calling upon the British to leave India. Almost immediately afterwards, Gandhi, Nehru and numerous other members of the Congress were arrested and imprisoned by the British Raj. Mass demonstrations broke out across India leading to thousands more arrests.

Britain's exploitation of Indian resources for the war effort continued during the Second World War and, largely due to British Prime Minister Churchill's antipathy of India, exacerbated a widespread famine which broke out the following year, causing the deaths of millions of people in Bengal.

1943   The armies of the Soviet Union defeated the Germans at **Stalingrad** (now Volgograd) in one of the bloodiest battles in modern history that lasted almost six months and claimed an estimated two million casualties. The battle turned the tide of the War in favour of the Allies.

1943   Prime Minister Churchill and President Roosevelt met at an allied conference in Washington at which they agreed on a date to recapture Europe: it was called **Operation Overlord** (or "**D-Day**") and was set to take place in the summer of 1944.

1944   Gandhi was released from prison for health reasons. Upon his release, he found that the Muslim League, led by **Muhammad Ali Jinnah**, was taking the centre stage politically. The League's policies went against Gandhi's idealistic notions. Gandhi (and Nehru) wanted a united, pluralistic and independent India, with Muslims and non-Muslims living side by side. However, many Muslims feared being ruled by a Hindu majority. In places like Lahore, for example, Muslims claimed to face frequent discrimination at the hands of Hindus. For these and other reasons, Jinnah rejected unity and insisted instead on partitioning the Indian subcontinent on religious lines to create a separate Muslim India (soon to be Pakistan).

1944   On 6 June, **Operation Overlord** commenced. Early in the morning, US paratroopers had already landed behind enemy lines. At 6:30am, the first wave of soldiers from amphibious landings hit several targeted beaches along Normandy. American troops had arrived at what they codenamed "Utah Beach" and linked up with the paratroopers. There were considerable difficulties for the American soldiers at "Omaha

Beach" where they faced heavy casualties at the hands of stubborn German defences. Despite setbacks, though, they held the beachhead. Meanwhile, British troops arrived at "Gold Beach" and "Sword Beach"; and Canadian soldiers arrived at "Juno Beach". By early afternoon, the Allies had successfully established footholds at all of the beachheads.

Hitler was completely taken by surprise by the invasions and, caught off guard, the German response was delayed allowing for the beaches to be completely secured. The Allies would use the invasion of Normandy as a launchpad to recapture and liberate France and the rest of Western Europe.

1945   The End of the Second World War

Roosevelt died of a heart attack. Vice President **Harry S. Truman** succeeded him to become the **33rd US President**. Not long afterwards, **Hitler committed suicide** in his bunker in Berlin. Subsequently, Germany signed an unconditional surrender on 8 May (known as Victory in Europe Day or simply "**VE Day**"). The Allies' war against Japan, however, raged on.

President Truman then received the results from the top-secret Manhattan Project. From several years of research by Allied scientists working on the development of an atom bomb, two radioactive materials seemed to offer the most promise as fuels for the new destructive weapons. One was a naturally occurring form of uranium (Uranium-235). The other was plutonium (Plutonium-239), which was human-made in a nuclear reactor. The scientists employed by the Manhattan Project made bombs from each. In July, Operation Trinity took place, marking the birth of the **Atomic Age**: the US government had successfully dropped a plutonium bomb in a desert in New Mexico.

In August, B-29 bomber "Enola Gay" took off from a US base in the Pacific carrying a uranium bomb nicknamed "Little Boy" and dropped it on the city of **Hiroshima** in Japan. The temperature beneath the mushroom cloud caused by the bomb reached 5,000 degrees centigrade. The city was completely destroyed and around 140,000 people were presumed killed. Thousands more died from radiation poisoning. The next day, President Truman addressed the world about the uranium bomb and issued Japan with a warning. But no Japanese surrender was received. Three days after Hiroshima, B-29 bomber "Bockscar" dropped a plutonium bomb nicknamed "Fat Man" on the major Japanese military port of **Nagasaki,** killing approximately 50,000 people. Again, many more would die from the after effects of radiation and burns.

The Truman Administration defended the nuclear attacks by arguing the ends justified the means. They persuaded the world that they had hastened the end of the War and thus spared human lives: Truman claimed half a million casualties were prevented as a result of the bombs. On 14 August, Truman announced that Japan had surrendered unconditionally. This day was known as Victory in Japan Day (or "**VJ Day**").

The Aftermath of the Second World War

In April, the **United Nations** was formed at San Francisco. It consisted of a small council of eleven members called the Security Council, of which six were non-permanent and five were permanent. These five permanent members were (and still are) the USA, USSR (or Russia today), UK, France and China. They had (and still have) the power to veto any measure put before the Council regardless of how popular it was with other representatives. The UN also includes a large assembly (called the General Assembly) consisting of representatives of all its member states (currently 193). The General Assembly met for the first time in 1946 in London.

Between July and August, the leaders of the Allies met at Potsdam in Germany after an initial meeting earlier in the year at Yalta in the Crimea. It was agreed that **Germany would be divided** into four zones of occupation: one zone operated by the Soviet Union, the other controlled by the British, the other would be American and the final zone would be French-occupied. Berlin, despite being deep in the Soviet zone, was divided up into four territories in the same way.

The Second World War had taken its toll on Britain and France, left economically devastated along with the rest of Europe. The USSR and USA, meanwhile, emerged as powerful military states, replacing Western Europe as the seats of dominance on the world stage. The US economy, now a well-oiled capitalist machine, experienced huge growth after the War. American factories were able to quickly pivot from producing weapons to churning out consumer goods as the country's new thriving middle class searched for more convenience and luxury in their lives.

The governments of the US and USSR were already suspicious of one another and their contrasting ideals. Even as the Second World War was drawing to a close, they were both racing in the final year to grab as much territory as possible, each fearful of the other becoming too powerful. The Soviets had managed to create a sphere of influence engulfing the countries in Eastern Europe where their armies had pushed back the Nazis during the War. Immediately after the War ended, Truman cut off aid to the USSR, where people were said to be starving, and Stalin took great offence to this. This was the first of a series of acts that would increase tension between these powers and usher in the **Cold War Era**.

During the Second World War, with the men away fighting, women took on traditionally male jobs on the home front. Some became engineers and mechanics, working in factories to help build weapons, ships and planes among other things. Others took to public services, driving buses, trains and fire engines. However, wherever they worked, women faced discrimination, particularly when it came to salary. After the War, women were forced to give up their jobs to the returning men but, determined to continue working and to receive equal treatment, they become more determined to fight for equality in the decades to come.

Yugoslavia

A year after Soviet forces liberated Yugoslavia, communist **Marshal Josip Broz Tito** was installed as its leader. Non-communists were removed from government and Tito was elected Yugoslav Prime Minister in an election reserved only for candidates from the communist-led People's Front. At the same time, the Federal People's Republic of Yugoslavia was proclaimed under a new constitution. It comprised the Balkan states of Serbia, Croatia, Bosnia and Herzegovina, Montenegro, Slovenia and Macedonia.

Vietnam

During the Second World War, Japan had been exploiting Indochina's natural resources to support its military campaigns, culminating in a complete takeover of the country and a large-scale famine in the region, which had already started in late 1944 and caused around two million deaths. The US army had met influential Vietnamese nationalist **Hô Chí Minh** and supplied weapons to his army, the **Viêt Minh**, to fight the Japanese.

When the War ended in August 1945, a power vacuum opened up, allowing Hô Chí Minh's Viêt Minh to seize power. Soon afterwards, he declared Vietnam's independence. At the Potsdam Conference earlier in the year, the Allied leaders agreed that British troops would occupy South Vietnam to oversee the Japanese surrender and restore law and order whilst the Chinese would do the same in the North. But when the British arrived in September, the Viêt Minh were already in control. Soon after this, French troops began to arrive in the city of Saigon in the South, and the British handed over control to the French who were intent on reasserting pre-war French dominance in the region. After the French swiftly took control of Saigon, an agreement was made with China which saw the Chinese withdraw from the North and the French moved in there as well.

Korea

After the surrender of Japanese forces, Korea was divided between the Soviets and the Americans. It was partitioned along the 38th parallel, forming the two states of the Democratic People's Republic of Korea (North Korea) and the Republic of Korea (South Korea).

India

Due to the economic strain caused by the War, together with growing international pressure, Britain was unable to maintain its empire and it would only be a matter of time before it would end its occupation of India. The question remained, though, as to how this would happen. In March, a British government delegation led by Viceroy Lord Wavell convened a conference at Shimla (the summer capital of the British Raj) to negotiate matters between the Muslim League and the Indian National Congress, India's two major political parties. However, negotiations broke down and the conference ended in failure. At this time, the majority of India's population was Hindu. The Muslims were mainly concentrated in the northwest and northeast of the country. The Sikh minority lived mostly in the Punjab with Lahore as its ancient capital, though Hindus and Muslims also resided there. The Sikhs were opposed to a partition of India, concerned that a such a divide would mean they would end up being ruled and persecuted by Muslims.

1946   The Great Calcutta Killings (or Direct Day Action) took place on 16 August. Thousands representing the Muslim League gathered in the city (now Kolkata) following calls from Jinnah for nationwide protests demanding a separate Muslim India. The gathering soon turned violent and radicals began attacking Hindus, who then retaliated. After three days of rioting, around 5,000 people were killed. The violence then spread to places like Bihar and Noakhali in north-east India.

1946   Hô Chí Minh visited Paris in an attempt to persuade the French to give up colonial rule. Whilst he was away, back in Vietnam, army general Võ Nguyên Giáp, in charge of the government in Hanoi, began consolidating communist rule and conducted a merciless purge of non-communist rivals. Hundreds were shot, drowned or buried alive. In December, fighting broke out in Hanoi between the Viêt Minh and the French military after months of building tension. Hô Chí Minh, Giáp and their comrades were driven out by the French to their mountain stronghold in the North. Hô called for nationwide guerilla war as the French government began to pour thousands of troops into Vietnam.

1946   Syria's independence from France was recognised whilst Britain took steps towards recognising independence for Jordan. The last of the French troops later withdrew from Lebanon, which had already established independence in 1943.

1946   Out of the wreckage of post-war Tokyo, two Japanese physicists Masaru Ibuka and Akio Morita founded electronics business Tokyo Tsushin Kogyo K.K (later renamed "Sony"). They would license the transistor, after it had been patented by US company Bell Laboratories, and soon produced one of the world's first portable transistor radios.

1947   In February, the British government declared it would definitely leave India by June 1948. Lord Mountbatten replaced Lord Wavell as Viceroy to oversee the transition. Heavy negotiations followed between Mountbatten, Jinnah, Nehru and Gandhi over the future of India. With tensions running high between the different religious sects, there was an urgency to strike a deal quickly. Despite dreams of a united India, Nehru and other Indian party leaders reluctantly accepted compromise and acquiesced to Jinnah's demands for partition. Gandhi, however, remained opposed to partition.

On 3 June, Mountbatten, Jinnah and Nehru broadcast that they would divide India into two nations: India and Pakistan (the latter consisting of West Pakistan and East Pakistan, located on either side of India). Those provinces with a Muslim majority would be controlled by Pakistan and those with a Hindu and Sikh majority would be controlled by India. Jinnah and Nehru gave special recognition to the Punjab and Bengal regions, which would be carved in half between India and Pakistan. The border, though, had not been agreed. Mountbatten also pushed forward the exit plans and announced that Britain would instead be leaving India on 15 August 1947 (which was only less than three months away).

In July, British lawyer Sir Cyril Radcliffe arrived in India and was faced with the daunting task of drawing the borders for the new nations of Pakistan and India in a way that would leave as many Hindus and Sikhs in India, and as many Muslims in Pakistan, as possible. British presence was minimal as troops were being sent home. Tension was particularly running high in Lahore in Punjab because people inside did not know on which side of the border they would fall. The Hindus were already leaving Lahore, fearing rumours that the city would be part of Pakistan and murder was becoming an everyday occurrence there. Some communities in the Punjab were taking up arms and attempting religious cleansing so that their village would fall on the side of the border they desired. The British, short in numbers, could do very little. On 9 August, Radcliffe had finished drawing up the border. However, Mountbatten decided to keep the border a secret until after the partition, arguably so Britain would not be blamed for any ensuing violence. In reality, it increased the uncertainty and the violence carried on.

On 14 August, **Pakistan was officially created**. Jinnah became Pakistan's first Governor-General. On 15 August, **India was declared officially independent**. Nehru became India's first Prime Minister. Mountbatten then announced the border:

Lahore would belong to Pakistan with the Punjab and Bengal to be effectively carved in half. In the immediate aftermath, millions of Hindus and Sikhs on the Pakistani side of the border, and millions of Muslims on the Indian side of the border, began a mass migration. It was an incredibly dangerous trek with no clean water, little food and the threat of armed bandits and violent gangs waiting for the vulnerable migrants on the trail. In the coming months, around 15 million people made the perilous journey from one side to the other. At least a million died.

Jammu and Kashmir, in close proximity to the Punjab province, was directly affected by the disturbances taking place there. Among India's 565 princely states, only Jammu and Kashmir had a Hindu Maharaja ruling over a majority Muslim population. India claimed the region as its own whilst Pakistan disputed this. The Maharaja chose to remain neutral. In October, Pakistani-backed armies moved into the region. The Maharaja appealed to India for help. India sent troops into the region but were ill-prepared for the climate. India eventually appealed to the United Nations to broker a ceasefire. The fighting, however, would continue for another year until the ceasefire came into effect in January 1949.

1947   In what became known as the **Truman Doctrine**, President Truman declared in an announcement to US Congress the government's foreign policy of countering Soviet geopolitical expansion and the 'containment' of communism, thus setting the scene for the Cold War. In his announcement, he particularly pledged to contain the threats of communism in Greece and Turkey, which could no longer be supported by Britain. Later that year, he signed off on the establishment of the **Central Intelligence Agency** - or **CIA** - amid growing tension with the USSR.

In a speech, newly-appointed US Secretary of State George Marshall proposed a European recovery programme that would come to be known as the "**Marshall Plan**". Billions of dollars would be invested into propping up the economies of war-torn Western European countries. The Americans feared that, without such support, these countries would be more susceptible to communism. The Marshall Plan would soon prove effective.

1947   After the Second World War, the British government, unable to control the violence in Palestine, handed the problem over to the United Nations. In 1947, the UN proposed to partition Palestine into separate Palestinian and Jewish states with Jerusalem given special international status. Whilst the proposal was generally acceptable to Jewish settlers, the Palestinians viewed the partition as another scheme to push them out of their land and rejected the proposal.

1948   The government of South Africa - under the newly-elected National Party - adopted **apartheid**: a system of racist segregation laws. "Apartheid" is translated from Afrikaans (the language of the first Dutch colonists) and means "separation" or "setting apart". Under this system, whites in South Africa (making up just 10% of the population) would be in certain areas and non-whites in others. The latter group would have no voting rights and were to be treated as second-class citizens with limited freedom. They could only live in certain areas set aside for them, consisting of townships around urban centres and Bantustans (territories specifically carved out by the government). Among other repressive measures, non-whites were required to carry an internal passport to move around the country.

1948   **Mahatma Gandhi was assassinated** in New Delhi by Nathuram Godse, an advocate of Hindu nationalism, apparently lamenting the outcome of the partition of 1947. Godse and his conspirator would be executed a year later.

1948   Ceylon (now Sri Lanka) was granted independence from British rule.

1948   Amid continuing tension between the USSR and its former Allies, the Soviets blockaded the western sections of Berlin to force the other Allies to relinquish control of the whole city. The blockade did not work for the Soviets because the western Allies instead airlifted supplies into the city.

Meanwhile, Josip Broz Tito's Yugoslavia split from Stalin's Soviet Union and Tito began his own separate communist government, though it would accept economic aid from the US. Five years later, Tito was elected Yugoslav President and was repeatedly re-elected until 1963, when his term was made unlimited.

1948   In the US, the first cable transmission compressed over-the-air broadcast signals into wires, sending out these signals to connected homes. Cable was introduced to get broadcast television to places - particularly rural areas - that could not otherwise pick up television signals using rooftop antennas (because they were too distant from the TV networks, which concentrated their towers in more heavily populated urban areas).

1948-   As the British Mandate for Palestine ceased, and the British
1949   rulers vacated, **an independent Jewish state, Israel, was declared** by Jewish leaders. Modern Hebrew, derived from the old Aramaic written script, was established as the official language of the Israelis. The Arab states of Egypt, Jordan, Iraq and Syria - rejecting the creation of Israel and viewing it as an encroachment - all declared war on the new state, triggering the **Arab-Israeli War,** which the Israelis managed to win. In the 1949 armistice that followed, Israel ended up occupying a third more land than they would have received under the UN's proposal (including the western part of Jerusalem). A ceasefire line was drawn and, as a result, Jordan controlled East Jerusalem and the West Bank (so called because it was territory west of the Jordan River) and Egypt controlled the Gaza Strip. Over 700,000 Palestinian civilians were forced to flee their homes and became refugees. This mass exodus is

known to the Palestinians as "Al Nakba" (Arabic for "the Catastrophe")

1949   On 1 January, a ceasefire between India and Pakistan over Kashmir came into effect. A "Line of Control" was established, with Pakistan controlling part of the region and India controlling the other part. However, no final border was agreed.

1949   The North Atlantic Treaty Organization (or "**NATO**") was formed. It formalised a treaty between the European and North American countries to defend one another in the event of a Soviet attack. Later that year, the Soviets called off their blockade of Berlin.

After the USA, Britain and France consolidated their western-occupied zones in Germany, a new Federal Republic of Germany (or **West Germany**) was created. A few months later, in response to the creation of West Germany, the Soviet-backed state of the German Democratic Republic (DDR for short (or **East Germany**)) was made. Berlin was also divided accordingly into West and East Berlin.

1949   In August, the USSR successfully exploded an atomic bomb in a top-secret test location in Kazakhstan. They would announce the news of possessing atomic weapons a year later.

1949   In September, **Communist Party Chairman Mao Zedong** proclaimed the establishment of the **People's Republic of China**, ending a brutal civil war in the country that had broken out after the Second World War between the Communist Party and the American-backed Nationalist Party. Under Mao's China, everyone shared the nation's wealth and the collective community would be represented by the state. China chose to be completely self-reliant with regards to finance, food and products, which meant cutting off diplomatic relations with the capitalist western governments.

1950   Mao Zedong formally recognised Hô Chí Minh's government and began to train its army. The Soviets recognised the Viêt Minh as well and offered their assistance in Hô's struggle against French rule. In response to Chinese and Soviet aid to the Viêt Minh, President Truman approved a multi-million dollar aid programme for the French. The US government quietly dispatched transport planes and jeeps to Vietnam, marking the beginning of their involvement in the region.

The Korean War also began when North Korean soldiers crossed the 38th parallel. As part of his containment policy, Truman soon poured in American soldiers to fight alongside the South Korean army.

1951   The **European Coal and Steel Community** was established under the Treaty of Paris. It was designed to integrate, and provide a common market for, the coal and steel industries in Western Europe. The original members of the ECSC were France, West Germany, Italy, Belgium, the Netherlands and Luxembourg.

1951   The USA and Saudi Arabia signed the Mutual Defense Assistance Agreement: the United States agreed to supply Saudi Arabia with arms in exchange for American training of the Saudi military. Relations between the governments centred around the production of oil in Saudi Arabia, significantly profitable for both countries, and ensuring security within the region to allow for that production.

1952   After a brief spell away, Fulgencio Batista returned to Cuba to run for President again. American mafia boss Meyer Lansky, having previously bribed Batista to allow his organisation to run its gambling operations unchallenged in Cuba, funded Batista's election campaign. Batista's opposition, by contrast, vowed to clean the corruption in Cuba.

Batista was certain he would not win the election so he used his influence in the military to stage another uprising and subsequently took power in an almost bloodless military coup. He swept aside the 1940 Constitution that he himself had brought in, violently repressed opposition and ruled as a dictator. In the late 1940s, a young **Fidel Castro** was studying law at the University of Havana, which at the time was a hotbed for activism and opposition against the sort of government condoned by Batista.

1952   Since the end of the 1940s, political activist **Nelson Mandela** had been a proactive member of the **African National Congress**, the main anti-apartheid opposition group in South Africa. The ANC organised a campaign of civil disobedience, which included thousands of demonstrators publicly destroying their passports in protest against the repressive measures imposed on non-whites. But the ANC's strategy of non-violence was impeded by the brutality of repressive measures imposed on them by the South African government.

1953   Republican **Dwight David "Ike" Eisenhower**, a key military commander during the Second World War (namely Operation Overlord), was inaugurated as the **34th US President**.

The same year, **Joseph Stalin died** and the influential **Nikita Khrushchev** worked his way via shrewd political manoeuvring to become head of the Communist Party of the Soviet Union and Stalin's successor.

1953   **The Korean War ended** in stalemate with no recognised peace treaty, but instead an armistice agreement. Millions of people, including an estimated three million civilians, lost their lives in the conflict and North and South Korea had been left in ruin. A demilitarized zone was created that still exists to this day.

1953   Cuba had become a police state under Batista. Arbitrary arrests, tortures and assassinations were commonplace. The mafia remained influential and the US government supported Batista in exchange for American corporate control over Cuba's economy. Fidel Castro, a lawyer at the time, tried to sue the government for being unconstitutional but the courts rejected his case. He and his brother Raúl decided to resort to more extreme measures and tried to capture Cuba's second largest army barracks (called Moncada) based in Santiago. Their attempt failed and the Castro brothers were forced to surrender. They were sentenced to 15 years in prison.

1953   There was a coup d'état in Iran, orchestrated by the CIA and British MI6, where elected Prime Minister Mohammad Mossadegh was overthrown in favour of Shah Mohammad Reza Pahlavi.

Mossadegh had been elected as Prime Minister in 1951. With the support of parliament, he nationalised the Anglo-Iranian Oil Company (recently renamed from "Anglo-Persian Oil Company"), angered by the fact that the majority of the company's revenues fell into British pockets and so little of it went towards Iran itself. The British government panicked: its teetering post-war economy was over-reliant on foreign imports, particularly from the AIOC. They also gave reason for their US counterparts to worry, persuading them that Mossadegh's government could easily sway towards Soviet influence if nothing was done. The British and American governments forcefully persuaded the Shah to play his part in the plan (codenamed "Operation Ajax") to overthrow Mossadegh. As part of the operation, apparently the CIA paid men in Tehran to stir up trouble. The ensuing coup led to Mossadegh's arrest and exile, in which he remained until his death in 1967.

The Shah, now heavily under American influence, would continue to rule Iran with increased monarchical powers. The US government, keen to prop up Iran's economy so that it would not fall into the hands of the Soviets, increased its financial aid to the country and encouraged American oil companies to invest in the region (which the Shah agreed to). The AIOC, which would change its name to "British Petroleum" (we know it as BP) in 1954, was required by the US to enter into a consortium of other oil companies.

1953   Scientists James Watson and Francis Crick, with the help of invaluable research contributed by chemist Rosalind Franklin, published their discovery of the double helix: the twisted-ladder structure of deoxyribonucleic acid (**DNA**), a fundamental breakthrough in the history of science. The DNA molecule contains our genetic code. Its double helix structure holds all the information and instructions that a living organism needs to grow and develop. Short sequences within our DNA - called genes - determine particular characteristics, such as height, muscle strength and fertility.

1953   Mountaineers Edmund Hillary from New Zealand and Tenzing Norgay from Nepal became the first people to reach the **Everest** summit at 8,848.86 metres (or 29,031.7 feet) above sea level.

1954   *Brown v. Board of Education of Topeka* was a landmark civil rights case in the US in which the Supreme Court declared state laws establishing separate public schools for black and white students to be unconstitutional.

1954   The Battle of Dien Bien Phu was fought between the French and the Viêt Minh. After two months of fighting, the French surrendered. The day after, diplomats from various nations met in Geneva to settle the future of Vietnam. China - reluctant to fight after losing so many of its men in the Korean War - and the USSR - keen to ease tension with the West - urged Hô Chí Minh to agree to a partition of Vietnam, much like Korea. Therefore, Vietnam was temporarily to be divided at the 17th parallel. The French were to withdraw from the North and head South and the Viêt Minh were to re-group to the North. With regards to the middle, the plan was for there to be a demilitarized zone until an election would be held in 1956 in Geneva to reunify North and South Vietnam.

1955   In reaction to West Germany joining NATO, the Warsaw Pact was formed. It was a military defence treaty between the Soviet Union and its European satellite states: Albania, Poland, Romania, Hungary, East Germany, Czechoslovakia and Bulgaria.

1955   In May, the last unit of the French expeditionary force left Vietnam, officially ending French colonial rule in the region. In October, anti-communist Ngô Đình Diêm, having won an election over control of South Vietnam (with a highly questionable 98.2% of the vote), named himself the first President of the brand-new **Republic of Vietnam**. He ruled like a dictator, ordering the imprisonment and execution of thousands of communists in the South. The reunification election that was supposed to be held in Geneva would never take place.

The American government saw South Vietnam as a key ally in containing the threat of communism in the region and were determined to help rebuild the country. Future President John F. Kennedy, a Senator at the time, referred to the Republic of Vietnam as America's "offspring".

1955   Batista agreed with his advisors that releasing the Moncada attackers would bring him good publicity. As a result, Fidel and Raúl Castro were released from prison. They then travelled to Mexico to meet other revolutionaries. Together, they forged the "**26 July Movement**" (named after the date of the Moncada attack). One of the revolutionaries they met was a doctor from Argentina called Ernesto (better known as **"Che"**) Guevara.

1955   The renowned **Montgomery Bus Boycott** began when an African American woman called **Rosa Parks** was arrested for refusing to surrender her seat to a white person. The event triggered a year-long civil rights protest campaign against the policy of racial segregation on the public transport system of Montgomery, Alabama's capital. In 1956, a federal court ruling, in the case of *Browder v. Gayle*, took effect and led to the US Supreme Court affirming that the Alabama and Montgomery laws which segregated buses were unconstitutional. Young civil rights activist and Baptist minister **Martin Luther King Jr.** played a pivotal role in the boycott.

1956   An uprising in Hungary against communist rule was quashed by the Soviet army, killing thousands of Hungarians.

1956   In what would become known as the **Suez Crisis**, President Gamal Abdel Nasser of Egypt, a staunch nationalist, seized control of the Suez Canal and nationalised the Suez Canal Company (in which both the British and French owned shares). He took great offence when the British and American governments went back on their promise to finance the construction of a high dam at Aswan (perhaps due to Egypt's financial ties with the USSR), which he saw as the final straw in a series of acts by the West to undermine and exploit the Middle East.

The British and French feared the canal would be closed and would cut off petrol shipments from the Persian Gulf to the Mediterranean, which would be detrimental to their economies. Britain and France, with the help of Israel, sent troops to occupy the canal. However, due to military threats from the USSR, international condemnation and President Eisenhower's threat of economic sanction, Britain ceased hostilities and, soon after, France and Israel agreed to a ceasefire. The UN sent in peacekeepers to monitor the end of the crisis. It ended in political victory for Nasser and embarrassment for the British and French (the crisis had ruthlessly exposed their diminishing influence on the world stage).

1956   Fidel Castro, undeterred by the size of Batista's forces, loaded his 82 men into a small boat called the "Granma" to head to Cuba. They sailed for seven days until they reached the island. Batista, anticipating their arrival, sent planes to bomb the rebels. 50 of the 82 rebels were killed but the rest fled to the mountains. Amongst the survivors were Che, Raúl and Fidel.

1957   The **Treaty of Rome** created the **European Economic Community**, the precursor to today's European Union. It consisted of, and created a common market between, Belgium, France, Italy, Luxembourg, the Netherlands, and West Germany. The ECC had the goal of enhancing political, economic and trade relations between its member states. The same members also signed a treaty that established the European Atomic Energy Community (or "Euratom"), the purpose of which was to the create a market for the peaceful development of Europe's nuclear resources.

1957   The Soviet Union ushered in the **Space Age** by launching "Sputnik 1", the first artificial satellite, into space. Sputnik 1 was closely followed by Sputnik 2, carrying a dog named Laika, who would not survive the mission. The first US satellite, "Explorer", would follow a few months later in early 1958.

1958   To rapidly industrialise China's primarily agricultural nation, Chinese leader Mao Zedong coerced millions of peasants to work on state-controlled collective farms. Others were forced to leave their farms and work in steel production. This has been referred to as China's "**Great Leap Forward**", though the experiment was nothing but a monumental disaster and led to large-scale famine and, over four years, tens of millions of deaths caused by execution, torture, forced labour, starvation, murder and suicide among other ways. Estimates at the higher end suggest as many as 50 million people died.

1958   Threatened by the recent advancements made by the Soviet space programme and its potential implications for national security, the US government founded the National Aeronautics and Space Administration (or **NASA**).

1958   A violent uprising in Iraq led to the overthrowing, and eventual execution, of the British-influenced King Faisal II (grandson of Faisal I) and his royal family. The Iraqi Prime Minister was also shot dead. The Iraqi Republic was established and its government was keen to separate Iraq from its recent historical ties with British imperialism.

1958-
1959

The survivors of the 26 July Movement in Cuba slowly grew in support. When Che Guevara joined the army - having started off as a doctor - he set up a radio station called "*Radio Rebelde*" to spread the revolutionary message. Fidel Castro's popularity grew due to his charisma, and led to Batista's policies of corruption and brutality being viewed by Americans in a negative light. In response, US Congress agreed to cut off arms shipments to Batista and when Castro launched an offensive against Batista's army, they were forced to retreat. On the radio, Castro - as ever manipulating the media to his advantage - called it a glorious victory. The rebels slowly gained territory in the eastern part of Cuba. The US could see Batista's position was weak and put pressure on him to resign which he did on 31 December 1958.

On 1 January 1959, Castro captured Santiago in the East without any resistance. Batista had fled the country. Meanwhile, Che Guevara's units marched to Havana and reached on 2 January. Batista's military had disintegrated by this time. The soldiers chose to surrender and most of the people in Havana openly welcomed the revolutionaries. The wealthy landowners, many of them Americans, fled out of fear of repercussions. On 8 January, Castro arrived in Havana and delivered a victory speech. He then formed a government of intellectuals but gradually dismissed them and replaced them with his own people, particularly Raúl and Che. The alleged worst offenders of Batista's armed forces (an estimated 3,000) were summarily executed by Castro's men. In February, **Castro made himself Cuba's Prime Minister**. In April, he made a visit to the USA in an attempt to open trade talks. However, President Eisenhower refused to meet with him and, instead, Castro met with Vice President Richard Nixon. After the meeting, Nixon expressed his concerns about Castro and what he saw as communist ideals. Soon after this, US-Cuban relations between would deteriorate.

Back in Cuba, Castro soon began an extensive reform programme, which included the expropriation and nationalisation of American companies in Cuba. Many of the expropriated properties were divided up and given to Cuban farmers. Castro lowered the rent to help improve the lives of the poor (which hit property owners hard). Those who were unwilling or unable to live under Castro fled the country. The US government, in reaction to US-owned properties being nationalised, cut off diplomatic relations with Cuba and much of its trade ties; it also tightened its trade embargo, which it had originally imposed on Cuba towards the end of Batista's regime.

1959   A politician called Lê Duân was emerging as an influential person in North Vietnam, becoming Hô Chí Minh's second-in-command. He began to change the country's policy and help southern revolutionaries to remove South Vietnam's President, Diêm, by force. Their soldiers crept back into the South - using carefully created trails - and accelerated the violence against Diêm's forces.

1959   Alaska was granted statehood in the US, followed by Hawaii, making Hawaii the most recent territory to join the US a state.

1960   On 1 February, four young black students staged a peaceful sit-in at a Woolworth's in Greensboro, North Carolina which served only white customers. The act launched a wave of anti-segregation sit-ins across the South in the US and ignited a national awareness of the prevalence of segregation in American society.

1960   In South Africa, demonstrations against the requirement for non-whites to carry passports led to a massacre at Sharpeville, near Johannesburg. Police fired into the crowd killing 69 people and wounding 180. Soon after this, the African National Congress, backed by Nelson Mandela, turned to a strategy of armed struggle, rather than peaceful protests, against apartheid.

1960   Castro turned to the USSR for aid and negotiated a trade deal. In March, a freighter stationed at a port in Havana unloading ammunition mysteriously exploded killing at least 75 people. Castro accused the Americans of sabotage.

1960   In May, an American U-2 spy plane was shot down whilst on a reconnaissance mission in Soviet airspace, increasing tension between the superpowers. The pilot, Gary Powers, was captured and taken prisoner but he would be returned to the US two years later as part of a prisoner exchange that took place on Glienicke Bridge (connecting East Germany to West Berlin).

1960   President Eisenhower ordered an operation to overthrow Castro. The CIA began arming and training militia groups of Cuban exiles. As the invasion of Cuba was being planned, the American public was gripped by the presidential election campaign: John Fitzgerald Kennedy (or "Jack Kennedy" or simply "**JFK**") of the Democratic Party ran against then-Vice President Richard Nixon of the Republican Party. On 8 November, **Kennedy won** the closely-fought election. After the election, the new President was briefed about the plans to invade Cuba.

1960   A month or so after Kennedy's election, in Vietnam, representatives of southern revolutionary groups met to discuss plans to overthrow Diêm. It was called the National Liberation Front. Its enemies in Saigon and America adopted the term "Communist Traitors to the Vietnamese Nation" or (put more simply) the "**Viêt Công**".

1960   The contraceptive pill was approved for commercial use in the USA. The introduction of the pill meant that, for the first time in history, women had an easy, discrete and reliable method of birth control. It was liberating for women, who previously had been reliant on men to use effective contraception. Those with the pill could take more control over their reproductive health and choose when they wanted to have a baby. By 1962, over a million American women were taking the pill.

1960   During this year, the **world population** surpassed **three billion**.

1961   **JFK was inaugurated as the 35th US President**. Aged 43, he is so far the youngest person ever to be <u>elected</u> as US President (Theodore Roosevelt was a year younger when he automatically assumed office after McKinley's assassination in 1901).

By Spring, over a thousand exiled Cubans, trained by the CIA, were ready to invade Cuba. Kennedy, allegedly under pressure from his advisors, had finally approved the military plan, albeit under two conditions: the troops would land at a remote location (the chosen location was the **Bay of Pigs**) and only eight US bombers - disguised as Cuban bombers - would accompany the invaders. The attempted invasion failed and the Cuban exiles were either killed or captured. Thousands of Castro's men were also either killed, captured or missing. Castro nonetheless announced the Bay of Pigs as an unmitigated triumph.

After the victory, Castro declared that his revolution was a socialist revolution, therefore confirming his government as socialist. He then formally allied with the Soviet Union. Over the years, the CIA would make frequent attempts to assassinate Castro but to no avail (he managed to evade all attempts).

1961   On the back of the Greensboro Sit-ins, the Freedom Riders, a multi-racial group on a bus tour of the southern US states challenging racial segregation, were growing in influence. But their campaign trail was dangerous. Their presence was met with violent white mobs in various places along their journey, including Rock Hill in South Carolina and Montgomery in Alabama.

1961   Kuwait, formerly a British protectorate, became an independent nation. The Iraqi government did not support this. It claimed that Kuwait was an extension of Iraq, though it had been created by British imperialism.

1961   **Yuri Gagarin** of the USSR, aboard the "Vostok 1", became **the first man in space**, beating the Americans to the race. In 1963, Valentina Tereshkova, aboard the "Vostok 6", became the **first woman in space**.

1961   In August, **the Berlin Wall was built** all around West Berlin by the communist German Democratic Republic (or East Germany) in an attempt to prevent defections from East to West.

1961   Che Guevara - under Castro's orders - and head of the Soviet Union, Nikita Khrushchev, met in Moscow to formally negotiate trade deals. Behind the scenes, the Soviets and Cubans agreed a military pact where the USSR agreed to secretly store nuclear missiles in Cuba. Khrushchev wanted the missiles in Cuba as a self-defence mechanism in response to the USA having missiles in Italy and Turkey. Castro felt Cuba needed to protect itself against another American invasion.

1962   China attacked India in the Aksai Chin region of Kashmir, easily defeating India's poorly equipped Himalayan troops.

1962   Cuban Missile Crisis

In May, Khrushchev arranged for the secret deployment of nuclear weapons, as well as around 40,000 Soviet troops, in Cuba. In September, the missile deployment was completed. The eastern region of the USA was now in range of Soviet nuclear missiles.

When the US government came to know about this, it called emergency meetings, during which military advisors recommended a full scale invasion and strikes on Cuban missile sites. However, JFK ended up taking a more careful approach: he announced that the US navy would intercept all shipments to Cuba. Though a more measured approach than a full-scale military invasion, it was not without its risks and a naval blockade was technically an act of war. In an attempt to somewhat soften the action, the US government decided to call the policy a "quarantine" rather than a "blockade". Khrushchev, however, in heated written correspondence to Kennedy, nonetheless viewed this as an act of aggression.

The crisis escalated further when an American U-2 reconnaissance plane was shot down by a self-defence missile launched from Cuba, killing the pilot, Major Rudolf Anderson. On the same day - and this information did not transpire until long after the crisis had ended - a Soviet submarine was hit by a small depth charge caused by an American navy vessel trying to signal for it to come up to the surface. The Russian commanders inside the submarine - too deep to communicate with the surface - mistakenly thought war had begun and prepared to launch a nuclear torpedo. However, **Vasili Arkhipov**, one of the crew on board the Soviet submarine, vetoed the decision to launch, ultimately saving the world from nuclear warfare.

The crisis eventually subsided when the Soviet and American leaders agreed that the US would remove missiles from Italy and Turkey in exchange for the USSR removing its missiles from Cuba under UN inspection. Though the crisis had fortunately been resolved diplomatically, the incident demonstrated just how close the world could come to a nuclear war.

1963   In Iran, the Shah announced a series of reforms, known collectively as the "White Revolution", which would modernise Iran. They included privatisation of state-owned businesses, enfranchisement of women, a literacy programme, land reform and developments to infrastructure. The reforms, however, upset the traditional Shia Muslim community, which saw them as a threat to Islamic tradition and a submission to Western foreign influence. Also, many Iranians were becoming increasingly frustrated by the seemingly little benefits Western aid was bringing to them. In their eyes, there was little economic progress to show for the reforms. Wages remained low while the cost of living increased. By contrast, the wealth of the Shah continued to accumulate and allowed for a lavish lifestyle as American money lined his pockets.

Ruhollah Khomeini, a prominent Shia religious leader at the time, delivered a passionate speech denouncing the Shah's regime. He was detained by the government and put under house arrest. In response, riots broke out throughout the country.

1963 In South Africa, the main leaders of the ANC were arrested in Rivonia, a suburb of Johannesburg. **Nelson Mandela** and his comrades were charged with sabotage and high treason, offences that risked punishment by death. He and the others were instead **sentenced to life imprisonment**.

1963 Martin Luther King Jr, now a prominent figure in the civil rights movement which had gained momentum in America, led his followers in a non-violent march in Birmingham, Alabama. There, police stopped the protestors and attacked them using dogs and water cannons. King was arrested and imprisoned. From his cell, he drafted the now-famous *Letter from Birmingham Jail*: a passionate statement on the civil rights cause.

Later that year in August, King, together with other key civil rights leaders (including A. Philip Randolph, John Lewis and Roy Wilkins) and their respective followers, marched on Washington DC From the Lincoln Memorial, King delivered his revered "*I Have A Dream*" speech, calling for freedom and justice for African Americans in their struggle for equal rights. This was the largest public demonstration in American history up to that time. President Kennedy then followed up with an address to the nation: he called on Congress to pass a law that would ban discrimination in all public accommodations.

1963   In June, Kennedy signed into law the **Equal Pay Act**, which prohibited wage disparity based on sex.

1963   In November, **Kennedy** was travelling with his wife, First Lady Jacqueline Kennedy, in a motorcade in Dallas, Texas. During the journey, he **was shot (apparently twice) and killed**. Suspect **Lee Harvey Oswald** was arrested for the murder (and for the murder of a police officer he allegedly tried to evade afterwards). Vice President **Lyndon Baines Johnson** was immediately sworn in as the **36ᵗʰ US President**.

Two days after JFK's assassination, Oswald, whilst in police custody, was shot and killed by a local nightclub owner called Jack Ruby (who himself died three years later of cancer whilst awaiting retrial). Ruby had always claimed he acted alone. President Johnson set up a commission (known as the "Warren Commission") to investigate the assassination. A year later, the Commission concluded that Oswald and Ruby both acted alone in their respective murders.

1963   Back in May, South Vietnamese authorities under Diêm opened fire on Buddhist protestors in the city of Huê, killing nine people. In November, troops loyal to a coup successfully stormed key areas in Saigon resulting in Diêm and his brother being assassinated. Over the next two years, South Vietnam would be ruled by over ten different governments, each one replacing the previous one by a military coup.

1964   In a significant breakthrough for the civil rights movement, the **Civil Rights Act** was passed in the USA. The Act prohibited segregation in schools, hospitals and privately-owned public places like restaurants, hotels and theatres. It also banned discrimination in employment based on race, colour, religion, sex or national origin.

The Act also banned unequal application of voter registration requirements. Despite the prohibitions, however, African

Americans still faced barriers to voting. The Jim Crow laws, so heavily entrenched in the southern States, imposed literacy tests as a prerequisite for voting, designed to impede the black community which, over the course of generations, had not been presented the same opportunities in education as whites. On top of this, intimidation tactics and other discriminatory practices were used in the South to deter blacks from registering or voting.

1964   Nelson Mandela and his co-accused were transferred from Pretoria to a prison on **Robben Island**, remaining there for the next 18 years.

1964   At the end of July, South Vietnamese ships, under the direction of the US military, shelled two Vietnamese islands in the Gulf of Tonkin. At the beginning of August, the so-called **Gulf of Tonkin Incident** took place: North Vietnamese torpedo boats fired on the USS Maddox, which responded by heavily damaging the boats. President Johnson's advisors put pressure on him to retaliate (though the attack had been provoked by the South Vietnamese raids a few days earlier).

A few days later, the USS Turner Joy and the USS Maddox reported during the evening that they were being attacked by North Vietnamese gunboats, although it was uncertain whether the attacks actually occurred (the attacks were said to be "probable but not certain"). Nonetheless, in response to the reports, President Johnson began to propose air strikes on North Vietnamese bases. On 7 August, approving Johnson's proposal, US Congress passed the **Gulf of Tonkin Resolution**, which gave the President authorisation to take all necessary measures to defend the US against further North Vietnamese aggression.

In November, Johnson won the presidential election in a landslide victory. In December, the Battle of Binh Gia took place with the Viêt Công inflicting heavy losses on South Vietnamese forces.

1965   A second **Indo-Pakistan War** took place. Pakistan, encouraged by China's success in 1962, sent troops over the Line of Control in Kashmir. Again, after an inconclusive war, both countries accepted a UN-backed ceasefire, though the Line of Control remained the same.

1965   In February, controversial activist **Malcolm X was assassinated**. During his lifetime, he and Martin Luther King Jr were often at odds due to their contrasting principles and methodologies. Malcolm X had publicly denounced King's notion of non-violence and instead believed in blacks protecting themselves using "any means necessary".

In the same month, people peacefully demonstrating against the disenfranchisement of African Americans in Alabama were attacked. This led to the death of a protestor, Jimmie Lee Jackson, at the hands of an Alabama state trooper. In March, a large group of protestors, led by another prominent civil rights activist John Lewis, attempted a 54-mile march from Selma to Montgomery. The marchers, however, were stopped and brutally attacked by Alabama state troopers. The scenes were captured on television and caused outrage among the American public. A second march, this time led by King, was attempted but King turned the marchers around. He was concerned about the legal repercussions of breaching a federal injunction which outlawed the march. More violence and intimidation followed, leading to a white church minister being killed. Later that month, President Johnson publicly declared his support for the Selma campaign and ordered for US army troops to be sent in to accompany a third attempted march from Selma to Montgomery. This time it was successful for the marchers.

On 2 March, President Johnson had ordered **Operation Rolling Thunder**: the systematic bombing of targets in North Vietnam. He also ordered for the first time the deployment of ground troops in Vietnam. On 8 March, 3,500 marines arrived on beaches near Da Nang, marking **the beginning of US ground forces in Vietnam**. Back in the US, meanwhile, demonstrations protesting involvement in the war were beginning. Despite the protests, and despite the mounting casualties, Johnson's government continued to approve sending in thousands more American soldiers to support the struggling South Vietnamese army against the Viêt Công.

In August, riots broke out in the urban neighbourhood of Watts, Los Angeles in opposition to mistreatment by the police. 35 people were left dead. In the same month, following the successful Selma-to-Montgomery march earlier in the year, the **Voting Rights Act** came into effect: it gave the federal government the right to oversee voting in places where discrimination was prevalent. The Act prohibited discriminatory practices such as literacy tests (which had commonly been used as a way to prevent blacks from voting).

1966   As the year began, over 2,000 Americans had died in Vietnam along with over 35,000 South Vietnamese. A public hearing on the war revealed that there were strong doubts about the Americans being able to win at all. The government, however, resumed bombing after there was no attempt from the North Vietnamese to come to the negotiation table.

At the beginning of the Vietnam War, 10,000 US troops a month were called up to serve. But by 1966, due to the fresh demand for more soldiers, the number increased to 30,000 (ethnic minorities and those from poor backgrounds were disproportionately represented in the armed forces). By the middle of 1967, there were nearly half a million US soldiers in Vietnam. By the end of that year, 20,000 Americans had been killed.

The high American death toll can be attributed to a range of factors. One was that the American M-16 rifles were less effective than the Soviet-made AK-47 (the latter weapon named after its Russian developer: Mikhail Kalashnikov). The

M-16 was prone to frequent jamming when used and was in need of constant cleaning. By contrast, the AK-47's durability, reliability, ease of use and low manufacturing costs made it a popular weapon for the Viêt Công and ensured it would stay in production for numerous decades.

1966   After the horrors of the Great Leap Forward, Chinese Communist leader Mao Zedong launched the so-called **Cultural Revolution**, bringing in a new period of political and social instability, and much brutality, in order to strengthen his own position in power. The aim of the revolution was to re-emphasise the communist ideology and purge political opponents, particularly those leaning towards capitalism and who threatened the socialist system. Chinese youths were encouraged to join the Red Guard and spread terror over those continuing to adopt perceived old customs. Bourgeois intellectuals were attacked, universities and schools were shut down and private homes were looted. At least a million people died as a result of the chaos.

1967   By this time, Che Guevara was in Bolivia, trying to stage another revolution. He was captured, interrogated and then executed under the orders of the Bolivian government (with assistance from the CIA).

1967   Another Arab-Israeli War (known as the **Six Day War**) broke out with Israel fighting the Arab states of Egypt, Syria and Jordan. Winning the war with the help of weaponry supplied by its western allies, Israel came out of it gaining more territory: it captured the West Bank and East Jerusalem from Jordan, the Golan Heights from Syria and the Gaza Strip and Sinai Peninsula from Egypt. In occupying the West Bank and Gaza Strip, Israel took control of a population of a million Arab Palestinians, several thousand of which would later flee. From this moment on, Israeli citizens, claiming holy land they believed was rightfully theirs, started crossing over into the West Bank and began establishing settlements there, something which the UN did not approve. Today, around half a million Jews have settled in the West Bank (with almost a quarter of a million in East Jerusalem).

1967   A series of violent race riots broke out across various places in the US including Newark in New Jersey and Detroit in Michigan.

1967   The Treaty of Brussels, also known as the "Merger Treaty", merged the European Coal and Steel Community (ECSC), the European Atomic Energy Community (Euratom) and the European Economic Community (EEC) into one institution.

1968   **Martin Luther King Jr was shot dead** at a motel in Memphis, Tennessee. A criminal called James Earl Ray was later convicted for the murder. As a consequence of his death, riots erupted in major US cities like Chicago and Washington DC. Two months later, in the midst of running for President, **Robert Francis Kennedy** - JFK's brother - **was assassinated** by Sirhan Sirhan, a man of Palestinian descent, opposed to Kennedy's support for Israel and its disputed occupation of territory in the Middle East.

1968   The **Têt Offensive**, officially called the "General Offensive and Uprising of Têt Mau Than", began in the early hours of 31 January. 84,000 Viêt Công and North Vietnamese soldiers attacked the majority of South Vietnam's provincial capitals, dozens of American military bases and the six largest cities in the country including Huê, Da Nang and Saigon. The name of the offensive comes from the Têt holiday which celebrates the Vietnamese New Year.

In the months leading up to the offensive, Viêt Công troops had been infiltrating the South and smuggling in weapons whilst blending in with the locals. Militarily, the offensive resulted in failure for the Viêt Công. However, heavy losses were inflicted on both sides. In the aftermath of the offensive, around 9,000 American and South Vietnamese soldiers were killed whilst 45,000 North Vietnamese and Viêt Công were killed. Back in the US, strong anti-Vietnam War protests were escalating.

In May, there was another offensive (sometimes referred to as "Mini-Têt") but this also failed for the Viêt Công. It proved to be the bloodiest month in the Vietnam War for the Americans during which over 2,000 were killed. A similar number of South Vietnamese were killed whilst well over 25,000 North Vietnamese bodies were counted.

In the build up to the next US presidential election, President Johnson stopped the bombings in Vietnam and arranged for peace talks. He also announced he would not be seeking re-election. Hubert Humphrey, Johnson's Vice President at the time, became the Democratic Party's nominee and would take on Richard Nixon of the Republican Party. Meanwhile, Nixon's staff had secretly been contacting the South Vietnamese government to persuade them to withdraw from peace negotiations and stall until Nixon became President on the premise that Nixon would drive a harder bargain for them. The South Vietnamese government did withdraw. Subsequently, **Nixon won the election**. He and National Security Adviser, Henry Kissinger, vowed to the public that they would end the war in Vietnam. The plan - which was called "Vietnamization" - was to phase out American troops and phase in the South Vietnamese to continue engaging the enemy.

1969   **Richard Nixon** was inaugurated as the **37th US President**.

1969   Yasser Arafat became Chairman of the Palestine Liberation Organization, which had been founded five years earlier with the principal aim of liberating Palestine in Israel.

1969   In February, the North Vietnamese launched another offensive, leading to around a thousand American deaths in just three weeks. President Nixon could not afford to resume bombing North Vietnam at the risk of provoking the anti-war movement at home and derailing peace talks. Instead, in an act of callous aggression, he secretly ordered B-52 bombers to carpet bomb

North Vietnamese and Viêt Công bases in neutral **Cambodia**. The bombings - nicknamed **Operation Menu** - started in March and would continue for 14 months. To avoid protests or negative press, the American public were not told and even members of Nixon's cabinet were kept in the dark about Operation Menu. However, the story leaked two months later in the New York Times. Nixon then illegally ordered wiretaps on suspected individuals to determine the source of the leak.

1969   A series of violent demonstrations (known as the **Stonewall Riots**) took place in New York when members of the lesbian, gay, bisexual and transgender community rose up against a police raid.

1969   On 20 July, four days after launching from the Kennedy Space Center in Florida, astronaut **Neil Armstrong became the first man on the Moon** and Edwin (or "Buzz") Aldrin became the second. Both were part of the three-astronaut Apollo 11 flight mission to the Moon (Michael Collins was the third person on the flight, though never walked on the moon himself).

1969   Muammar al-Gaddafi (or Colonel Gaddafi) led a bloodless military coup against the pro-western monarch King Idris I of Libya and took control of the country. Once in control, Gaddafi closed down American and British bases in Libya and forced a renegotiation of oil contracts with foreign companies benefitting from Libya's oil resources.

1969   In September, **Hô Chí Minh died** of heart failure aged 79.

In November, it was reported that, 20 months earlier, a US army division brutally murdered approximately 400 innocent women, children and old men in the Vietnamese village of **My Lai**. At the same time, another company over a mile away murdered 97 more villagers. Women and children were raped and tortured before being murdered. Until this time, US army officers had covered up the massacre. Almost all of the army involved in the My Lai Massacre were acquitted. Only one soldier was convicted but President Nixon reduced his sentence to three years' house arrest.

1970 In April, Nixon ordered for US ground troops to enter Cambodia to fight against North Vietnamese forces. Soon after this, in May, the Kent State shootings took place: the Ohio National Guard shot and killed four unarmed students protesting the war in Cambodia. Hundreds of campuses across the US were closed down and demonstrations took place throughout the country. When American soldiers had withdrawn from Cambodia at the end of June, it was reported that they had killed over 11,000 enemy troops.

1970 The **North Tower of the World Trade Center**, still under construction, surpassed the Empire State Building as the world's tallest building. To the roof, it was 417 metres (or 1,368 feet) tall when completed.

1971 The Bengali-speaking population of East Pakistan demanded autonomy from Pakistani rule and eventually the struggle led to war. The conflict was triggered by elections which were won by an East Pakistani party called the Awami League that campaigned for greater autonomy in the region. Many Bengalis claimed to be culturally subjugated, and economically exploited, by West Pakistan and became convinced its government was intentionally blocking their ambitions for independence.

Eventually the situation turned violent in East Pakistan. The Awami League called for civil disobedience and its followers attacked non-Bengalis. West Pakistan sent in the army to put down the nationalist movement. The Indian government, led by Prime Minister Indira Gandhi, sent in its army to intervene and support the rebels in East Pakistan. This resulted in a devastating defeat for Pakistan, which lost control of half its population and a significant portion of its economy. East Pakistan would break away and become a new independent country: **Bangladesh**.

The war had led to **mass genocide of Bengalis** at the hands of the Pakistani military: independent researchers believe that between three hundred and five hundred thousand people died. The Bangladeshi government claims the figure to be around three million. In addition, millions of displaced civilians fled to India as a result of the genocide.

1971   In June, the press in the US released to the public top-secret correspondence exchanged between officials in the White House relating to government involvement in the Vietnam War. The correspondence, famously dubbed the "**Pentagon Papers**", revealed numerous inadequacies and dishonesties of the various administrations in relation to the war. The papers revealed concerns about the war being unwinnable; that the bombing campaigns were not effective; that the Kennedy administration had a hand in the overthrowing and assassination of Ngô Đình Diêm; that administration after administration had misled the American people about the true extent of the country's involvement in the war.

President Nixon was concerned that the journalists would have more dirt on him about the secret bombing of Cambodia. He created a private undercover investigative unit within the White House (nicknamed the "Plumbers") to find out who the conspirators were. One of them was whistleblower Daniel Ellsberg. Nixon's aide ordered a burglary of Ellsberg's psychiatrist's office in an attempt to dig up dirt on Ellsberg and blackmail him. The burglars were unable to find such files.

Nixon was also concerned there might be other documents which could reveal he had a hand in scuppering the Vietnam War peace talks (and thus prolonging the war) around the time of his election three years earlier. He wanted his men to break into the Brookings Institution - a think tank based in Washington DC - which held these documents, crack the safe, and remove the files. Despite Nixon's demands (which are revealed in tape recordings), the break-in never took place.

1972   In February, President Nixon, looking to take advantage of a rift between China and the Soviet Union, travelled to visit Chairman Mao. He became the first American President to visit China. It was an event which shocked the world due to China's policy of isolationism up to that point.

In March, Lê Duân - now heading up the Communist Party in North Vietnam in place of Hô Chí Minh - launched a new offensive, known as the Easter Offensive, on South Vietnam. Only around 60,000 US personnel were left in Vietnam (with only a few who were trained in combat). The offensive was therefore a huge test for the South Vietnamese army. But their (and the Vietnamization plan's) weaknesses were exposed. Nixon, in response, ordered Operation Linebacker: air attacks were launched on the advancing North Vietnamese. Nixon had originally promised to wind down the war but the ferocity of the bombings proved otherwise. The airstrikes proved effective and the North Vietnamese advances were checked. In May, the US and Soviet Union signed a historic Anti-Ballistic Missile Treaty: the first agreement to limit nuclear armaments since the Cold War began. This meant that, for the superpowers, Vietnam's significance on the world stage was beginning to decline.

During his presidential election campaign, Nixon ordered his "Plumbers" to break in to the Democratic National Headquarters in a Washington DC complex called **Watergate**. Their task was to install bugging apparatus at the Democratic National Committee. This time, unlike before, they were caught in the act. Nixon convinced the public his staff were not involved in the incident. It would later transpire that Nixon had a say in paying off the Plumbers to keep quiet. He also approved a plan for the CIA to obstruct the FBI's investigation into Watergate.

In November, the Republican Party convincingly won the election in a landslide and **Nixon was re-elected as President**

for a second term. Meanwhile, in relation to the Vietnam War, whilst he vowed to remove troops from Vietnam, Nixon still ordered the airlifting of weaponry and vehicles to the South Vietnamese, which hindered peace talks. In December, he ordered further bombings of North Vietnamese targets.

1972   A Palestinian militant group known as Black September broke into the Olympic Village where Israeli athletes of the Munich Olympics were housed, murdered two of the athletes and took nine others hostages. The group demanded the release of 230 Arab prisoners in Israeli jails. The Israeli government refused. What resulted was a shoot-out where five of the group members were killed along with all nine of the athletes and a German police officer.

1973   In January, Nixon announced that peace talks with the North Vietnamese government had been agreed. Later that month, a treaty was signed in Paris: a ceasefire would begin and American prisoners of war were to be released. In March, **the last American troops left Vietnam**. Over 58,000 Americans had been killed overall in the Vietnam War. As many as 2,000,000 Vietnamese civilians on both sides lost their lives together with over 250,000 South Vietnamese soldiers and over 1,000,000 North Vietnamese and Viêt Công fighters. Despite the American withdrawal, both South and North Vietnam violated the ceasefire and war carried on in the region.

1973   The **Sears Tower** (also known as the Willis Tower) in Chicago overtook One World Trade Center as the tallest building in the world at 442 metres (1,450 feet) high.

1973   In a follow-up to Israel's victory in the Six Day War of 1967, a combination of Egyptian, Syrian, Iraqi and Jordanian forces attacked Israel during the Jewish holiday of Yom Kippur seeking to recapture territory that had been lost in that war. Israel successfully defended itself against the attack. The UN then secured a ceasefire.

In response to American military aid to Israel in the so-called **Yom Kippur War,** the Arab members of OPEC (the Organization of the Petroleum Exporting Countries) imposed an oil embargo causing a stop on oil supplies to the USA. In the space of six months, one barrel of oil shot up from $3 to nearly $12. Due to oil being crucial for the economy to run, the increase in oil prices led to the cost of just about everything else going up. Almost overnight, western economies, including the US and the UK, were driven into recession. Though the embargo was lifted in 1974, the oil shock had a longer lasting effect. Oil prices remained significantly high during the 1970s, particularly in the US, which suffered an economic decline resulting in high unemployment and reduced energy consumption. Western governments were forced to seek and invest in alternative energy solutions.

In comparison, the wealth of the Middle Eastern countries around the Persian Gulf skyrocketed. They had taken back control of their most valuable commodity and those in power in the oil-producing countries became immensely rich. The economies of countries like Saudi Arabia and Iraq especially prospered in the 1970s.

1974   As a result of the **Watergate Scandal,** the House Judiciary Committee, a standing committee in Congress, recommended that President Nixon be impeached for abuse of office and obstruction of justice among other violations. Rather than facing impeachment, in August, **Nixon became the first President in American history to resign the presidency. Gerald Ford,** the Vice President at the time, took over to become **38th US President** and gave Nixon a pardon for any wrongdoings committed during his presidency.

Congress then significantly curtailed the military spend towards Vietnam and Nixon's personal pledge to provide continual support to the South Vietnamese army via airpower was not met. In December, North Vietnamese forces attacked Phước

Long, northeast of Saigon.

1974   During this year, the **world population** surpassed **four billion**.

1975   In March, North Vietnamese forces entered Da Nang, South Vietnam's second largest city. In April, rockets began to land in Saigon and Americans were evacuated. **The Vietnam War ended** with victory for the communist North Vietnamese after the **fall of Saigon**, which would later be renamed **Ho Chi Minh City**.

1975   Spanish dictator **Francisco Franco died** from ill health. Spain subsequently began its transition towards becoming a democratic state.

1975   Bill Gates and Paul Allen founded **Microsoft**, a company specialising in computer software.

1976   A brutal dictatorship seized power in Argentina in a military coup. In the face of a mounting economic crisis and civil unrest, the ruling generals ordered the arrest, torture and execution of tens of thousands of political opponents.

1976   The company **Apple Computers**, which originally specialised in making and selling user-friendly personal computers, was founded by Steve Jobs and Steve Wozniak.

1977   **Jimmy Carter** of the Democratic Party was inaugurated as the **39th US President**, having defeated Gerald Ford in the previous year's election. Later that year, Carter signed a treaty which transferred the Panama Canal back to Panama.

1978   In a bloody revolt, communist radicals took control of Afghanistan. At this point, things heated up between the US and USSR as both superpowers each had their motives for exerting influence over Afghanistan. The Soviet Union was fearful of Iran, Saudi Arabia and Pakistan (American allies at the time and frequent customers of US weaponry). The US feared the extent to which Russia would control the new regime in Afghanistan and what it might mean for the rest of the Middle East.

The communist government in Afghanistan sought to radically modernise the country: they wanted to improve healthcare and literacy; and they supported equality and education for women. In response, Muslim opposition groups, vehemently opposed to the changes being introduced, began to organsie themselves in rebellion, though the government brutally suppressed any such opposition.

1978   President Carter helped broker the **Camp David Accords**, which resulted in the governments of Egypt and Israel signing a peace agreement in 1979. Israel agreed to withdraw troops from the Sinai Peninsula and pledged for the establishment of Palestinian self-government in Gaza and the West Bank (though the UN never formally recognised the treaty as it was made without Palestinian participation).

1978   Tensions were running high in Iran. People were growing restless of the increased cost of living, cuts in pay, the widening gap between rich and poor and the heavy-handedness of the Shah. Resistance to the Shah's regime was put down, at times brutally, by his secret police, the SAVAK. Many Iranians were angered too by the extravagant lifestyles of those within the Shah's royal court, seen to be funded by the country's oil revenues and money flowing in from the West.

Though **Ruhollah Khomeini** was exiled at the time, support for him grew, particularly among students, intellectuals and religious groups. These groups were not necessarily Islamic fundamentalists but people who were dissatisfied with economic inequality, political repression and a corrupt regime. There was also widespread anger at the extent of foreign intervention, particularly from the US, which yielded little benefit for the people.

In September, mass marches erupted in protest against the Shah. In response, the Shah used tanks and helicopters to break up the demonstrations. Protestors were shot at and killed as a result.

1979   As the protests became increasingly violent, the Shah fled Iran - never to return - and sought refuge in the US. He was replaced, however, by a regime equally (if not more) autocratic and despotic, though this may not have been obvious at first. Khomeini returned to Tehran 14 years after going into exile. He was greeted by numerous key supporters who very swiftly took control of the government in Iran. Within a few months, a **new Islamic Republic of Iran was formed** and Khomeini would be named its Supreme Leader. He ruled on the basis of what he believed an Islamic government should be. Whilst the new regime may have looked democratic, in reality it gave the Supreme Leader extensive powers. For example, he could overrule decisions of the government, start wars, and appoint heads of media.

In a similar fashion to 1973, the **Iranian Revolution** caused global oil prices to jump, leading to an oil crisis and inflation across western economies. BP's assets in Iran were nationalised by Khomeini's new government, meaning that the company immediately lost 40% of its global oil production and was forced into a major restructure.

Meanwhile, President Carter agreed to allow the exiled Shah to enter the USA to receive medical treatment for his cancer. This resulted in a backlash: a group of Iranians stormed the US embassy in Tehran and took 53 Americans as hostages. Khomeini fully supported the act and demanded the return of the Shah. After discussions between the governments on the matter had broken down, Carter ordered for a helicopter rescue operation in 1980, though it failed spectacularly resulting in the accidental deaths of eight Americans. Only when Ronald Reagan took office in 1981 were the hostages finally released.

1979   **Deng Xiaoping** of the People's Republic of China became the first Chinese leader ever to tour the USA, marking an end to thirty years of isolation for China. When Deng became paramount leader of China in 1978, he made clear that, whilst his Communist Party would not relinquish any power, China would consider opening up its markets to the West.

The country would embark on an ambitious economic reform programme, creating a series of special economic zones (or SEZs). These zones would be allowed certain privileges, which differed from the rest of communist China. In an attempt to attract foreign investment in these zones, and power the rest of the country's economy, their factories were permitted to export products to the West.

Villages soon transformed into industrial cities. What started off as an experiment in global trade for China ended up being a resounding success economically. The SEZs' factories were able to tap into China's massive cheap labour force that could churn out high quantities of products at low cost. Over the next 30 years, the Chinese government would begin designating more of these special economic zones and China's economy would grow to be one of the largest in the world.

1979   The Afghan communist rulers were facing growing unrest and lots of rebellions, the first of which took place in Herat in March and then spread to places like Jalalabad and Kabul. The Afghan president, Nur Muhammad Taraki, visited his ally, Soviet leader **Leonid Brezhnev**, requesting that he supply troops to Afghanistan to restore order. The USSR were providing financial aid, food and weapons to support the Afghan government but were reluctant to intervene themselves militarily. However, when Taraki was overthrown by, and later killed at the order of, his number two, Hafizullah Amin, Brezhnev ordered an invasion (Amin was too closely aligned to the Americans for his liking).

In December, Soviet troops poured into the Presidential Palace, shot Amin dead and installed a Soviet puppet leader. They then proceeded to **invade Afghanistan**. The **Mujahedeen**, Muslim rebels, would rise up against the Russians. They saw this as a holy war in which fellow Muslims were fighting against communist atheist oppressors. The US government covertly supplied weapons to the Mujahedeen across the Pakistani border so long as the weapons could not be traced back to them. Pakistan also supplied safe havens and routes for the Mujahedeen. The US additionally provided billions of dollars in funding, which allies Saudi Arabia would match also.

At the beginning of 1980, President Carter proclaimed the Carter Doctrine: the Americans would use force if necessary to protect its interests in the Persian Gulf region. Additionally, the US government imposed a grain embargo against the Soviet Union and led a boycott of the 1980 Moscow Olympics.

Among the Mujahedeen was a university-educated young Saudi called **Osama bin Laden** who fought in and helped finance the war against the Soviets. In the late stages of the war, a petty street thug from Jordan called Abu Musab al-Zarqawi also joined. Zarqawi would rise to notoriety in the late 2000s, leading a faction that would eventually come to be known as "ISIS".

1980   By the 1970s, Cuba had fully established itself as a socialist state, aligning its policies with those of the USSR. Castro had accordingly brought in significant reforms to Cuba, including free education and healthcare. In addition, the state controlled and planned all aspects of agriculture, industry and trade. Even the smallest private ventures were prohibited after 1968. Cuba's economy relied heavily on trade with the USSR, particularly as the US had imposed a trade embargo on them. To repay their socialist allies, Cuba would rely almost entirely on sugar production, much to the detriment of other industries which suffered as a result.

Castro lived a reasonably lavish lifestyle in a heavily guarded estate whilst a lot of people in Cuba were still living poorly. People were starting to reject his dictatorship and, by the 1980s, supply problems, the lack of consumer goods and sometimes even food - as well as travel restrictions - encouraged young people to leave Cuba and travel to the USA or Europe. 1980 itself saw a mass exodus of Cubans, particularly to Miami. Castro did not prevent this. Instead, he released people from prisons and asylums and allowed them to go to the US to become "their problem".

On top of this, Castro's government supported the drug trade with Colombia, in which drug manufacturers had been producing cocaine for the rest of the world. Since the 1960s, Cuba had been supporting communist rebels in Colombia. Some of these rebels would co-operate with drug barons in order to finance their rebellions. Machine guns and other weapons were smuggled into Colombia and the drug dealers then transported them to the rebels. Castro also allowed drug dealers to use Cuban territorial waters for their ventures. Planes would drop parcels of drugs in the water to be picked up by boats. Castro himself took a share of this business. All of this caused a huge headache for the US government.

1980   **Josip Broz Tito died**. Following his death, Yugoslavia's economy would take a turn for the worse and ethnic tensions in the area re-emerged as nationalist groups became more vocal about demanding independence for their respective regions.

1980   President **Saddam Hussein's** Iraqi forces invaded Iran, triggering the **Iran-Iraq War**. Saddam, insecure, paranoid and ambitious in personality, felt threatened by the Iranian Revolution, which had brought Ayatollah Khomeini to power in the previous year. Khomeini, in turn, saw Saddam as a brutal Sunni tyrant, oppressing his country's Shia majority, and did not hide his intentions to see him overthrown.

Saddam believed that Iran was in disarray and that his forces could achieve swift victory. However, he was mistaken and the war would drag on for eight years. It was no secret that the US government supported Iraq in the war: they poured in billions of dollars of non-military resource and worked to influence their allies in the region to provide financial aid to Iraq's military. They also sought to try and hinder the sale of weapons to Iran (now anti-American after the revolution). The CIA would even become aware of the use of chemical weapons by the Iraqi military but the US government mostly turned a blind eye to avoid the risk of damaging relations with Iraq.

1980   After a large scale global vaccination campaign, smallpox was the first virus ever to be declared eradicated. For thousands of years, it had plagued humans globally over the course of numerous deadly outbreaks. In the 20th century alone, it claimed the lives of hundreds of millions of people.

1980   In December, lone gunman **Mark David Chapman shot John Lennon** (formerly of *The Beatles*) four times in the back at close range. The shooting took place outside the Dakota building in New York where Lennon had an apartment. Lennon was rushed to hospital where he was pronounced dead on arrival. Earlier that evening, he had autographed a copy of his album *Double Fantasy* for Chapman.

1981   **Ronald Reagan** of the Republican Party was inaugurated as the **40th US President,** having defeated Jimmy Carter in the 1980 presidential election.

1981   The first official report on AIDS came in June, although the term "AIDS" was not given until 1982. It was not until 1983, when the disease was spreading rapidly across the globe, that scientists discovered the culprit behind AIDS. **HIV** - short for "human immunodeficiency virus" - is a virus that leads to immune system deterioration. The human immune system can clear many viruses within the body, but that is not the case with HIV. Acquired immune deficiency syndrome (or **AIDS**) is a condition that the virus may cause. Contracting HIV can - but does not always - lead to the development of AIDS. AIDS, otherwise known as stage 3 HIV, means that the HIV infection is at a late stage.

In the late 1970s, the HIV strain started an epidemic in North America having made its way to the US via Zaire (now the Democratic Republic of Congo) and Haiti. It spread mainly through homosexual men who were, and still are, disproportionately impacted by HIV because it transmits more easily through anal sex than through vaginal sex. The virus also heavily affected haemophiliacs (those with a rare disorder where blood doesn't clot normally so they bleed for longer) and injection drug users. Despite people dying from AIDs, particularly those in the gay community, the US government failed to take the issue seriously. Instead, discrimination and homophobia associated with HIV stigma were allowed to fester.

1981   General Galtieri, President of Argentina, ordered an **invasion of the British-owned Falkland Islands** (or Islas Malvinas) despite economic crises at home. Since the 1830s, Argentina had been claiming the Falklands, although their claim had been peaceful. However, the newly established dictatorship of Argentina concluded that, if they took the islands by force, their popularity would be boosted and they would be viewed as heroes.

The international community opposed the invasion, viewing Argentina as the aggressors. Argentina lost the war to Britain in 1982 and the humiliation of the defeat led to the eventual end of military dictatorship in Argentina in 1983 and a subsequent transition to democracy.

1982   Nelson Mandela was transferred to Pollsmoor Prison in Tokai, Cape Town.

1982   The US government issued the Boland Amendment, which made it illegal for the US to assist a group of rebels called the

Contras who were fighting against the socialist Sandinista government in a civil war in Nicaragua. The basis of this was pressure from the American public which was opposed to government assistance to a group known to be largely funded by the drug trade. The Boland Amendment, however, did not stop the Reagan administration which contravened this law in 1985.

1984   **AIDS had become a global epidemic**. In Africa, an estimated 970,000 people were infected with HIV. The Health and Human Services Secretary in the US announced the development of an AIDS test and forecast that a vaccine would be available by 1986. But no vaccine ever came. By 1985, over 12,000 Americans had died and the virus began to spread quickly through haemophiliacs and injection drug users.

1985   **Hezbollah**, a radical Shia Islamist militant group from Lebanon known to have ties with the Islamic Republic of Iran, started a policy of sponsoring attacks on Western civilians. In a clandestine deal, the US agreed to sell weapons to Iran in exchange for facilitating the release of seven American hostages (despite an arms embargo imposed on Iran at the time and Reagan publicly denouncing negotiating with what they saw as terrorist organisations).

In addition, in contravention of the Boland Amendment, prohibiting support for the Contras in Nicaragua, the CIA used a portion of the proceeds of sale from the Iran weapons deal to pay the Contras. The affair was made public in 1986 and turned into a political scandal for Reagan who denied knowledge of the deals.

Many US officials were indicted and convicted, though they would all be pardoned by future President George H.W Bush in 1992. Saddam Hussein was incensed when he learned about the so-called Iran-Contra Affair. The episode convinced him not to trust the Americans and relations between the US and Iraq would turn sour. Though the US did try and make several attempts to win back his trust, Saddam would look upon them with suspicion.

1985 **Mikhail Gorbachev** became General Secretary of the Soviet Union. In 1989, he went on to become its President. He made the decision to withdraw the Russians from Afghanistan and set a deadline of three years. Nonetheless, he continued to pour in resources towards the Soviet-Afghan War during this period.

1986 In the early hours of 26 April, one of four nuclear reactors (specifically nuclear reactor number 4) exploded at the **Chernobyl** power station in Ukraine. Two key reasons for the nuclear meltdown were managerial negligence and government failures. Reactor number 4 had been operating since 1983, though shortcuts were taken to get it operational. Safety tests, which should have been completed prior to being in operation, had failed on previous occasions and there was pressure to satisfactorily complete the tests in 1986. The disaster occurred during the conducting of one of these safety tests. In addition, cost-cutting measures were used to build the power plant. In taking such shortcuts, there were design flaws in the key components of the reactor making the plant more susceptible to a meltdown.

Those conscripted by the government to contain the incident were required to work tirelessly and swiftly, often in life-threatening conditions, to prevent the spread of nuclear radiation. Following the disaster, there was a significant increase in cancer rates in Ukraine and Belarus, with children being the worst affected. The actual human cost of Chernobyl is difficult to ascertain. Contamination is still a problem and disputes continue about how many will eventually die as a result of the accident. According to estimates, thousands upon thousands of people are believed to have died from it. However, the official Soviet death toll had the number at around the 50 mark. The contaminated region of Ukraine and Belarus, known as the Exclusion Zone, encompasses around 2,500 square kilometres. Around 300,000 people were displaced from their homes and it is still forbidden to enter without permission.

The costs required to rectify the damage caused by the disaster, and ensure future prevention, were enormous. Five years later, Mikhail Gorbachev said that the nuclear meltdown at Chernobyl "was perhaps the true cause of the Soviet Union's collapse".

1987   Zidovudine, or AZT, became the first drug approved to treat AIDS. Whilst being a first positive step, it was not the end of the road. The drug would slow progression of the disease but it did not cure it or prevent death.

1987   In the 1980s, Palestinians, increasingly aggravated by growing Israeli settlers in the West Bank and Gaza Strip, began boycotts of Jewish products and services and refused to pay Israeli taxes. However, demonstrations soon turned violent and Israeli authorities responded with heavy force. As the situation became more violent, the militant Palestinian organisation, **Hamas**, formed and carried out its first attack in 1989.

1987   During this year, the **world population** surpassed **five billion**.

1988   Mandela was moved to Victor Verster Prison in Paarl (west of Cape Town).

1988   A UN-brokered ceasefire was reluctantly agreed by Iran **ending the Iran-Iraq War**. The result of the war was inconclusive with neither side achieving a clear victory. It had, however, claimed between half a million and a million lives on both sides.

1988   South Korean electronics company **Samsung** launched the SH-100 mobile phone. In previous years, companies Nokia, Siemens and Motorola had each already launched their first mobile phone.

1989   **George Herbert Walker Bush** of the Republican Party became the **41st US President**, having defeated Michael Dukakis in the presidential election the previous year.

1989   **The Soviet-Afghan War ended**. An estimated 25,000 Soviet troops died during the war. Ten years of Soviet occupation had left Kabul largely intact. But when the Mujahedeen seized the capital, inter-fighting among various factions tore the city apart. This commenced a civil war lasting several years and created a breeding ground for extremism.

Out of the chaos, the radical Islamic political group, the **Taliban**, emerged. Life under the Taliban regime would be oppressive and dangerous as numerous human rights were violated, particularly against females. Opponents to their doctrine often faced harsh punishment, including imprisonment and execution. After the Soviets withdrew, Osama bin Laden returned to Saudi Arabia. Over the next couple of years, he would grow the recently-established international organisation, known as **Al-Qaeda**, into a large-scale terrorist network.

1989   In Spring, student demonstrations erupted in Beijing's Tiananmen Square. Despite China adopting certain capitalist characteristics in the early 1980s, a large portion of the population were still not seeing the benefits. The protestors demanded more political rights such as freedom of speech and press. On 4 June, in what became known as the **Tiananmen Square Massacre**, Chinese government soldiers began firing on the protestors.

Hundreds or even thousands may have been killed in the massacre, though the Chinese government would never release an official death toll. The Tiananmen Square Massacre would not change things politically for China, which continued its one-party system of government, suppression of political rights, censorship and denial of human rights. Despite this, China's economy would continue to grow as a result of its more liberal trade policies.

1989   British computer engineer, Tim Berners-Lee (now **Sir Tim Berners-Lee**), published a proposal for an information management system. In the same year, Berners-Lee implemented the first successful communication of "hypertext" (a term coined by a man named Ted Nelson in 1965 to describe text which contains links to other texts) via the Internet. In doing so, Berners-Lee had **invented the World Wide Web**, the first web browser.

The Internet is a communication network with the ability to connect servers around the world. The World Wide Web, by comparison, is the platform that allows for easy access of information on, and made possible by, the Internet. Prior to Berners-Lee's discovery, the various components of the Internet were already in place but the World Wide Web, using the Internet, now allowed for the sharing of hypertext between people around the world on different computers. Information could now be shared in a way that was not previously possible.

1989   Following a series of liberal reforms introduced by Gorbachev to improve his country's struggling economy, the socialist ideologies which had originally underpinned the power of the Soviet Union were weakening. **The Cold War was coming to an end.**

On 9 November, the East Berlin Communist Party announced that its citizens were free to travel to the West. The two sides of the city then united to **knock down the Berlin Wall**. Millions of East and West Berliners celebrated the fall. As a result of decreased Soviet military presence in Warsaw Pact nations, communism in other countries, like Poland, Czechoslovakia and Romania, began to collapse. The Baltic states of Estonia, Lithuania and Latvia soon broke away from the USSR and declared independence.

1990   On 11 February, on the order of President F.W. de Klerk, keen to overhaul the political system in South Africa, **Nelson Mandela was released** from Victor Verster Prison after a total of 27 years of captivity.

1990   West and East Germany officially reunited to form a single **united Germany**.

1990   After the conclusion of the Iran-Iraq War, the oil minister of Iraq suggested increasing oil prices as a means of paying off its war debts. Around the same time, Kuwait increased its oil production. With abundant oil supplies on the market, Iraq was prevented from increasing its oil prices and the country's economy continued to struggle.

Saddam Hussein accused Kuwait's refusal to reduce its oil production as being an act of aggression. This was followed by the allegation that Kuwait was drilling in Iraq's Rumaila oil field. Saddam's government insisted that Kuwait had developed advanced drilling techniques, capable of slant-drilling. According to Iraqi officials, Kuwait's use of slant-drilling allowed it to steal over two billion dollars' worth of oil.

In 1989, Iraq demanded repayment for the lost oil. By mid-1990, Kuwait agreed to a decrease in oil production. However, tensions still remained high and Saddam ordered the invasion of Kuwait, which was captured within 12 hours of a surprise attack. The UN opposed the invasion and, when Saddam refused to withdraw his troops, sanctioned withdrawal by force. The US government led a coalition of 34 nations and sent troops to Saudi Arabia out of fear that Iraq might try and take Saudi oilfields.

Operation Desert Storm then began, commencing a huge air bombardment of Iraqi airfields. The coalition successfully pushed Saddam's forces out of Kuwait, winning the war. However, President Bush decided against taking Baghdad or toppling Saddam, who remained in power after the war (perhaps due to the potential political backlash Bush might face if accused of mission creep and meddling in Iraqi affairs for too long).

An American ambassador had met with Saddam Hussein only a week before Iraq invaded Kuwait. Transcripts of the meeting could suggest, though not definitively prove, that Saddam was misleadingly given a green light to invade Kuwait or at least that the US had no interest in Iraq's border disputes with Kuwait.

In the aftermath of the so-called **Gulf War,** the UN adopted resolutions that imposed heavy trade sanctions on Iraq. This led to economic hardship for the country throughout the nineties which mainly affected the poor and caused many Iraqis (including a significant number of children) to starve to death.

1991   Pursuant to the Strategic Arms Reduction Treaties, the US and USSR agreed to reduce the number of nuclear weapons in their possession.

1991   The End of the Cold War

The Soviet Union dissolved when Gorbachev resigned as President. He was eventually replaced by the popular **Boris Yeltsin,** the **new President of the independent Russian Federation**.

The dissolution of the Soviet Union led to Russia's neighbouring countries such as Ukraine, Belarus and Georgia breaking away to become independent states (Latvia, Lithuania and Estonia had already done so within the last year). The dissolution had a knock-on effect globally, too. It was bad news for Cuba, which was heavily reliant on trade with the USSR. Electricity, coal, gas and oil, together with the most basic necessities, had to be rationed and infrastructure collapsed. In 1993, Fidel and Raúl Castro ordered for the army to take control of Cuba's economy, allowing them to remain in power.

After the collapse of communism, ethnic tensions resurfaced in the Balkans. Slovenia and Croatia had declared independence from Yugoslavia. The most dominant state within Yugoslavia was Serbia, led by Slobodan Milošević, who attempted to keep ethnically Serbian areas in other republics under Yugoslav rule. He demanded that Yugoslavia be controlled centrally with Serbia at the forefront. A Serb-dominated Yugoslav army entered Slovenia and Croatia. Despite quickly withdrawing from Slovenia (Serbia was less interested in Slovenia due to the Serb population in it only being a small minority), a major conflict erupted in Croatia where Serbian rebels, backed by the Yugoslav army, fought against Croatians who were holding out for independence.

1992   The people of Bosnia, which had a population consisting of Serbs, Muslims and Croats, began an independence movement of their own. Again, this was strongly opposed by Bosnian Serbs, who had the support of other Serbs within Yugoslavia including Slobodan Milošević's Serbia. In April, war broke out between the Muslims and Croats on one side and the Bosnian Serbs on the other. The Bosnian Serbs, led by Radovan Karadžić, bombarded Sarajevo, Bosnia's capital, and went on to occupy large amounts of the country. Terrible atrocities (including murder and rape) on an appalling scale were carried out against Muslim people by Serb forces.

1992   The **Maastricht Treaty** was signed, establishing the European Union (previously the ECC). At this time, it had 12 Member States.

1992   An all-white jury acquitted three out of four police officers in Los Angeles charged with beating up a black motorist, Rodney King. The jury failed to reach a verdict on the fourth officer. The decision was made despite the incident being recorded on video. The outrage of the decision led to riots in Los Angeles, during which 52 people were killed, over 2,000 were injured and over a billion dollars in property damage was caused.

1993   **William Jefferson Clinton** (or **Bill Clinton**) of the Democratic
        Party was inaugurated as the **42nd US President**, having
        defeated George H.W. Bush in the presidential election held
        in the previous year. At 46, he became the third youngest US
        President in history. He would go on also to win the next
        presidential election in 1996, defeating Bob Dole, the
        Republican nominee at the time.

1993   Hamas began suicide bombings. In the meantime, peace talks
        took place between Israel, led by Prime Minister Yitzhak Rabin,
        and the Palestine Liberation Organization, led by Yasser
        Arafat, which culminated in the **Oslo Accords** being signed.

        The Oslo Accords were a set of agreements where Israel
        recognised the legitimacy of the PLO and the PLO formally
        recognised the state of Israel. The Israeli government also
        agreed for Palestinians to have some form of limited self-
        governance in Gaza and the West Bank. Unfortunately, the
        peace talks, whilst a potential step in the right direction, failed
        to address key issues and would leave many Palestinians to
        feel disappointment with the outcome. In addition, Israeli
        settlements on occupied Palestinian territory continued,
        undermining the spirit of the Oslo Accords. Extremist groups on
        both sides also sought to undermine the peace and, in 1995,
        an Israeli extremist who opposed the Oslo Accords
        assassinated Rabin.

1993   There was a terrorist bombing attempt on the World Trade
        Center. Although the bombing failed to do more damage than
        intended, six people were killed and thousands were injured.

1994   The first multiracial elections in the history of South Africa took
        place. **Nelson Mandela won the election**, becoming **South
        Africa's first democratically elected President**.

1994   A horrific **genocide** took place in **Rwanda** in Africa. Over a
        hundred-day period, between 500,000 and 1,000,000

people were massacred. Those who committed the genocide, belonging to the Hutu majority, targeted an ethnic minority group known as the Tutsi people.

As part of the late 19th century "Scramble for Africa", Germany acquired Rwanda and neighbouring Burundi in the Berlin Conference back in 1884. By the time the Belgians had claimed the colonies during the First World War, racial divide had already began: the colonists promoted the elite Tutsis as racially superior to the Hutus. The Belgians exacerbated the divide by introducing identity cards, essentially implementing a caste system with the Tutsis at the top of the group. Hutu resentment eventually boiled over when violent riots broke out in 1959. Hundreds of thousands of Tutsis were forced to flee the country. Rwanda became independent from Belgium in 1962. Tutsis outside Rwanda would build up militia groups and carry out attacks on the Hutu government.

Fast forwarding to 1994, when the Hutu-born President of Rwanda was assassinated (his plane was shot down over the country's capital, Kigali) the Hutus retaliated and initiated a full scale systematic ethnic cleansing of the Tutsi minority (as well as Hutu moderates) committing dreadful atrocities. Despite warnings of the genocide, the UN did not intervene. Eventually, the Rwandan Patriotic Front, consisting of Tutsi rebels, with the help of the Ugandan army, were able to seize territory in Rwanda and capture Kigali.

1994   The company **Amazon** was founded by entrepreneur Jeff Bezos in his garage in Seattle, Washington. Originally, the company began as a business selling books online.

1995   The US government approved the first drug that, when combined with the therapies existing at the time, proved effective enough to halt and reverse the progression of AIDS. But the epidemic would still continue amongst poor and ethnic minority communities, many of which could not afford the treatment.

1995   Bosnian Serbs took over the UN-protected "safe area" of Srebrenica in eastern Bosnia and massacred more than 8,000 Muslims, mostly men and boys. Other similar safe areas were attacked by Bosnian Serb forces during the war. NATO ordered airstrikes on Bosnian Serb strongholds.

The Croatian army launched an offensive against Serb-occupied areas in Croatia and successfully won the country's independence.

Later that year, the **Dayton Accords** were signed, putting an **end to the Bosnian War**. Bosnia was divided into two entities along ethnic lines: Republika Srpska and a Muslim-Croat Federation. Bosnia and Herzegovina is today divided in the same way (in accordance with the Dayton Agreements) into the two entities of Republika Srpska and the Federation of Bosnia and Herzegovina.

1996   The Taliban in Afghanistan provided a safe haven for Osama bin Laden's Al-Qaeda, which had declared war against the USA and its allies. The terrorist group was particularly opposed to American support for Israel, military intervention in the Gulf War and US involvement in the affairs of Saudi Arabia.

1997   The British government officially and peaceably **returned Hong Kong to China**. As part of the handover, it was agreed that Hong Kong's capitalist system would be preserved.

1998   Both India and Pakistan announced the conducting of nuclear tests.

1998   Two almost simultaneous explosions occurred outside the US embassies in Nairobi, Kenya and Dar es Salaam, Tanzania respectively, killing 224 people and wounding several thousands more. Bin Laden was blamed for orchestrating the attacks and, within weeks, President Clinton ordered missile attacks on four suspected Al-Qaeda bases in Afghanistan.

| 1998 | The **Petronas Towers** in Kuala Lumpur, Malaysia overtook the Sears Tower and became the tallest building in the world at 452 metres (or 1,483 feet). |

| 1998 | Stanford University students Larry Page and Sergey Brin founded the company **Google**, which provided to its users an online search engine. |

| 1998-1999 | When Kosovo, a region with 95% Albanian Muslims, tried for independence, Milošević's Serbia sent in armed forces and began a campaign of ethnic cleansing. Albanians were targeted by Orthodox Christian Serb troops. With the 1995 Bosnian genocide still fresh on everyone's minds, NATO intervened, eventually launching a series of air strikes against the Milošević regime. |

Despite the intervention, around 15,000 Albanians were murdered in the genocide. In October 2000, Milošević was overthrown in a popular revolution. He was then arrested and charged with crimes against humanity and genocide. He eventually died in 2006 in prison in the Hague before his trial ended.

After a decade of heated discussions that began at the end of the war, Kosovo would eventually declare its independence in 2008. Since then, over half the world, including Turkey, Albania and the US, have recognised Kosovo as an independent state (though other nations still do not).

| 1998 | **President Clinton was impeached by the House of Representatives**. In 1994, a former Arkansas State employee called Paula Jones sued Clinton for sexual harassment. In 1995, Clinton began a two-year relationship with then-intern Monica Lewinsky. In 1997, Paula Jones' lawyers learned about the affair with Lewinsky and subpoenaed her (that is, presented her with a legal summons to give evidence). Jones' lawyers wanted to strengthen their client's case by arguing Clinton had |

a pattern of behavior in sexually harassing employees. Lewinsky lied under oath, denying the affair. Allegedly, Clinton had persuaded her to lie. Clinton himself then also denied the affair in his testimony in the Paula Jones case.

When it transpired both had lied, Clinton admitted the truth and gave a televised statement admitting the affair. One of Clinton's political opponents at the time, Kenneth Starr, who had already been trying to build a case against him, outlined a case for impeachment on grounds of perjury and obstruction of justice among other things. However, insufficient votes were obtained in the Senate to convict Clinton. He was acquitted and he therefore remained in office for the remainder of his term.

1999   **War broke out between India and Pakistan** when Pakistan's military infiltrated the Indian-controlled region around Kargil. Eventually, though, the Pakistani government withdrew its forces from all captured positions along the Line of Control and India regained control of Kargil.

1999   Yeltsin announced his resignation as President of Russia and named prime minister **Vladimir Putin as acting President**. In early 2000, he won the presidential election, properly securing his position as president, and was re-elected for another term in 2004. He was barred by the constitution from serving a third consecutive term though still served as prime minister in 2008 before being re-elected as president once again in 2012 (and again in 2018).

1999   During this year, the **world population** surpassed **six billion**.

1995-   In the late 1990s, there was a stock market bubble (known as
2000   the "**Dot-Com Bubble**"), which revolved around speculative investments in internet companies. Investors were so excited about the progress of the Internet that they invested in any technology company, not necessarily checking whether that company was profitable.

Not all companies focussed on sound business models. Many incurred net operating losses as they spent heavily on advertising and promotions to build their market share as quickly as possible, adopting a "get large or get lost" mentality. Some companies offered their services or products for free or at a discount with the expectation that they could build sufficient brand awareness to charge profitable rates in future. Their perceived invincibility led them to engage in lavish spending on elaborate business facilities and luxury vacations for employees. But this did not seem to matter to investors who were sucked into the excitement of the Internet.

Competition and speculation pushed investors to pay significantly more for dot-com stocks than their fundamental value, which sent IPOs soaring. The difference between the perceived value and actual value of companies created a market bubble. That bubble eventually burst and the market experienced a downturn. Many companies (famously pets.com) lost millions of dollars. Other businesses, now household names (like Amazon and eBay), incurred heavy losses but survived and managed to recover from the crash.

2000   In the **presidential election of 2000**, then-Vice President Al Gore of the Democratic Party ran against Texas Governor George W. Bush - son of former President George H.W. Bush - of the Republican Party. It was one of the closest presidential races in history.

In the US, the winner of the presidential election is determined using a system called the Electoral College. Each state (plus Washington DC) is designated a set amount of electoral votes, roughly based on the state's population. In 2000, the very populous California had 54 electoral votes (now it has 55) whereas, by contrast, Alaska, much less populated, had (and still has) 3. With the exception of Maine and Nebraska, the candidate who gains the most votes in each state is awarded all of the electoral votes for that state. For example, Gore won the popular vote in California and therefore received all 54 electoral votes in relation to California. At the time, there were (and today still are) 538 electoral votes and the winning candidate would need 270 electoral votes in order to win the election.

The 2000 presidential election was incredibly close because everything hinged on Florida's 25 electoral votes and which way they would swing. The winner of Florida would win the presidential election. The final result in Florida was so tight that it triggered an automatic recount by machine. After that had completed, Bush appeared to have gained more votes by the slimmest of margins.

Gore then demanded a recount by hand in four counties, as permitted under Florida State law. The Bush campaign sued the Gore campaign in the Supreme Court, which ultimately decided in Bush's favour and that the recount be stopped. The majority in the Supreme Court held that the different standards of counting ballots across Florida violated the equal protection clause of the 14th Amendment in the constitution. As a result of the recount being ceased, **Bush** won Florida's electoral votes and **won the election overall**.

The Supreme Court decision in *Bush v Gore* has been viewed controversially because the 5-4 vote to stop the recount was arguably along partisan lines, meaning the justices appointed by Republican presidents (with the exception of one) ruled in favour of Bush, and the justices appointed by Democratic presidents argued in favour of Gore. The recount also revealed deficiencies in voting procedures. For example, voting cards that required a hole punch, but were not punched properly, would not be registered correctly on machines and so those votes were discounted altogether.

Bush would go on to win another presidential election in 2004, after defeating Democratic nominee John Kerry, giving him a second term as President.

2000   After peace talks broke down between Israel and the PLO, violence once again broke out between Israelis and Palestinians, this time much bloodier than the demonstrations that occurred in the late 1980s. Known as the **Second Intifada** (the first had occurred in the 80s), thousands of Israelis and Palestinians died as a consequence.

2001   Following his controversial win in 2000, **George Walker Bush** was inaugurated as the **43rd US President** in January.

2001   On the morning of **11 September**, four passenger planes were hijacked mid-air by 19 terrorists linked to Al-Qaeda, with the intention of crashing them into chosen targets in America. Fifteen of the hijackers were citizens of Saudi Arabia, two were from the United Arab Emirates, one was from Lebanon and the other was Egyptian. Two planes hit the twin towers of the World Trade Center, one hit the Pentagon outside Washington DC and a fourth - intended for the White House - crashed instead in Pennsylvania after the passengers onboard struggled with the hijackers in an attempt to overpower them. The terrorist attacks claimed 2,977 lives. Osama Bin Laden was immediately declared the number one suspect behind the attacks.

Soon afterwards, President Bush declared a "**War on Terror**". He then issued an ultimatum to the Taliban, demanding the handing over of Osama bin Laden and all other leaders of Al-Qaeda. The Taliban rejected the ultimatum. Soon afterwards, Bush and British Prime Minister Tony Blair ordered air strikes on targeted bases in Afghanistan. An American-led coalition then began a ground invasion of Afghanistan to drive out the Taliban and fight Al-Qaeda operatives. Bin Laden evaded capture, went into hiding and eventually ended up in Pakistan.

2002   The Bush administration transformed the naval base at **Guantanamo Bay** into a prison for alleged enemies captured during America's War on Terror, particularly from Afghanistan (and later Iraq). It would go on to hold just under 800 men from across 35 different countries.

The lease of Guantanamo Bay from Cuba to the US, granted in the early 20th century, is said to have created legal uncertainty regarding which country has lawful authority over the base. Whilst Cuba retains ultimate sovereignty over Guantanamo Bay, the US has complete jurisdiction. Therefore, the land is not technically US territory but nevertheless the US has sufficient control over it. Some writers have described it as a "legal black hole" where the US government is able to operate outside the confines of domestic and international laws and detain prisoners without the proper due process they would be given if they were on actual American soil.

Despite government reassurances that the prison system at Guantanamo Bay was humane and legitimately run, reports and accounts of abuse and torture of prisoners surfaced. When President Obama came into office, he made a commitment to close the detention centre but, due to political and legal complexities, this would not happen during his administration. Around 40 people continue to be detained there, the vast majority of which were never charged with a crime. More recently, President Trump since ordered the military prison at Guantanamo Bay to remain open, reversing the Obama administration's intention to close it.

2003   In March, a US-led coalition, which included British armed forces, launched a **War on Iraq**. The alleged justification for the war, according to both the British and American governments, was that Saddam Hussein possessed, or was building, weapons of mass destruction. The war went ahead without authorisation from the UN Security Council.

Air strikes were followed by a ground invasion, shortly after which Saddam went into hiding. Later that year, he was captured by US troops, arrested and put on trial for crimes committed during his regime. He was subsequently executed in 2006.

Despite the initial justification, according to a report issued by the CIA, weapons of mass destruction were never found nor was there any evidence of concrete plans to develop such weapons. This led critics of the American and British governments to question whether the public had been misled as to the real motives for the war. In 2004, the UN Secretary-General at the time, Kofi Annan, described the war as illegal and not in conformity with the UN charter.

2003   The Human Genome Project, a global scientific research project started in 1990, was completed. The project announced it had identified the whole of our genetic code (that is, the make up of human DNA and of identifying and mapping all of our genes: the blueprint for the human body).

2004   Harvard University student Mark Zuckerberg launched the social networking site, **Facebook**.

2004   **Taipei 101** in Taipei, Taiwan became the tallest building in the world at 509 metres (1,670 feet).

2005   Israel withdrew its troops and around 7,000 settlers from the Gaza Strip. Hamas grew in power and, in 2006, won elections in the legislature.

2006   Twttr - later renamed **"Twitter"** - was launched by a podcasting company called Odeo. It was originally set up to allow users to share short updates via SMS among friendship groups.

2007   Apple CEO Steve Jobs revealed the new smartphone: the **iPhone**. It gave users the ability to browse the web on their mobile phone as they would do on a personal computer.

2007-   The causes of the Recession
2008

Traditionally in the US, it would have been difficult for someone to obtain a mortgage if they did not have a steady income or had a poor credit rating. Lenders did not want to take the risk that a person might default on their loan. But this would change at the beginning of the millennium when global investors, seeking a low-risk, high-return investment, turned their attention to the US residential property market.

Investors saw that they could receive a better return from the interest rates homeowners paid on mortgages than they could from investing in other markets. The drawback for global investors, however, was that they did not want the hassle of dealing with each proprietor and his or her mortgage individually. To overcome this, large financial institutions designed for the market attractive financial products known as **mortgage-backed securities** (MBSs), which involved buying up thousands of individual mortgages, pooling them together and selling shares of that pool to the investors.

The housing market was booming in the 2000s. Houses prices were rising and demand for homes was high. Lenders thought, at worst, if a borrower defaulted on their mortgage, they could just sell the house at a profit to a new buyer. Investors, meanwhile, enthusiastically bought these MBSs, which saw a suitably high rate of return. Credit rating agencies in the US, such as Standard & Poor's and Moody's, were often giving MBSs triple A ratings. In other words, they gave investors the best ratings to show that they were financially sound and safe investments. This made sense as mortgages traditionally were only reserved for those borrowers who were creditworthy.

However, investors began to demand more and more of these MBSs. Therefore, mortgage lenders, desperate to capitalise on the housing boom and meet the demand from investors, created more. But creating more MBSs required more mortgages. So lenders lowered their restrictions on the type of borrower able to borrow. They handed out loans to buyers with lower credit ratings (that is, people who were less likely to pay back the loans). These risky loans were called **subprime mortgages**. Some lenders got into the practice of issuing loans without even verifying the borrowers' income. They also adopted predatory lending practices and lured borrowers into agreeing repayment terms and interest rates that were affordable in the short term but in the longer term escalated beyond what they could afford.

The subprime mortgage was new. Therefore, credit rating agencies could not rely on historical information to determine whether they were safe to invest in. Regardless, they issued high credit ratings and so investors continued to rely on these ratings and throw their money into the mortgage market. Meanwhile, similarly risky instruments (for example, **collateralized debt obligations** (or CDOs)) were being sold, again with similar credit ratings attached to them. All seemed well, though, as the prices of homes were climbing. The combination of relaxed credit requirements and low interest rates caused house prices to increase further, which made MBSs and CDOs seem even more attractive. There seemed no reason to question them. If the borrowers defaulted, investors thought, the banks would still have very valuable houses returned to them.

All this created a **housing bubble**: the sharp increases in home prices were based on over exuberance. Low interest rates and predatory lending practices encouraged more people to buy homes. This increased demand and raised house prices. Confident in the housing market, buyers took more risks to enter it.

Then, the bubble burst. Eventually, borrowers could not pay for their overly expensive homes or keep up with their escalating mortgage repayments. They started defaulting on their loans, leading to foreclosures (where the banks stepped in and took ownership of properties to recover their debt) and causing more homes to go back on the market. This time, though, they were not being bought, which meant demand for property went down whilst the supply went up. Consequently, house prices started falling. As house prices fell, the large financial institutions ceased buying subprime mortgages and lenders which had granted subprime mortgages were no longer able to sell them on, getting stuck with bad debt. By 2007, some very large lenders had declared bankruptcy. The big investors, which had heavily bet on MBSs and CDOs, started losing money on their investments.

In addition, there was another financial product that exacerbated all of these problems: the **credit default swap**, which was essentially sold as insurance against the default of CDOs and MBSs. The global insurance powerhouse AIG, for example, sold billions of dollars of these insurance policies without money to back them up if something went wrong, considering the risk of default to be low. A considerable number of pension funds, hedge funds and other institutions invested in AIG and looked set to suffer from AIG's oversight.

Panic set in as financial markets froze and the stock market crashed. Major banks like Lehman Brothers, which was heavily invested in the subprime mortgage market, declared bankruptcy whilst others (like Bear Stearns) were forced into mergers or buyouts. The resulting economic downturn was felt around the world as financial institutions globally had been intertwined in a complex web consisting of MBSs, CDOs, credit default swaps and the like. The global economy found itself in a disastrous recession. **To avoid the failure of banks around the world, governments were required to step in and bail the banks out using taxpayers' money**.

2008   Raúl Castro became President of Cuba and would continue his brother's regime.

2008   **Blockchain** was born out of the work of the mysterious Satoshi Nakamoto on the crypto-currency Bitcoin.

2008   In December, Israel launched a major offensive in Gaza. More than a thousand Palestinians were killed in the violence (compared to a dozen or so Israelis) which lasted 22 days.

2009   **Barack Hussein Obama** of the Democratic Party became the **44ᵗʰ US President, and made history in becoming first ever black US President**, after defeating Republican John McCain in the presidential election the year before. Obama would go on to serve a second term after winning another presidential election, defeating Mitt Romney, in 2012.

2009   The **Burj Khalifa** in Dubai became the tallest building, and tallest structure, in the world at 828 metres (or 2,716 feet).

2010   In December, a street vendor in Tunisia named Mohammed Bouazizi had his products arbitrarily confiscated by the police for failing to obtain a permit. After his complaints of police harassment failed to be heard, in an extreme display of protest, he stood outside a government office building and set himself on fire, eventually killing himself. This incident is considered to be the catalyst for the "**Arab Spring**": a series of uprisings in the Middle East and North Africa. Tunisia had been under the allegedly corrupt and authoritarian rule of President Zine El Abidine Ben Ali for more than two decades.

2011   Protests erupted in Tunisia and spread rapidly through the use of social media, leading to President Ben Ali's abdication. Later that year, parliamentary elections were held in Tunisia.

Protests had also broken out in Algeria, Jordan and Oman. The movement then quickly reached Egypt and Yemen among other countries. In Egypt, President Hosni Mubarak was forced to step down. Yemen's government was also overthrown. In Libya, Colonel Muammar Gaddafi was captured, tortured and executed. However, when Gaddafi was gone, Libya fell into lawlessness and infighting continued between local factions.

In Syria, peaceful Arab Spring demonstrations began to take place. The demonstrators protested high unemployment, lack of political freedom and corruption under President Bashar al-Assad. The demonstrations turned violent when Assad's forces fired shots at the protestors. As a result, rebel groups formed and, together with groups of soldiers who had defected from the Syrian army, began fighting back against government forces, causing a bloody **civil war to break out in Syria**.

2011   In May, a top-secret operation was carried out by US Navy SEALs, which located a private compound in Abbottabad, Pakistan where **Osama bin Laden** was hiding. He **was shot and killed**.

The US began to complete the withdrawal of its soldiers from Iraq, thus concluding its war there. As well as causing an estimated half a million deaths overall, and leaving the country's infrastructure and economy in ruin, the aftermath of the Iraq War created an instability in the region that cultivated the conditions for an insurgency and violent extremism to follow. In particular, one of the major consequences of the Iraq War was the rise of the extremist militant group **Islamic State** (otherwise known as "IS", "ISIL", "ISIS" or "Daesh").

In 2003, in a speech addressed to the UN justifying military intervention in Iraq, US Secretary of State Colin Powell spoke on numerous occasions about Jordanian radical **Abu Musab al-Zarqawi** being the crucial link between Al-Qaeda and Saddam Hussein's regime in Iraq. In reality, Zarqawi, though he fought alongside the Taliban and Al-Qaeda in 2001, had at this point been operating a separate terrorist network in and around the Middle East (including Syria, Iran and Afghanistan). He had no link to Saddam and little connection with Al-Qaeda. In fact, Zarqawi and bin Laden were known to have disagreed on the fundamental principles of their respective ideologies (particularly that Zarqawi advocated the execution of all Shia Muslims in Iraq).

However, by being named in public by the US government, Powell's speech arguably gave Zarqawi the platform to rise to notoriety and become the leading figure in the insurgency in Iraq (to where Zarqawi was believed to have moved at some point in 2003). After the American-led invasion of Iraq in 2003, Zarqawi's group, having built up a following of Sunni extremists, carried out a series of bombings, particularly targeting Shia mosques and neighbourhoods, leading to hundreds of deaths.

It was not until 2004 when Zarqawi pledged allegiance to Al-Qaeda. In 2006, a US bombing raid killed Zarqawi. In 2010, a man called Abu Bakr al-Baghdadi emerged as the new leader of the group - later to be called the Islamic State of Iraq (or ISI). The aim of Islamic State was to establish a separate state, or 'Caliphate', that, according to their rhetoric, adhered to the strict code of Islam. In the upcoming years, the group would become notorious for its ruthless violence, terror and coercion in spreading its message and crushing those opposed to it, whether Muslim or non-Muslim.

2011   At the end of this year, the **world population** was over **seven billion**.

2012   In Florida, 17-year-old black American Trayvon Martin died after being shot by neighbourhood watch captain George Zimmerman during a physical altercation. Martin was unarmed and walking back from a convenience store. In his trial in 2013, the jury found that Zimmerman was not guilty of second degree murder and was acquitted of manslaughter. As a consequence, campaigners Alicia Garza, Patrisse Cullors, and Opal Tometi founded the **Black Lives Matter** movement after a series of impassioned social media posts adopting the hashtag **#blacklivesmatter**.

The movement gained a lot of traction, particularly in 2014 after African American Eric Garner was choked to death by a New York police officer and black teenager Michael Brown was shot dead by a white police officer in Ferguson, Missouri.

Like Martin before, Brown was also unarmed. Despite this, a grand jury declined to charge the officer.

What has arguably underpinned the success of BLM as a recognised movement has been the power of technology and social media and the ability for messages, together with videos and photographs of the injustices, to be spread rapidly across the world. The video of Garner being put in the chokehold, for example, went viral very quickly allowing people around the world to see and react to the incident first hand.

2012   Fighting in Syria reached the capital Damascus and also Aleppo, Syria's largest city. By this time, extremist networks from around the Middle East, including Al-Qaeda, had poured into Syria to join the war. Iran, in support of Assad's Shia regime, was believed to have provided troops to fight the war against the rebels. To counter Iran, Saudi Arabia provided money and weapons to the rebels. Assad's government was meanwhile accused of using chemical weapons against civilians - including children - sparking outrage within the international community against the Assad regime.

2014   After Pope Francis' attempts to mediate relations between Cuba and the US, Raúl Castro and President Obama agreed to warmer relations between their respective governments. In 2016, Obama became the first US President to visit Cuba since Calvin Coolidge in 1928.

2014   Exploiting the chaos of the Syrian War, the "Islamic State of Iraq and Syria" (ISIS, formerly ISI) took centre stage and carved out a mini-state of its own, which it called its 'Caliphate'. ISIS soldiers captured the Syrian city of Raqqa and then spread to Iraq, occupying Mosul and other cities in Iraq's eastern provinces. The US government began air strikes targeting ISIS bases. A coalition of US allies also followed up with strikes. Over the next few years, numerous terrorist attacks, which ISIS would claim responsibility for, would be carried out in various places around the world.

2014   A series of incidents triggered another Israeli military offensive on Gaza. At least 2,000 Palestinians (which included around 1,500 civilians) were killed. 67 soldiers and 6 civilians were killed on the Israeli side.

2015   At the United Nations Climate Change Conference in Paris, 196 countries adopted the Paris Agreement, which subsequently came into force in 2016. The principal aim of the agreement was to limit the rise in global temperature to well below 2°C (preferably to 1.5°C) above pre-industrial levels.

Human-made climate change is the biggest issue facing the planet. Such has been the impact of human activity that we, as opposed to natural causes, are now evidently the primary drivers of climate change. It also means we have the power to prevent it, or at least curb its effects.

What is climate change, what has caused it and why is it such a serious problem for us? The Earth's climate is naturally warmed by greenhouse gases. Greenhouse gases are vital for the Earth because they help trap heat from the sun (thereby creating a 'greenhouse' effect) and keep the planet at the warm habitable levels which allow living things to survive. One of main greenhouse gases is carbon dioxide. Carbon dioxide is produced naturally through respiration by animals after inhaling oxygen. It is also released by plants (though plants absorb more of it than they release making them nature's ideal moderators of CO_2 levels).

Since way before human beings arrived on the scene, the average temperature of the Earth had more or less remained constant alongside the concentration of carbon dioxide in its atmosphere. This trend continued when humans arrived and began to civilise. But the Industrial Revolution changed all that. Since then, in order to keep up with the demands of the modern economy - to power our homes, offices, factories, aeroplanes and cars - and a swiftly increasing global population, humans have been burning more and more fossil fuels (namely oil, coal and gas) which have released unprecedented amounts of carbon dioxide into the atmosphere. Prior to the Industrial Revolution, CO^2 levels in the atmosphere were at around 278 parts per million (PPM). In 1988, that number passed 350 PPM. In the middle of 2020, it hit 417 PPM (to put this into perspective, the last time CO^2 levels exceeded 400 PPM was several million years ago).

As humans have continued to allow for excess greenhouse gases to be released into the air, therefore trapping excess energy from the sun, the temperature of the Earth has increased considerably in such a short period: it is predicted to have risen so far by 1°C since pre-industrial times. This may not seem like much but it is enough to have a profound impact on the planet's climate and threaten life on it. Increasing global temperatures present more extreme heatwaves, a further rise in sea levels, flooding, more severe storms, long droughts and devastating forest fires. These events are already happening. There will come a moment, though, where the changes to the planet caused by rising temperatures reach a tipping point (some scientists say that a 1.5°C rise will trigger that tipping point) and become irreversible, sending the planet past the point of no return towards an unpredictable and precarious path.

Agriculture, food production and deforestation (particularly the cutting of trees in the Amazon rainforest at a rapid rate for livestock and soya products) are also major drivers of climate change. Now, over half the world's habitable land has made way for farmland. People continue to demand products from livestock for consumption. Farming animals on such a huge scale has meant the release into the atmosphere of an abundant level of methane (another major greenhouse gas and far more powerful than carbon dioxide at warming the Earth).

As the forests are reduced, their ability to recycle water and produce the rain for the dry season diminishes. This has the knock-on effect of killing more trees and further disrupting carbon moderation levels in the atmosphere. With these natural habitats being destroyed, biodiversity has already suffered and we are heading towards a mass extinction of a range of wildlife. This has an impact on humans who are so reliant on a balanced ecosystem to feed our growing population. And that population is growing quickly. Global industrialisation, particularly ramped up in the 20th century, has caused a population explosion. The number of people in the world has trebled in the past 70 years. More people means more mouths to feed and therefore an increasing demand for food, water and shelter.

Then there are the melting ice sheets (namely, Greenland and Antarctica). Ice sheets serve the crucial purpose of reflecting back the sun's excess energy in order to cool the planet and maintain a status quo in terms of keeping the Earth's temperature stable. However, with less ice on the Earth's surface due to swathes of it melting, less of the sun's excess energy can be reflected back and it becomes trapped within the atmosphere. As global temperatures increase, more of the glaciers will melt and the excess water will cause sea levels to rise to dangerous levels, which would particularly affect coastal regions and expose many major cities to the risk of flooding.

The window is still open for us to avoid passing a post-industrial temperature rise to $2°C$ and is even open to avoid hitting the $1.5°C$ mark. But that window is closing quickly. Since the beginning of the Industrial Revolution, we have emitted 2,400 billion tonnes of carbon dioxide. To stay below $1.5°C$, at the time of writing, we must not emit any more than 300 billion tonnes. But if we continue to emit carbon dioxide every year at the rate we currently do, our 'budget' will run out within the next decade and that $1.5°C$ will be surpassed.

Despite the 2015 Paris Agreement, CO_2 levels unfortunately since continued to rise. Under President Trump, the US, historically one of the world's biggest polluters, pulled out of the Paris Agreement and Russia and China have since been criticised for not setting ambitious enough targets to reduce carbon emissions. President Biden since rejoined the US with the

Paris agreement in 2021.

2016   A referendum was held in the UK to decide whether the country should leave the European Union. 51.9% voted in favour of leaving. In January 2020, the UK officially left the EU.

2016   After Russia began military intervention in Syria in 2015, coming to the aid of Assad (though they claimed to be targeting ISIS), the Syrian War turned in Assad's favour. Assad's Syrian army, backed by Russia and Iran, recaptured Aleppo, delivering a devastating blow for the rebels.

2017   Two *New York Times* reporters, Jodi Kantor and Megan Twohey, published a series of articles about how the powerful Hollywood producer Harvey Weinstein had, on numerous occasions, sexually assaulted dozens of women. It transpired that, for decades, Weinstein had threatened his victims, and silenced them with confidentiality and/or settlement agreements, so that they would not go public about his behaviour. But when the story of his widespread abuse broke, it became the catalyst for further similar stories to break out and for famous female actors to come forward and expose Weinstein publicly.

This subsequently brought to the forefront the **#MeToo** movement following a tweet by actor Alyssa Milano (the hash tag came in 2017, though the movement had already existed for ten years: it was originally founded by activist Tarana Burke). It turned into a global social movement that denounced sexual harassment and abuse worldwide and created a public forum for victims and survivors of abuse, not just celebrities, to come forward.

2017   As of 2017, the AIDS epidemic had infected an estimated 77 million people globally, and killed 35 million, according to the group UNAIDS. There are currently 38 million people living with HIV around the world. If an HIV infection develops into AIDS, life expectancy drops significantly. With successful antiretroviral therapy, many people with stage 3 HIV are able to live long and healthy lives. However, the battle continues to reach those people, especially children, in need of diagnosis and treatment but do not have access to it.

2017   Since military intervention in 2014, forces from around 60 countries had taken the fight to Islamic State. By the beginning of 2017, ISIS had been driven out of almost all of the territory they used to hold in Iraq (at one point, they occupied about a third of the country). Their last remaining stronghold was Mosul. In Syria, they had been driven out of almost every region except Raqqa, the Islamic State's de facto capital. By December, the ISIS Caliphate had lost around 95% of its territory, including Mosul and Raqqa.

2017   After an acrimonious presidential election campaign in 2016, **Donald John Trump** of the Republican Party was inaugurated as the **45ᵗʰ US President** after, in a surprise upset, he defeated Democrat Hilary Clinton (despite Clinton having won the national popular vote). At the time, at 70 years old, Trump was the oldest person to be elected President (a record which has since been surpassed by his successor).

At the end of the year, Trump formally recognised Jerusalem as Israel's capital, reversing decades of US policy on the issue, which saw the fate of Jerusalem as a matter to be decided between Israel and Palestine. Trump's declaration enraged Palestinians - who claim East Jerusalem as their own - as well as other leaders of the Muslim world. The following year, Trump relocated the US embassy from Tel Aviv to Jerusalem.

2019   Baghouz in Syria, the last holdout of ISIS, fell in March, **ending the Islamic State's claim to any territory**. In October, Abu Bakr al-Baghdadi was confirmed dead.

2019   **The House of Representatives impeached Donald Trump.** The impeachment investigation was sparked by an anonymous CIA whistleblower complaint about a phone conversation between

Trump and his Ukrainian counterpart Volodymyr Zelensky. Trump used the call to urge the newly-elected Ukrainian leader to investigate unfounded allegations against his political opponent, former Vice President Joe Biden, one of the Democratic party frontrunners to take on Trump at the next presidential election.

Evidence showed US diplomats were concerned that a meeting between the two leaders, and the granting of military aid to Ukraine, was conditional on the Biden investigation. Ukraine was desperate for the aid to fund its conflict against Russian-backed rebels having seized control of the eastern part of the country. The Trump administration denied the threat of withholding military aid was used as leverage against Ukraine in order to get information to discredit Biden.

Trump, accused of various offences and misdemeanours, particularly his seeking help from a foreign nation to interfere in the upcoming presidential election, was impeached by the House of Representatives. However, as was predicted by experts, the Republican majority in the Senate cleared him. He was therefore acquitted and remained in office to run again in the next presidential election.

2019-
2021

COVID-19

A **coronavirus** (referred to as "**COVID-19**" by the World Health Organization) broke out into the human population causing a new virus pandemic on a scale not seen for many years. It was believed to have originated from a wet market in the city of Wuhan, the capital of the Hubei Province in China.

Studies have predicted that bats were the original carriers of the virus, which since evolved before then coming into contact with other animals in one of these wet markets. Such markets, especially popular in South-East Asia, often house a wide range of exotic wild animals, many of which are still alive at the point of sale. As the theory suggests, this variety of animals and their proximity to one another, combined with lack of hygiene, are believed to have created the conditions for the virus to jump from animal to animal (for example, when the fluids from slaughter or excrements are mixed), mutate in the process and then jump over to humans.

The official name of the virus is **SARS-CoV-2**: the disease this virus causes is called COVID-19, which stands for Coronavirus Disease 2019. SARS-CoV-1 (the 'predecessor' to SARS-Cov-2) broke out in the Guangdong Province of southern China in 2002, infecting more than 8,000 people globally (and killing nearly 800). "SARS" stands for "Severe Acute Respiratory Syndrome".

"Corona" takes its name from the Latin word for "crown" because of the virus' crown-like spikes. The spikes are capable of locking onto the protein found on the outside of human cells. It then breaks in to the inside of the cell and gives instructions to produce more copies of itself. The viruses then do the same with other human cells causing symptoms to develop. The symptoms of COVID-19 have varied but include fever, cough, fatigue and shortness of breath. It is also possible that someone can be asymptomatic (that is, having the virus without showing any symptoms) making it easier for the infection to spread.

According to studies, COVID-19 mainly spreads through droplets generated when an infected person coughs, sneezes or speaks, or through droplets of saliva or discharge from the nose. It can enter another person through his or her eyes, nose or mouth. The virus can live on a range of surfaces for hours, the number of which varies depending on the material of the surface. Therefore, people can infect themselves by touching the surface and then touching their face. According to studies, a human touches their face on average 23 times an hour.

Initial reports of the virus in Wuhan were suppressed and whistleblowers were detained by the police. Three weeks before the Chinese government implemented containment measures, a doctor called Li Wenliang, working at the Wuhan Central Hospital, sent a group chat to his fellow doctors warning them of the virus. However, the Wuhan police told him to stop spreading these messages, threatening him with repercussions. In early February 2020, Wenliang tragically died having contracted the very virus he tried to warn the world about.

Many world leaders initially downplayed the new virus. But soon, most governments came to terms with the severity of the situation and hastened to try and control its spread. Eventually, strict lockdown measures were implemented on citizens worldwide throughout 2020. In a major, and impressively swift, breakthrough in November 2020, German biotechnology company **BioNTech and** US pharmaceutical cooperation **Pfizer announced in November 2020 a vaccine**, BNT162b2, which was more than 90% effective in preventing COVID-19. At the start of December, the UK became the first country to formally approve this vaccine. Within a week, it began its nationwide immunisation campaign and other countries soon followed.

As of May 2021, the total number of people worldwide who had died so far from COVID-19 surpassed 3.5 million and the number of confirmed cases exceeded 170 million.

2020   The Black Lives Matter movement took centre stage in the middle of 2020 after the killing of George Floyd, a 46-year-old black man, by Derek Chauvin, a white police officer, who knelt on Floyd's neck for over nine minutes during an altercation. Floyd suffocated to death as a result. The video that captured the incident went viral and waves of protests swept the US and across the world.

In April 2021, in a Minnesota state court, Chauvin was found guilty of murder by the jury.

2020   After several days of vote-counting following the **2020 presidential election**, Joe Biden (full name **Joseph Robinette**

Biden Jr.), former Vice President during the Obama presidency, defeated the incumbent Donald Trump to become the next US President.

The delay in vote-counting was mainly caused by the record number of mail-in votes due to the COVID-19 pandemic. Trump and his team tried to stop the vote-counting and accused the mail-in voting process as fraudulent, though there was no evidence of any election fraud or wrongdoing. The Trump campaign launched a series of lawsuits in an attempt to halt the vote-counting process or disqualify ballots. But their attempts made little to no success.

2020   The world population measured at approximately 7.795 billion.

2021   In January, as members of Congress were meeting to formalise Joe Biden's election win, a mob of far-right Trump supporters stormed the Capitol in Washington DC, forcing Congress members to evacuate the building. Four Trump supporters and a Capitol police officer were killed in the chaos. A reported 60 further police officers were injured.

Despite the setback, Biden's victory was confirmed the next day. A few weeks later, he was sworn in as the **46th US President**. At 78, he is currently the oldest person to assume the presidency (overtaking Reagan who was 77 when he left office). Biden's running mate, Kamala Harris, made history as the first female, first black and first Asian-American to be sworn in as Vice President.

Trump also made history, being the only President so far to be impeached twice after the House of Representatives delivered their charge of impeachment. He was accused of inciting the insurrection at the Capitol. However, he was acquitted after the Democrats failed to secure the votes required to convict him.

Printed in Great Britain
by Amazon

67193576R00200